University Life

Life the essential guide for students

SAGE

Los Angeles | London | New Delhi
Singapore | Washington DC

SAGE Publications Ltd
1 Oliver's Yard
55 City Road
London EC1Y ISP

SAGE Publications Inc.
2455 Teller Road
Thousand Oaks, California 91320

SAGE Publications India Pvt Ltd
B 1/1 1 Mohan Cooperative Industrial Area
Mathura Road
New Delhi 110 044

SAGE Publications Asia-Pacific Pte Ltd
33 Pekin Street #02-01
Far East Square
Singapore 048763

Library of Congress Control Number: 2010923737

British Library Cataloguing in Publication data

A catalogue record for this book is available from the British Library

ISBN 978-0-85702-372-8

Typeset by C&M Digitals (P) Ltd, Chennai, India
Printed on paper from sustainable resources

University Life

Contents

Acknowledgements

The chapters collected here have been selected from key texts in the field published by SAGE. We would like to thank the following authors for their permission to reproduce their work in this volume.

Burns. T. and Sinfield. S., *Essential Study Skills: The Complete Guide to Success at University*, 2nd edn, 2008.

Davey, G., *The International Student's Survival Guide: How to Get the Most from Studying at a UK University*, 2008.

Felton. S.P., in G. Hall and J. Longman (eds) *The Postgraduate's Companion*, 2008.

Hall, G. and Longman, J. (eds) *The Postgraduate's Companion*, 2008.

Lowes. R., et al, T*he International Student's Guide: Studying in English at University*, 2004.

McIlroy. D., Studying at University: How to be a Successful Student, 2003.

Palmer. S., and Puri. A. *Coping with Stress at University: A Survival Guide*, 2006.

Rugg, G. et al., *The Stress-Free Guide to Studying at University*, 2008.

Smale. B. and Fowlie. J., *How to Succeed at University: An Essential Guide to Academic Skills and Personal Development*, 2009.

Turner. J., *How to Study: A Short Introduction*, 2002.

Williams. N., *How to get a 2: 1 in Media, Communication and Cultural Studies*, 2004.

Introduction

JERRY WELLINGTON
University of Sheffield

Going to university is the start of a great adventure. You've worked hard to get here, so now you need to make the most of your opportunities at university. As well as achieving your chosen degree, you need to get the most out of the experience of being at university, facing new challenges and meeting new people. I know this has become something of a cliché, but it really is the start of a new life and it will open up new horizons. It's also great preparation for the world beyond university. I still vividly remember my first evening at university (admittedly quite a posh one) when I met two very friendly fellow 'freshers' who had both been to a well-known, expensive public school. It was my first time away from a fairly sheltered life in a state school in the south west of England. They looked at me strangely every time I spoke and eventually (very politely) asked if I was an American. It dawned on me the next day that they had never met anyone with a regional accent before – and I had met very few people without one. We have been friends ever since.

This book brings together practical advice and tips based on years of experience by SAGE authors who have helped students like you.

Part 1 Going to University sets out what to expect, especially if you are perhaps the first in your family to study at university. *How to Prepare Yourself for Higher Education (HE)* sets out a programme of useful activities for the period before you start your course. This involves examining your own motivations for embarking on HE, your own feelings and emotions about it and the importance of confronting any 'social phobias' that you might have. Similarly, the second chapter, *Going to University*, provides useful guidelines on exploring your own 'hopes and fears', both academic and social. *Starting University Life* offers essential tips for settling in. Most people will experience some form of 'homesickness' – the cliché that you are starting a new life means that you will be away from your own social, home and academic environment. You will meet people with different accents from varied academic backgrounds, with a wide range of social skills. You may feel inferior, socially and academically, as I did to some extent in my first semester in HE. This is to be expected and it may cause anxiety and stress. The first 3 chapters will offer you a tool for overcoming these anxieties, presenting a way of engaging 'stress-alleviating thinking' as opposed to stress-inducing. Finally, in your first few weeks, it's fairly common to have second thoughts about your course – *Are You on the Right Course?* will help you work your way through this issue. Everyone has doubts about the course they have chosen, especially when it becomes tough, boring or difficult. Learning is often a struggle and makes your head hurt. This chapter shows you how to weigh up in detail the pros and cons of changing course before you make any hasty decision.

Part 2 shows you *how to Develop Your Personal Skills* – communication, assertiveness and organizational skills are all important if you are to succeed in your chosen course. This part, like the first, has useful tips on handling the stress and anxiety which every student feels from time to time. *What Makes a Good Communicator?* provides practical advice on presenting yourself and your work in both writing and in person. It discusses the importance of know-ing your 'audience', addressing them clearly, and using structure and style in communicating via the written or spoken word. The next chapter, closely related to the first, explains how to 'cultivate' good organizational skills in plan-ning, studying and writing. Having these skills, and using them, can help to prevent some of the stress and anxiety which are discussed in the next two chapters. One of these, *Relaxation Skills* presents four techniques (all new to me) of 'imaging' situations in your mind's eye which can help you to deal with difficult situations or challenges. Finally, two chapters discuss the importance of being assertive – in the nicest possible way of course. Assertiveness is not the same as rudeness or aggressiveness – it is an important quality or skill to have in dealing with many situations as an HE student, both academically (in seminars and in group work, for example) and in your social life, as part 3 discusses.

Looking After Yourself, Part 3, focuses on your health, wealth, welfare and social networking – you can't study effectively unless you keep yourself healthy and have some leisure time. Both involve a 'delicate balancing act' and both can be difficult if you're not used to looking after yourself, studying inde-pendently, working to tight deadlines and are away from home for the first time. One chapter focuses on basic advice about alcohol and drugs to help you understand the risks these present to effective achievement at university. *Staying Healthy* emphasises the importance of a healthy diet, exercise, regu-lar relaxation, adequate sleep and drinking plenty of water whilst studying. There is growing evidence from neuroscience research that all these factors play a vital role in the development of your brain – which is one of the main reasons for being a university student!

Managing Your Money is a useful list of tips on this essential subject. A growing number of students have part-time jobs, often to make ends meet but also for social reasons. These should never take up more than 15 hours of your week (the absolute maximum) and again are part of the delicate balanc-ing act that is university life: everything in the right proportions.

If you've come to the UK to study, then *Part 4 Overseas Students* is essen-tial reading. Every student will be required not only to read and write in English but also to speak English. This will occur in seminars and tutorials of course, but the increase in small group work in many disciplines has raised the impor-tance of working and speaking together, often with fellow students from differ-ent backgrounds and cultures. The chapters contain sections on understanding and speaking English, as well as dealing with daily life and culture. Guidance is even given on the English climate (unpredictable), English customs (unpredictable) and English manners (even more unpredictable). There is a guide to such delicacies as fish and chips, Shepherd's pie and Yorkshire pudding, with rhubarb crumble to finish. You might be well advised to read the chapters on healthy eating alongside these descriptions! Mature and part-time students' concerns are also covered. The authors call them 'the forgotten army' but in HE they are hardly a minority now. Helpful advice is given on work-life balance (many mature students will have families), using support networks and time management.

Last, but certainly not least, *Part 5 What's Next*? focuses on life after university. Producing a clear and succinct CV for potential employers is vitally important, as are the letter of application and the job interview. Guidance is given on all three. There are numerous other tips on how to prepare yourself for the jobs market. Some of you will take the option, as I did, of moving into postgraduate study, perhaps a masters or even a doctorate. Are your reasons for this choice extrinsic e.g. to get a better Job? Or intrinsic e.g. your love of your subject? What will the benefits be? The chapter on Why do a *Postgraduate Degree?* gives a helpful framework for examining your motivations for postgraduate study and the benefits it might provide to you.

Each chapter in this book is an extract from a larger work published by SAGE, and each of these longer works is available to buy should you wish to go into the subject in more detail. Visit www.uk.sagepub.com/studyskills.sp to find out more.

We hope that *University Life: The Essential Guide for Students* will be useful to you.

Part 1

GOING TO UNIVERSITY

1 How to Prepare Yourself for Higher Education

BOB SMALE AND JULIE FOWLIE

> Overview – what's in this chapter?
>
> - Why do you need to upgrade your personal skills?
> - Handling the transition into higher education
> - Recognising your own motivation to learn, grow and develop
> - Understanding your emotions in the developmental process
> - Self-efficacy and self-confidence
> - Follow-up activities, further reading and websites to look up
> - Time for review and reflection

Why do you need to upgrade your personal skills?

Try completing this short self-scoring test, to assess your own level of confidence in relation to developing your own personal skills in order to complete your course successfully.

Activity: Why do you need to read this chapter?	
You need to self score each question on a scale from 0 to 10, where 0 is low and 10 is high.	
1. How confident do you feel about starting your course?	
2. How confident do you feel about meeting new people?	
3. How organised do you feel you are in terms of your studies?	

(Continued)

(Continued)

4. How confident do you feel about your study skills?	
5. How motivated do you feel about completing your course?	
6. How confident do you feel about overcoming any barriers?	
7. How able are you to handle the emotional side of your course?	
8. How clearly can you visualise your next role after your course?	
9. How well do you think you present yourself to other people?	
10. How confident do you feel that you can complete your course?	
Total score	

Interpretation

What did you score?

- Less than 50%   You definitely will find a lot of help in this chapter.
- 50%–75%   There is still plenty to learn in this chapter.
- 75%–100%   You are very confident – read on to confirm your understanding.

What do you want to achieve by studying in higher education?

What do you want to achieve by studying in higher education? This is a question that you may already be asking. Understanding your answer will have a lot to do with you successfully completing your course.

There is a considerable drop out rate during the first year for most undergraduate courses, which is a tragedy for all those concerned. After all the new students had worked hard, got good grades, got there and yet failed at the first hurdle. Why does this happen? More importantly, why should you let it happen to you?

This chapter is first about helping you make a successful transition into higher education. How was your induction? You may have felt confused or overloaded by the end of day one. Then there are the problems of meeting new people and getting your studies organised.

[...]

Handling the transition into higher education

How did you feel on the first day?

The first day in higher education can be quite traumatic for many new students. There will almost certainly be an induction programme organised for you and it could last for a whole week or even for two. Many people feel that they are subject to *information overload* as a series of well meaning 'talking heads' supply endless information – all of which, they tell you, is absolutely essential.

Activity: How did you feel at the start?

1. Write a paragraph expressing how you felt on the first day in higher education.

2. Write another paragraph about how you felt at the end of the first week. Was it better or worse?

3. Write a paragraph about how you felt at the end of the first month. You might need to make a diary date to do this.

What is culture shock?

Culture shock is experienced when people are first exposed to a new and alien culture. They may feel confused and disorientated. When people enter higher education there is always an element of culture shock, because virtually everyone was somewhere else with a different culture before they arrived. International students are often more prone to suffering from culture shock, not only because of differences in the education system, but also because of language and cultural differences. Indeed it is generally true to say that the greater the difference between where you came from and where you are now, the more likely you are to feel the effects of culture shock.

There are good and bad ways to help overcome culture shock. Consider the following two lists.

Good ways …	**Bad ways …**
Become more socially integrated (see next section).	Avoid everybody, especially from your course.
Eat in the refectory.	Eat in your room.
Visit the Students Union and see what is on offer.	Cut classes.
Join student societies, attend meetings and activities.	Don't do any work.
Read and file away all that 'stuff' from induction.	Deny what is really happening.
Get your studies organised, check out your timetable, etc.	Resort to drink or drugs.
Log onto the computer system and check student websites, blogs, etc.	Drop out.
Visit the library and check out the facilities and the nearest book shop.	Go home for good!

Activity: Overcoming culture shock

1. Have a look through the 'good ways' outlined above and make a list of things that you need to do over the first few days and weeks.
2. Keep the list in a place where you can see it and tick off things as you achieve them. It's important to record your successes!

Do you feel homesick or like dropping out?

Culture shock can lead to homesickness, and you may feel like packing up and going home. It's very common to feel like this, particularly if you feel overwhelmed by the workload, the place or the people – perhaps all three!

Dropping out of your course is a big decision. It is life changing and so deserves thorough consideration. Knowing *why* you want to leave or stay will be really important if you are going to make the right decision for you.

Activity: Thinking of leaving your course?

1. Try making two lists to consider your reasons for going or staying.

Reasons for going...		Reasons for staying...	
•		•	
•		•	
•		•	
•		•	
•		•	
•		•	
•		•	
•		•	

2. Now consider:

• Are your reasons more emotional or rational?

• Are any of your reasons short term and likely to change?

• What help and support could you access? (See next section).

Here are some more things you really should do before dropping out:

- Talk it over with your friends / other people on the course. You may be surprised at how much they want you to stay.

- Talk it over with your course leader, personal tutor or any other member of the academic staff you feel comfortable talking to.

- You may have accommodation problems or just be unhappy where you are. There should be an accommodation officer or department you can talk to about this.

- You may have special needs that can be accommodated by the institution and there should be someone to talk to about this, probably a whole department called 'student services' to check out.

- You may actually feel depressed or be suffering from anxiety problems. This is not a reason for leaving, but rather a reason for staying and working through your problems. You should be able to get support through a student counsellor who will probably be accessed through your student services department or student medical centre.

- Your students union can also help with welfare and academic problems and will be experienced in giving advice and support.

Finally, if you have worked through the two lists in the previous activity and accessed the support you need, you will know if you are making a rational or emotional decision to leave. It's very easy to make a snap decision and then regret it. While it may be harder to stay and work through your reasons in the short term, it will be more rewarding in the long term.

 A student told us...

One student told us that, having arrived from one of the remotest corners of the world, she found she had no friends and felt nothing in common with anyone in her halls or on her course. She was so homesick that she just wanted to get on a plane and go back home. We encouraged her to hang in and join some student societies in order to meet more people. By the end of the first year she felt sufficiently confident that she didn't even go home for the summer vacation.

How are you with meeting new people?

Meeting new people tends to happen quite naturally for most people in the first few days at university, but maybe you found it difficult or met the wrong people, or maybe it has all gone a bit quiet now. This could be an area that you need to work on in order to integrate and settle in happily at your university or college.

The first time you meet someone is very important. First impressions really do count. People can sense intuitively in the first thirty seconds of an encounter what basic impression they will have of the other person after fifteen minutes – or half a year. For instance, when people watch just thirty-second snatches of staff giving a lecture, they can assess each teacher's proficiency with about eighty per cent accuracy (Ambady, 1993). Almost the same level of accuracy has been found from brief observations in forty-four other studies, including one of people's interactions with bosses, peers and subordinates (Ambady and Rosenthal, 1992).

> ## Activity: Meeting new people
>
> Take a few minutes to reflect upon the following questions:
>
> - Who was the first person you met on your first day?
>
> - What were your first impressions?

Some people find it particularly difficult to talk to strangers and will tend to avoid making new connections. This is known as a *social phobia*, but it can be overcome with perseverance.

[…]

Here are some 'golden rules' for overcoming a fear of talking to new people:

- You have a perfect right to speak to strangers.

- It doesn't matter what they think of you, because you are still you.

- It doesn't matter how many rejections you get because eventually you will get into meaningful dialogue with someone.

- The more you do it, the better it will go and the more your fears will reduce.

- You are OK!

Not believing in the last of these 'golden rules' – you are OK – underpins our fears and phobias. If you can't truly believe it, try pretending that you are OK, acting a role, when you speak to someone. You may be surprised how quickly you begin to believe it!

Activity: Overcoming social phobias

1.   Put yourself in a social situation such as a common room at lunch time or student union bar in the evening. Avoid one that is so loud you can't talk or so quiet that you are feeling self-conscious.
2.   Think about what you will say to open a conversation. Open questions such as 'how is it going?' are a good start (see also Chapter 3 on questioning and listening skills).
3.   Look out for someone who looks friendly and is also on their own.
4.   Try out your opening question and try to back this up with friendly questions, exploring what they told you and then perhaps sharing something of your experience.
5.   Make sure you keep doing this until you get into a meaningful conversation.
6.   Review how it went and try again another time – soon. Avoidance breeds more anxiety, so it's better to keep at it.

How well focused are you on other people?

You can improve the quality of the conversations you have with other people. Three critical factors are: energy, openness and mind focus. These largely determine the presence we can muster and maintain in any given interaction.

Activity: Presence assessment

1.   Ask yourself the following questions to measure your current ability to offer others your full presence:

   • On a scale of 1 to 10 (with 10 indicating a mind homing in like a laser beam of pure attention and 1 being a state of total mind-meandering), what is **your focus level** right now?
   • On a scale of 1 to 10, what is your level of **open-mindedness and open heartedness** at this very moment towards other people?
   • On a scale of 1 to 10, what is your energy level right now, in terms of the reserves of **mental and physical vitality and vigour** you can bring to the moment?

2.   Now consider how you can use these techniques:

- You can perform the above simple self-awareness exercise at any time, mentally calculating your score in order to gauge your current level of presence.
- Consider using it just prior to an interaction with others, initially to prepare yourself emotionally, then midway through an interaction to increase your mindfulness and alertness, and finally as you leave an interaction to assess your overall presence throughout.
- Used with regularity, the assessment becomes a self-correcting mechanism. Conscious attention to self-awareness can increase your ability to get on with other people.

Orientating yourself to your studies

What is your attitude to work and study? How do you approach study? Although you may be new to higher education, you will know how you were at school or college.

Activity: How were you at school or college?	
Did you:	**Tick**
attend classes regularly?	
participate enthusiastically when you were there?	
do all the work that was set?	
read to support the work in class?	
file your notes away neatly?	
revise thoroughly for exams?	

Whatever you did before, it's now time to get organised for higher education. The emphasis will be much more on independent study, so being organised will be much more important – and if you don't get organised it is going to get very tough.

Contact time with staff may be much more limited in higher education than you were used to in school or college. The emphasis will probably be much more on you becoming an **independent learner**. Therefore knowing what you are supposed to be doing, when and where, and how to access the support facilities that you need, will become much more important.

Here are some ideas to consider:

- **Check your timetable** – sounds obvious, but you need to be in the right place at the right time. Not everything runs to timetable, so make sure you have a system for remembering what you should be doing such as a diary, personal organiser or mobile phone.

- **Full participation** – again it sounds obvious, but it's essential. It's usually true that failure rates correlate very closely to poor attendance patterns. You don't have to be especially gifted to pass, but you do need to turn up and to participate when you get there. Be there in mind and body!

- **Pre- and post-session work** – try to look upon pre- and post-session work as essential parts of the course and not as a nuisance or a 'bolt on'. Actual taught sessions in higher education tend to be relatively short, so post-session work will help to reinforce and extend what you have started to learn in a session and pre-session work or 'prep' will help you understand the next one.

- **IT facilities, library and bookshops** – get logged onto the computer system as soon as you can in order to access online information. Finding your way around the library and checking out the bookshops are all useful things to do in your first few days and will really help you when the pressure builds up later.

- **Notes / folders** – how are you with paper work? If it's all in a messy heap in the corner, it will be a serious setback to your studies. So the first few days is a good time to buy some files and start to learn to love filing! Taught programmes go by very quickly, with new material to take on board every week. Filing things away is good for revision as it helps to refresh your memory about what you studied. In addition it's all there waiting for you when you need material in order to complete assessments.

Activity: Getting organised for study

1. Make a list of things you think you need to do over the next few days and weeks.
2. Keep the list in a place where you can see it and tick off things as you achieve or complete them. It's important to record your success!

Recognising your own motivation to learn, grow and develop

Motivation is simply about motive, for example why go to work? Why study? Why get up at all? It is clear that people do not all have the same motivations, but each of us has to find what motivates us in order to complete a course, get a job or whatever. The questions are: what is going to motivate you to succeed in your course, then in finding a job and in life as a whole?

Try completing the activity box below in order to find out what is going to motivate you and why, what the barriers to your achievement are and what new skills you might need to learn.

Activity: Understanding your own motivation

Write down your thoughts concerning the following:

1. What do you want to achieve during your time at university?

2. Why do you want to achieve this?

3. What barriers do you think you might encounter in achieving your aims?

4. What new skills do you think that you will need to learn in order to overcome these barriers?

5. How anxious are you about your ability to achieve your aims? You can score your level of anxiety from 0 (low) to 10 (high) – please circle:

    0   1   2   3   4   5   6   7   8   9   10

Identifying what you want to achieve and why at the start of your course is important, because there will always be days when you wonder what you are doing it all for. Many people also feel seriously anxious about their ability to complete their studies. If you are considering dropping out, and many students do, remembering why you are studying and your motivation to achieve can pull you through on dark days.

> ### Activity: Comparing your motivation to succeed
>
> 1. Get someone else to complete the questions in the previous activity and then compare your answers. You might want to consider:
>
>   - Are your answers the same or similar?
>   - Do you think that they should be so?
>
> 2. Note down any differences which you feel are important.

Succeeding in higher education will require you holding onto your dream. Here are a few things you might want to try out:

- Try visualising yourself in a future time, perhaps at graduation or starting a new job. Paint the picture in your mind and put yourself clearly in it.

- Try using affirmations. An affirmation is something we say to ourselves because we need to say it. It is a lie until we don't need to say it anymore. It normally starts with 'I', so your affirmation could be as simple as 'I know that I can succeed in my course'. Try repeating affirmations every day until they become redundant. You'll know when that is!

- Try putting your affirmations on notes and put them up in your room to remind yourself what you are doing and why. This can seem quite daft when you are starting your course in the heady days of September or October, but by the dark days of November or February, they could be your salvation.

- Similarly, try putting up pictures or carrying them with you. Many people find friends, family or partners are an inspiration, or maybe it could be a car or a house you aspire to own. If you want to live in another part of the world, try carrying a picture of that place around with you to remind you of your dream.

A student told us ...

One student told us that his ambition was to be an accountant, but clearly this relied upon him completing his course successfully. He imagined himself in his new life, driving a black BMW. To remind himself, he put a picture of one from a magazine over the desk in his room.

Understanding your emotions in the developmental process

The science of moods

One of the biggest and perhaps least talked about factors in your development will be your ability to understand and work with your own emotions and those of others. At the core of this is the idea that, as human beings, we are 'hard wired' to respond to the behaviour and subsequent emotional reactions of other people. One person transmits signals that can alter hormone levels, cardiovascular functions, sleep rhythms and even immune functions inside the body of another. In all aspects of social life, our physiologies intermingle.

In recent years a science of emotion has developed which is known as **emotional intelligence**. This has been defined as:

> The ability to express emotion, assimilate emotion in thought, understand and reason with emotion and regulate emotion in self and others. (Mayer and Salovey, 1990)

and as:

> The capacity for understanding our own feelings and those of others, for motivating others and ourselves whilst using leadership, empathy and integrity. (Goleman, 1998: 82)

Why are our emotions a potential threat to our success?

Negative emotions can get in the way of our succeeding, not only in our studies but also in employment and life generally. When we are taken over by negative emotions, this is referred to as an **amygdala takeover**. This can be defined as an inappropriate and uncontrolled emotional response. It has four components:

- A trigger, which is a catalyst that stimulates because it generates an impulse.

- A strong emotion that is felt, such as anger, desire or frustration.

- An instant, impulsive, irrational or uncontrolled reaction that is usually inappropriate.

- A subsequent feeling of regret, after the feelings have passed.

When are we at risk of amygdala takeovers?

Predisposing factors	Triggers	Responses
• Tiredness	• Frustration	• Shouting
• Build-up of stress – 'the last straw'	• Value conflicts	• Crying
	• Personal criticism	• Shutting down
• Lots of effort into something	• Unfairness	• Swearing
	• Aggressive behaviour from others	• Physical violence
• Alcohol		

Activity: Amygdala takeover

Think about an amygdala takeover you have experienced.

1. What triggered it?

2. What was your response (that you regretted)?

3. Can you identify anything that made you predisposed to a takeover?

[...]

Self-efficacy and self-confidence

Self-efficacy is about our confidence in our ability to succeed, whether it is in higher education, employment or life generally. Spencer and Spencer (1993: 80) offer a more detailed definition of self-confidence:

> Self-confidence is a person's belief in his or her own ability to accomplish a task. This includes the person expressing confidence in dealing with increasingly challenging circumstances, in reaching decisions or forming opinions, and in handling failure constructively.

Activity: Recognising your success competencies

Spencer and Spencer (1993: 336) have also identified the following competencies that predict success at work and in life:

- **Achievement orientation** – the desire to attain standards of excellence and do better, improve performance.
- **Initiative** – acting to attain goals and solve problems before being forced to by events.
- **Information seeking** – digging deeper for information.
- **Conceptual thinking** – making sense of data and using algorithms to solve problems.
- **Interpersonal understanding** – hearing the motives and feelings of diverse others.
- **Self-confidence** – a person's belief in his or her own efficacy, or ability to achieve goals.
- **Impact and influence** – a person's ability to persuade others to his or her viewpoint.
- **Collaborativeness** – working effectively with others to achieve common goals.

1. Review the above list of success competencies, ticking those you feel competent in.
2. Add your findings to the SWOT analysis you made in the previous section.

[...]

Spencer and Spencer (1993) state that self-confidence is a component of most models of superior performers, although they also state that self-confidence may or may not be an independent variable: 'Is someone successful because they have self-confidence, or do they have self-confidence because they are successful?'. Both may be the case in a positive self-perpetuating cycle.

Building your self-confidence will mean doing new things and developing new skills. Whenever we step into new territory we are likely to feel anxious, but we develop confidence by keeping at it and pushing through. Your decision to enter higher education will inevitably mean doing new, different and sometimes difficult things, but the rewards will come from achieving them and from the increased self-confidence that you can take into employment and life.

Activity: Developing your self-confidence

1. Reviewing your SWOT analysis, think of something you could do to build your self-confidence. It may be something you would normally avoid doing or something you have been putting off.
2. Make a definite plan to do something different in your life and then activate it.
3. How did it go? Make a note of what happened.

Follow-up activities

It is quite common in the first couple of weeks of a course not to have much academic work to do, so this may be a good time to invest some effort in what will be important for you over your time in higher education.

TIME FOR ACTION – CHECKLIST

Have you:

- made good efforts to get socially integrated?
- checked out your academic timetable and located rooms?
- started dealing with the information overload by setting up files etc?
- checked out the library and bookshop?
- logged onto the IT facilities?
- accessed any other support services that you will need?
- considered your motivation and how it compares to that of a friend?
- recognised the role of your own emotions and self-efficacy in your development and success?

Further reading

Burns, T. and Sinfield, S. (2008) *Essential Study Skills: The Complete Guide to Success at University,* 2nd edition. London: Sage.

Cottrell, S. (2008) *The Study Skills Handbook*, 3rd edition. Basingtoke: Palgrave Macmillan.

Feldman, R. (2000) *Power Learning, Strategies for Success in College and Life*. Maidenhead: McGraw-Hill Higher Education.

Goleman, D. (2003) *Destructive Emotions and How We Can Overcome Them*. London: Bloomsbury.

Jeffers, S. (1991) *Feel the Fear and Do it Anyway*. London: Arrow.

Lee-Davies, L. (2007) *Developing Work and Study Skills*. London: Thomson.

Pedler, M. and Boydell, J. (1999) *Managing Yourself*. London: Lemos and Crane.

Race, P. (1995) *Who Learns Wins*. London: Penguin.

Race, P. (2007) *How to Get a Good Degree: Making the Most of your Time at University.* Buckingham: Open University Press.

Websites to look up

- Most universities and colleges of higher education will have pages on their own website with titles such as 'arriving at university', 'accommodation', 'dealing with homesickness', 'culture shock', etc.

- The National Union of Students also provides information at:

http://www.nusonline.co.uk/info/freshers/

- Information for international students is available from:

UKISA at: http://www.ukcisa.org.uk/

 # Time for review and reflection

This is your space to log your reflections on this chapter, to think about what you have learnt, how you will use it and what else you need to find out.

There will be more on reflection and why and how we can use it to learn, grow and develop in Chapter 2, in the sections on recognising strengths and planning personal development.

What were the key learning points of this chapter?

What are your strengths in the areas covered by this chapter?

What areas did you identify for development?

What have you learnt about yourself?

How will you use it?

What else do you need to learn or find out about in relation to this chapter?

Going to University

TOM BURNS AND SANDRA SINFIELD

AIMS

To examine what it feels like to be a student, and to outline our SOCCER or 'six steps to success' strategy that informs this book and the activities and information that we cover within it.

LEARNING OUTCOMES

After reading this section and engaging with the activities, you will have:

- reflected on what it feels like to be a university student
- gained an understanding of the premise of the book
- been introduced to the characteristics of successful study that inform the rest of the book.

Coming to university feels like . . .

Starting to study at university or college or returning to a higher level of study, especially after a break, can make you feel anxious: how will you cope with it all? How will you manage the reading, notemaking, organising your time, the assess-ments – essays, reports, presentations and exams? Everyone else looks as though they know what's going on, and you are the only one who looks, sounds and feels like a fool. Everybody else is a good student, and no one has the same fears and worries as you. What can you do? One thing that you can do right now is to reflect on how you are really feeling about going to university and being a student. So before reading on, we would like you to respond to the hopes and fears statements in the following activity.

Activity 1: Hopes and fears statements

We have gathered together some of the things that we have heard new students say. Have a look at these statements and jot down your own responses to them: note whether you agree or disagree with the statement, or even consider what advice you would give to the student concerned.

1 I'm not sure that I'll find enough time to study.
2 I'm apprehensive that my studies will affect the rest of my life.
3 I find it hard to concentrate for long periods.
4 I'm really looking forward to the challenge of studying again.
5 I haven't written an essay for ages and I'm anxious about putting pen to paper.
6 I was never good at school in the first place, so how will I cope with this?
7 My memory isn't as good as it used to be.
8 I'm worried that the work will be difficult and I won't be able to understand it.
9 I enjoy working with other people and discussing things.
10 I'm worried because English isn't my first language.
11 I'll find it hard to get down to work.
12 I'm not sure how my friends and family will react to my studies.
13 I'm good at organising my time.
14 I'm worried that I'll find it hard to cope with the difficult reading. I wish I could read faster.
15 I bet everyone on the course will be more used to studying than I am.
16 I'm not sure how to cope with the distractions at home.
17 I'm afraid that I'll fall behind with my work.
18 I'm glad that I have somewhere quiet to study.
19 I'm not sure how much to discuss my work with other people. Isn't that cheating?
20 Deadlines give me the energy to do things.
21 I get a real sense of achievement out of finishing things.
22 I'm not very good at spelling.

▶

23 I'm never sure when to use a comma or a full stop.
24 I've forgotten all the rules of grammar.
25 I can write letters but I don't know the sort of language you have to know to write essays.
26 I know what to say but I can't find the right words.
27 I don't have a wide enough vocabulary.
28 I have plenty of ideas but I don't seem able to put them together.
29 I'm all right once I get started, but I have a block about starting.
30 I just don't know how to set about writing an essay.

Discussion: Well, that was a long list. How do you feel now? Here are a couple of things that might have happened:

- just writing your fears down or saying them out loud made you see that they are not so bad after all
- seeing a list like this was reassuring – you are not alone!

Did either of these things happen for you? Why don't you try to find someone to discuss your list with? If you can find someone, move on to Activity 2.

Activity 2: Talking it over

Find someone to talk to about your responses, someone who is studying with you, a friend or colleague or a member of your family.

Tip: A study partner can make all the difference when studying. A partner can help break down some of your fears. A partner can share the study load. And, of course, a partner gives many opportunities for active learning, for you can talk about and discuss things all the time.

If using a study partner for this activity, it would help if they also completed their own list.

With your partner:

1 Look at the similarities and differences between your lists.
2 Consider whether any of the statements that express anxiety really matter.
3 Can you think of any solutions that are relevant to this stage of your work?

> *Discussion:* Has your discussion helped at all? Why don't you now look at some responses collected from other students?

Hopes and fears statements and responses

- I'm not sure that I'll find enough time to study.
  I realise that I will have to be very organised in order to work, study and maintain my family and friends. I will look at the Study Techniques section of the book.
- *I'm apprehensive that my studies will affect the rest of my life.*
  Well, being a student is going to have a dramatic impact on my life, I can see that. I will not have as much time for friends and family, nor to do the other things that I really like doing perhaps. But, there again, life does change; it's about changes and changing. I can see why they say that change can be very uncomfortable, as it already is.
- *I find it hard to concentrate for long periods.*
  I shall start by concentrating for short periods and try to build up to longer study periods. I don't have to get it all right straight away.
- *I'm really looking forward to the challenge of studying again.*
  So am I! It makes me feel good about me.
- *I haven't written an essay for ages and I'm anxious about putting pen to paper.*
  But that's why I'm using this book.
- *I was never good at school in the first place, so how will I cope with this?*
  I know what you mean, but I didn't like school – maybe that's why I didn't do well there. It's different now.
- *My memory isn't as good as it used to be.*
  I've heard that this isn't really true. As we get older, we pay more attention to what we forget. Apparently, we should notice what we are getting right instead. However, when it comes to studying, I have never realised before how much effort I will have to put in to remembering things. I thought that the brain just remembered stuff or it didn't. I can see now that I have to choose what to remember and how to remember it. It's different, but I hope that I can learn to do that.
- *I'm worried that the work will be difficult and I won't be able to understand it.*
  I noticed the point about being prepared to get things wrong, so I am going to try to be brave and be prepared to learn from my mistakes. I'm also going to ask questions if I don't understand. And I've bought an English dictionary and a subject dictionary to help me cope with the language of my subject.
- *I enjoy working with other people and discussing things.*
  I'm going to have to find a study partner, because I really do like talking things over. I've done some of my best learning in the canteen once class is over.
- *I'm worried because English isn't my first language.*
  My daughter is better at English than I am and she has said that she will help me. She also thinks that I'm being very brave studying in English, which makes me feel strong instead of foolish.

- *I'll find it hard to get down to work.*

  It is hard to study – for everybody. I have a special place to sit, and when I am there, I 'feel' like a student. Sometimes I trick myself into sitting there – I say, just sit there for five minutes and see what happens – before I know it, I have started to work and it is all right after all.

- *I'm not sure how my friends and family will react to my studies.*

  Yes, this can be a problem. I do know people who have a really hard time: their friends think they'll become snobs, or their children start to play up every time they try to get some work done . . . I guess if we want them to understand what we are doing – and support us – we have to explain what we are doing, and build some time for them into our study timetable.

- *I'm good at organising my time.*

  I find I have two approaches: one is to be very organised – I make lists of all the things that I have to do and I work through them. The other system is where I sit down amongst a pile of work, and just plunge in and get on with it. Both systems seem to work sometimes. This tells me that there is no one right way to do anything, but that I do have to keep on top of things or else everything feels worse!

- *I'm worried that I'll find it hard to cope with the difficult reading. I wish I could read faster.*

  I've heard that academic reading does get easier with practice – I certainly hope so. Still, I suppose it's got to take up some time – it's not a detective story, is it?

- *I bet everyone on the course will be more used to studying than I am.*

  I also bet that I'm the only one who's frightened, and I'm the only one whose family doesn't understand them . . . It's not true really, is it?

- *I'm not sure how to cope with the distractions at home.*

  Well, I've got a friend who works from home, so I know it can be done. She puts the answerphone on; she does not open the door, and things like that. The problem arises when we actually want to be distracted, because that is easier than doing the work.

- *I'm afraid that I'll fall behind with my work.*

  I'm hoping the section on organising my time will help me with that.

- *I'm glad that I have somewhere quiet to study.*

  Lucky you – I don't! Anyway, I've heard that this is another case where there is no one right way of working. Some people work best in the quiet, while others like noise.

- *I'm not sure how much to discuss my work with other people. Isn't that cheating?*

  I know the answer to this one. Talking isn't cheating, it's active learning. I like the sound of that.

- *Deadlines give me the energy to do things.*

  Without deadlines, I do find it difficult to finish things. At the same time, I know that I mustn't leave it all till the last minute – I must pace myself through an assignment.

- *I get a real sense of achievement out of finishing things.*

  I love it when I hand a piece of work in on time. But I do know other people who hate finishing things off. They just keep on reading and reading. I guess that sometimes it's difficult to know when you've done enough work.

- *I'm not very good at spelling.*

  I'm going to use the spell checker on my computer. I've also heard that it is a good idea to build up your own dictionary of difficult words. I've already bought a small exercise book to do this.

- *I'm never sure when to use a comma or a full stop.*

- *I've forgotten all the rules of grammar.*

Punctuation was not my strong point either. My trick is to write in relatively short sentences. This keeps my meaning clear. I use new words when it is easier to use the word, than explain what I am talking about without using that word. Like everything else, I hope it gets easier with practice.

- *I can write letters but I don't know the sort of language you have to know to write essays.*

  I think I'll try to do what that other person says – get the exercise book to jot down the new words, and use them when I understand them and if it makes sense to do so.

- *I know what to say but I can't find the right words.*

  I will try the little exercise book tip, too. I do know that it's not about talking as if you have swallowed a dictionary – it's about expressing yourself effectively. This usually means writing simply and clearly.

- *I don't have a wide enough vocabulary.*

  A friend of mine coped with this by writing new words on Post-its and sticking them up all over his flat. He said he got to learn them really quickly that way.

- *I have plenty of ideas but I don't seem able to put them together.*

  Apparently, planning helps us get our ideas together, and that's covered in here somewhere.

- *I'm all right once I get started, but I have a block about starting.*

  Yes, that is why sometimes you do have to trick yourself into starting, You know, I'll just give it five minutes . . . and see if that helps.

- *I just don't know how to set about writing an essay.*

  Again, I don't think that I have to know about this just yet. If I worry about too many things at once, then I get nothing done at all.

> *Query:* How do you feel now? Hopefully, you have found it useful to cover these things. Remember, there is often no right or wrong way to approach being a student. As long as you want to do well, and you are prepared to put some effort in, you should discover your own way of doing well.

The six steps to success

Our work with students, examiners and tutors has made us aware that there are certain study and academic skills and practices that, if learned and rehearsed, can help us all to be better students, and to be happier and more successful when studying. This book is informed by the following propositions, and we have called these the six steps to study success. We urge you to put the six steps into practice with all your studies, all the time.

By the way, just because these ideas are in a list does not mean that the first thing mentioned is more important than the last – they are all equally important if we want to do well.

The six-step propositions:

- Study techniques and practices can be learned – good students are made, not born.
- Overview is vital – everybody needs the big picture.

- Creativity is essential – and can be developed.
- Communicate effectively – in the correct form.
- Emotions rule – dealing with your emotions is crucial.
- **Review** – without reflection there is no learning.

You might trace the letters in bold, above, that take us from the six-step propositions to the mnemonic designed to help you remember these six steps – SOCCER:

> **S** – Study techniques and practices
> **O** – Overview
> **C** – Creativity
> **C** – Communicate effectively
> **E** – Emotions
> **R** – Review, review, review

We discuss these six steps briefly here, and refer to other sections of this book that develop the ideas even further.

Study techniques and practices can be learned – good students are made, not born

It is all too easy to think that we are not 'cut out' for studying. Often, negative experiences at school can lead many people to believe that studying is not for them – they are just not good students. Our work with students of all ages and 'abilities' leads us to believe that most of us can learn to become good students – what gets in the way is the belief that it should all come naturally, that if we don't just know what to do, then something is wrong with us.

Why should you think that you 'ought' to know how to study effectively? If you wanted to be a fire fighter or a farmer or a chef or a carpenter, you would know that you would have to learn how to be one. You would guess that you could also learn certain tricks of the trade that would make the job easier or more effective. If we think of studying like this, it can become easier. All the way through this book we will look at the constituent study and academic skills that can help you to succeed.

In terms of developing your study techniques, consider:

4 How to learn effectively
5 How to organise yourself for independent study
6 How to use computers and e-learning . . .
7 How to succeed in group work
11 How to research and read academically
12 How to make the best notes
20 How to understand and pass exams.

'Why didn't they tell us this before? I left school feeling like a complete failure, but it was just that
I didn't know how to learn. These techniques have given me such a boost. I feel really confident now.'

Overview is vital – everybody needs the big picture

While it is true that we tend to learn things in pieces, one step at a time, this process is helped
if we have the big picture first: if we know what we are learning and how the subject area will
be covered. To use a simple analogy, it is like a jigsaw puzzle – it is much easier to put the pieces
together if we have the picture on the box to guide us.

The institutions in which we study have specific shapes and functions – they are organised
and work in particular ways. If we can understand how universities work, we will be able to
negotiate our time at university more successfully, and more swiftly.

Further, programmes of study – from GCSE to university courses – have all been designed
to have an overall shape and structure. If we can understand the structure of our courses, if we
work to get the big picture before we start, this will help us as students to make sense of our
learning. Our argument is that each lecture and each piece of reading that we encounter will
make more sense if we fit them into a picture of the course as a whole.

In order to get an overview of your university and of your course, have a look at:

2 How universities work
3 How to understand your course.

'I really hated school, not knowing what was going on and why. Using the "overview" has made all
the difference. I'm on top.'

Creativity is essential – and can be developed

There is a lot of 'common sense' about being a successful student – it is common sense to have
resources to hand, to be well organised, to make time each day for study and so forth. We do not
want to criticise common sense, as we know students who have gained good 2:1 degrees with
common sense and sheer hard work. However, if you want to do that little bit more, if you want
studying to be a little bit easier and more interesting, then a touch of creativity is needed.

If you give back to lecturers what they have told you, if you just use their examples and
read the books that they recommend, then you will be a strong, average student. To get a little
further, you have to be creative, you have to go somewhere or think something different, but
how can you do that? We discuss creativity generally, and explore creative ways to approach
assignments and notemaking in *ESS2*, as ways of bringing creativity into learning and studying.
These are techniques that in their various ways encourage a different or more original approach
to your studies. Look at:

 8 How to be creative in your learning
12 How to make the best notes (especially the section on pattern notes).

'At school, I was told to go away and get a job in a shop [sorry, shop workers!], that I would never be
able to learn anything. Putting colour and life into my university work has made all the difference;
now I get As for my assignments.'

Communicate effectively – in the correct form

Just as we cannot 'know' how to study, we cannot 'know' what an essay, report or presentation is. These things have specific shapes to them (what), they have specific learning and assessment purposes (why), and there are tried and tested ways of approaching them that can be developed (how). In order to help you develop successful assessment techniques, we devote a whole, long section to effective communication, where we look at essays, reports, presentations and seminars and other assessment engines.

[…]

> 'They used to write things like "there's no introduction" or "there's no conclusion" on my essays. But no one ever told me what these were, or why they wanted them. Now, I only have to worry about my ideas; I know how to present them.'

Emotions rule – dealing with your emotions is crucial

Studying and learning may be cognitive or intellectual activities, but for most of us, they are also fraught with emotion. Typically, when we first start a course or go to a new college, we are apprehensive, nervous or even terrified. Certain tasks exhilarate us while others will bore us. If we do not acknowledge and address our own emotional responses to the different things that we encounter as students, we will never be able to benefit from our positive responses or overcome our negative ones.

We explore the emotional dimension of study and the roles of fear and self-confidence in the academic environment, in order for you to think about your own emotional highs and lows as a student, and what you intend to do about them. Note that positive thinking is useful for all our studying and learning activities, but you may draw on positive thinking tips and tricks even more when approaching your first presentation and your exams. If this is a big issue for you, first read:

9 How to deal with your emotions.

> 'You ask what the first day was like? I was het up, frightened, terrified . . . I thought "Why the hell have I done this to myself?" I just wanted to run away . . . Oh I love it now, I don't want to leave!'

Review – without reflection there is no learning

There is much evidence to suggest that learning involves an active selection of what to learn, and how to learn it. Throughout the book, we will be examining different revision and review strategies: memory and revision strategies, reflective learning logs and Personal Development Planning (PDP). You might also notice that each chapter ends with 'Review points' that encourage you to explore not only what you have learned but how you learned it.

Learning and remembering are not necessarily automatic or simple, but we can learn how to do these effectively, and we have structured the book to reinforce this. To explore this in more depth, go to:

10 How to be a reflective learner
15 How to write a great reflective essay
19 How to build your memory and revise effectively
20 How to understand and pass exams
21 How to make the most of Personal Development Planning

> 'I love doing my learning logs, as it helps me make sense of what I'm doing. If I didn't do my logs, I don't think I'd understand anything at all.'

Conclusion

In this brief chapter, we have covered your hopes and fears about becoming a university student, our six-step propositions and the six steps to success. We have argued that good students, like you, are made, not born. If you build SOCCER into your study habits every day, you will have real progress in your study habits.

Review points

By reading this six-step chapter, you should now have an:
- awareness of your own hopes and fears about becoming a student
- awareness that developing your potential as a student will involve you in change
- awareness of the six steps to success, the propositions that shape and inform the rest of the book itself.

Tips checklist

- ☐ Look forward to becoming a student. Enjoy being a student.
- ☐ Help your family and friends to see how important being a student is to you.
- ☐ Have a regular place to study: when you sit there, your body will learn to work.
- ☐ Make some time to study every day: turn off the phone, don't answer the door. Focus.
- ☐ Concentrate for 15-minute blocks at first and build up.
- ☐ Move out of your comfort zone.
- ☐ Practise writing every day.
- ☐ Develop your memory with the revision cycle (pages 274–5).
- ☐ Discover if you like working alone or with other people.
- ☐ Discover if you like working with noise or quiet.
- ☐ Discover if you like working in the morning, afternoon, or evening, or at night.
- ☐ Buy an English dictionary, a subject dictionary and a dictionary of sociological terms.
- ☐ If English isn't your first language, join an academic English class.
- ☐ Buy an exercise book and make your own list of all the new words that you encounter.
- ☐ Buy an exercise book and make your own subject dictionary. Put in the key people of your subject. Put in new theories. Put in the key words, phrases and terms that you will have to use.
- ☐ When you encounter new theories, theorists, words and phrases, write them on Post-its and stick them up all round your home. Take them down when you know them.
- ☐ Practise organising your time: prioritise, make lists, use a diary, use a 24/7 timetable. Sometimes be very organised, and sometimes sit amongst a pile of work and plunge in.
- ☐ Find a study partner, or use online discussion boards.
- ☐ Enjoy studying – do not see it as 'work'.
- ☐ Use deadlines to keep you on track.
- ☐ If unhappy with your spelling, punctuation or grammar, buy a simple grammar book and use it.
- ☐ Keep a small notebook with you at all times. When you have a bright idea or an insight into your subject, write it down.

 **Starting University Life**

STEPHEN PALMER AND ANGELA PURI

What this chapter covers
In this chapter we will briefly look at how leaving for university can impact on family dynamics and affect other relationships you currently have with friends and partners. Going to university is something to look forward to, but it can be stressful if the change is not managed adequately. This chapter addresses ways of maintaining contact with family and friends, and also looks at how to tackle homesickness.

On your way to university!

You did it! After all the hard work and effort you put into getting to university the time has finally arrived! There is a lot to be excited about – it's a new place, with new people and new challenges. However, as with all change and with any adventure, in order to move forward there are always some things you have to leave behind …

… the folks

This may well be the first time you are leaving home and it's likely that there is a part of you that's dying to finally have the freedom and autonomy to do what you want, when you want and where you want. However, you are also leaving the security of what you know, the comfort of your home and the familiarity of your surroundings. There is nothing wrong with feeling a little overwhelmed. Change can feel like a scary place.

In all the excitement, it is also easy to forget how the folks are feeling. It is a big transition for them as well. Whether they joke about it, '*finally we get the spare room we've always wanted*', or lay on the emotional bit, '*I don't know how we are going to manage without you*', it is possible that they are also going to find it a bit strange when you leave. Do keep in touch with them as it may give them some peace of mind.

… the friends

University enables you to meet a variety of different people from all walks of life and this will only help to expand your network of friends, rather than reduce it.

Although you may be anxious about losing touch with your friends, it is likely that they feel the same way as well. So don't forget to take their mobile numbers, email addresses and new contact details to keep in touch.

'Uni is a great place to make new friends but, personally, there is something special about friends that you've known for a long time – they understand you, warts and all! Even now, if I'm really excited about something or if I'm upset or feeling lonely, the first thing I'll do is call my best mate in London. The familiar voice is great to hear and she normally knows what to say to make me feel better!'

Nadia, 19 years, Bristol

… the partners

Leaving behind a loved one is hard, especially if they are not going to university. It's common to hide your excitement or to keep plans about nights out from your partners out of a sense of guilt.

'I'm sure she will feel bad if I talk to her about the party, especially as I had such a great time without her.'

Tom, 19 years, Leeds

It is never wise to make assumptions and an open and honest discussion with your partner about how your relationship may change whilst at university will be far more beneficial. Many couples find that university does not necessarily cause a break-up in relationships, especially if your partner is included in your future plans.

'I had been dating this guy for about six months before starting uni. It wasn't that serious so we agreed to see how things would develop. He was at a London university as well so it wasn't that difficult to meet up. But we made sure we did our own thing too. I think it worked out pretty well … 10 years on and we are now married!'

Amber, 30 years, London

It is not unusual for students to be in a relationship when they join university. But whether a relationship lasts the course of university depends on the strength of your relationship, how you both handle the change and the emphasis you place on being together.

'Clare never went to university and wasn't really that happy when I got my place at Warwick. Once I started uni, we stayed in touch and met up, but as time went on we seemed to have less and less to talk about. I also felt that I was making all the effort to see her, as she never felt that comfortable coming to see me. I think we broke up three months into my first year. I did really like her ... but we both changed and had moved on.'

Jack, 23 years, Warwick

Starting university after completing your gap year

If you have just completed your gap year, leaving home may not cause as many anxieties for you, especially if you went travelling or stayed away from home during that period of time.

However, some gap-year students find it difficult to re-adjust to student life after their year out, feeling they have less in common with the other first-year students. Whether this is because you have been working in an office environment over the past year, or backpacking across Europe, it may feel like you have been experiencing a life that other students may not be able to relate to.

'I'm sure I alienated lots of people when I came back from travelling. Looking back I was really full of myself! I wanted to tell everyone about my adventures in India, Thailand and Australia, and to be honest, whatever they had to say about their summer after A Levels just paled into insignificance! I wasn't trying to be arrogant, I guess I was a bit immature, and I think I was still overwhelmed and excited about what I had actually done. I did eventually stop going on about my travels – but not until I noticed someone rolling their eyes when I said 'when I went travelling ...'

Paul, 21 years, Kingston

Although it is good to share your experiences and there is nothing wrong about being excited about your gap year, it is important to remember that not all first-year students have been in a similar position to yourself and may not share your enthusiasm, so try to limit the number of times you mention your year out, at least until you get to know your friends a bit better!

Some gap-year students also find that settling back after a year of not reading or even touching textbooks, can also cause them stress!

'I'd had one year where I barely wrote anything except the odd email and coming back to an environment where I sat in lectures and wrote notes was completely weird to me!

Marieke, 20 years, Portsmouth

Be prepared for the shock of putting pen to paper again! You may find it useful to get into a studying routine fairly early on. This will reduce the stress and anxiety when the assignments begin to come in, as you will be more prepared to deal with them.

Feeling homesick?

So you have been at university for a while now. The excitement of the freedom and independence might be wearing off a little. Are you fed up washing your own clothes and cleaning up after yourself? Are you missing home-cooked food? Your friends? Or have you just run out of money?

It is quite natural to miss home and adjusting to a new way of living does not happen overnight. It will take time and probably a few trips home to feel more settled.

Here are a few tips to help you along the way:

✓ Ensure that you have a regular method of contacting home which won't dip into your finances (possibly arrange a call card or a pay-as-you-go mobile phone which is used just to call home).

✓ Plan meetings. Arrange dates and times for meeting up with family and friends back home. This will help you to make sure that everyone is free to meet when you go back and gives you a date to look forward to.

✓ Learn a few of your favourite home-cooked recipes so you can make them during term time.

✓ Keep yourself busy. Initially, you may find it a bit of an effort to make friends and to join clubs and societies, yet it is very important to do so. Too much time on your hands can lead you to feel isolated and lonely.

✓ If you are feeling very homesick, it's worth making a trip back home. Many students find that they go home a bit more frequently in their first few terms than they do for the rest of their university years. However, if you find that you feel even worse after you make a trip home, you may benefit from making a conscious effort to stay at university and settle into a routine before going home again.

✓ Make your room feel like your own. Your room is probably very bare when you move in so decorate it in your own style. Display your favourite memorabilia and put up some posters and photos to make the room feel more personable to you. (Check the rules of your accommodation before putting things up on the walls.)

If you're finding it increasingly difficult to adapt to your new surroundings and are becoming depressed, you are not alone! This anxiety is not uncommon for many new students at university. However, if the symptoms of depression appear to be getting worse (such as complete fatigue, losing weight, tearfulness or feelings of hopelessness) and you do not feel you are able to cope, it is advisable to contact you local GP or your student counsellor.

Changes in relationship dynamics when you go to university

In some instances students find that they feel homesick because they are worried or concerned about friends and family back home. This leads to feelings of guilt or anxiety when at university. Whether you are worried about your partner being unable to cope with you being at university or your family falling apart when you leave, it is important to tackle the problem rather than feeing the unwarranted guilt.

Case study **Changing dynamics**

Ian had never lived away from home before moving to university. Although he was enjoying his first few weeks at university, he was very concerned about how his parents would manage without him. His parents had a rocky relationship and this was intensified by his mother's heavy reliance on alcohol. Ian had always been the mediator when they argued and without his presence, Ian was very worried about how they were coping. These thoughts kept him awake at night, and often made him think of packing up and going home.

Ian went home every weekend and called home everyday. However, he often found his mum crying down the phone. Ian was becoming depressed and anxious about what he could do.

Ian wrote down his stressful thoughts and then worked on how to think more positively about the situation. The SIT (stress-inducing thinking) and SAT (stress-alleviating thinking) form that Ian created is shown below.

PROBLEM: Leaving home	
Stress-inducing thinking (SIT)	**Stress-alleviating thinking (SAT)**
• Mum and dad can't manage without me	• They managed before I was born and when I was younger
• I'm being selfish by enjoying myself at university, when they are so upset – I have a duty to look after them!	• They are both adults, and they both went to university – I would resent them both if I went home without completing my degree
• They may end up getting a divorce	• Although I would find that very difficult to cope with, it is their lives and if they are not happy why should I try to keep them together
• Mum is drinking more alcohol and it's my fault. She would be okay if I was at home	• Mum is making her own choices. I will go home this weekend and talk to her again about getting some help. But she shouldn't be that dependent on me. I will call her just once a week. I will be there to support her all the way, but I can't ruin my life just because she is adamant on ruining her own
• Things will change when I go back home	• I am already changing! I'm seeing my family in a new light and enjoying my own independence. I don't even know if I would want to go back to that environment again

© Centre for Stress Management, 2005

Once Ian had clarified his thoughts he was able to tackle the problem more confidently. He discussed the form with his parents, explaining his concerns with them. He explained that he would only call home once a week, although his mother could call him on the mobile if she felt she really needed to. He also explained that he was there to support her if she decided to get help for her alcohol problem.

After the first month, which was very emotionally draining for Ian, things calmed down. His mother stopped calling him as often and was beginning to seek advice for her drinking with his father. When Ian went home over the Christmas holidays, he noticed that his parents had formed a stronger relationship whilst he was gone and they no longer relied on him to sort out their problems.

Ian admitted that he did feel slightly rejected that his importance was now diminished, but he knew they still loved him and he felt less guilty about living his own life at university.

Problems like Ian's are not uncommon. Leaving home can impact on the family dynamics in a number of different ways. If you are concerned about how things will change, you may find it useful to fill in the stress-inducing thinking/stress-alleviating thinking form below. This may help you to clarify your thoughts and can be a useful starting point to discuss your concerns with family or friends.

Have a go! Stress-inducing thoughts/stress-alleviating thoughts

If you are worried about how friends, partners or family members are going to cope without you at home. Or if you are concerned about how moving to university will impact on your relationships, you may find it useful to write down your concerns in the form below and dispute the stressful thought (SIT) with a more rational and helpful response (SAT).

(Continued)

(Continued)

PROBLEM:	
Stress-inducing thinking (SIT)	*Stress-alleviating thinking (SAT)*

© Centre for Stress Management, 2005

Chapter summary

This section deals with the transition from home to university. A few useful tips to help you acclimatise include:

✓ Good communication methods with family and friends back home

✓ Planning ahead

✓ Staying busy at university

✓ Adapting your university environment to make it as comfortable and homely as possible

✓ Confronting concerns about how university will change existing relationships and dynamics

Learning points from the chapter

Use the space below to write down any thoughts or comments you have about this chapter.

Helpful resources

The Site.Org

This website provides factsheets and articles on all the key issues you may face when starting university, including: sex and

relationships; drinking and drugs; work and study; housing; legal and finances problems; and health and well-being.
Weblink: www.thesite.org.uk/workandstudy/studychoices/whatcourse/thewrongcourse

Depression Alliance

Tel: 0845 123 2320 (all calls charged at the local rate)

Depression Alliance is a self-help organisation for people suffering from depression. It provides information, understanding and local self-help groups for the benefit of depression sufferers. Depression Alliance has three offices within the UK:

England

212 Spitfire Studios, 63–71 Collier Street, London N1 9BE
Email: information@depressionalliance.org

Wales

11 Plas Melin, Westbourne Road, Whitchurch, Cardiff CF14 2BT
Email: wales@depressionalliance.org

Scotland

Depression Alliance Scotland, 3 Grosvenor Gardens, Edinburgh EH12 5JU
Email: info@dascot.org

The Samaritans

The Upper Mill, Kingston Road, Ewell, Surrey KT17 2AF
If you are in crisis you can write to the Samaritans: Chris,
PO Box 9090, Stirling FK8 2SA
Use this web address to locate the closest Samaritans branch to you: http://www.samaritans.org.uk/talk/local_branch.shtm

The Samaritans national helpline

UK: 08457 909090 (open 24-hours)
Republic of Ireland: 1850 609090 (open 24-hours)
(All calls charged at local rates)

***How to Cope with the Stress of Student Life.* MIND (2003*).
London: MIND.***

A document with information on the different types of stress you may encounter as a student and how to cope with them.

Weblink: http://www.mind.org.uk/Information/Booklets/How+to/ How+to+cope+with+the+stress+of+student+life.htm

4 Are You on the Right Course?

STEPHEN PALMER AND ANGELA PURI

What this chapter covers
This chapter gives advice on what to do if you realise that you are on the wrong course. Some students find that the course they have chosen does not meet their expectations and this can be a very stressful experience. This chapter offers practical advice and illustrates techniques to help you make the right decision.

Was it the right decision?

So you are beginning to settle down in your accommodation and have had a great few weeks getting introduced to student life. Now it's time to concentrate on the reason you are here – your degree course. But what happens if you find that it is not quite what you were expecting? Statistics show that about one in six students either drop out of university or seriously consider doing so. The primary reason for this was disappointment with their course and that it *wasn't what they expected it to be* (42 per cent). After all the hard work of getting to university, coming to the conclusion that it may be the wrong course for you can be very stressful.

However, if you genuinely feel that your course or your university isn't right for you, you will need to think carefully and act quickly to rectify the situation. Otherwise you may have to wait for the next academic year before you can make any changes.

'I started my course on Business IT and hated it! I couldn't believe how boring it was. Whilst everyone else was settling into their courses and getting to know their way around, I was running around to see what else I could do. The worst part was that I didn't know what I wanted – it was an important decision to make and I didn't have much time. What made it even more stressful was that when I tried to get on to different degrees at my university and at others, the places were all taken! It got sorted out eventually, so it was worth it. But it was horrible at the time.'

Simran, 23 years, Kingston

Talk to parents, friends and tutors to discuss your concerns and work through the possible alternatives. Contacting a trusted teacher from your old school for a chat may also be helpful.

Do your own research as well. Find out about what other courses are available and whether you are eligible for transfer on to a different or more appropriate course. The worst possible approach you can take is to pretend that there isn't a problem (sticking your head in the sand approach) or running around in a constant state of panic (the headless chicken approach), as neither tactic is likely to assist you in making the right decision.

Questions to ask yourself

If you are in a quandary about changing your degree course, ask yourself a few questions to assist you in making your decision.

- Am I feeling homesick or do I actually dislike the course?
- Would I mind taking a year out and attempting to get a place on a more appropriate course next year?
- Do I know what I would like to do instead of this course?
- Have I spoken to the lecturers on my current course to see whether I am overreacting (being the first few weeks of term you may not be into the main part of your syllabus as yet)?
- What other courses are available?
- Do I have enough time to transfer on to another course this year?
- Is there time and spaces available to transfer elsewhere to another university or college?
- Could I have an informal chat with a student in the year above me, who is on this course, to get a better idea of what my course is really like?
- If I decide to change my course, I will need to act quickly. Do I know who are the right people to talk to?

If you feel you have made the wrong choice, it is important to stay positive and think about how you can improve the situation. By staying in a positive frame of mind, thinking constructively (see Chapter 3) and keeping your goal in sight, you are likely to be more successful in achieving your desired outcome.

It is also useful to keep an open mind, remembering all the alternatives that are open to you. A choice form may be a useful way of helping you clarify the situation, as shown in the case study below.

Case study Was it the right decision?

George had been at university for a month before he began to question his motives for being there. The course he was on was not what he had expected but he wasn't sure whether his perception would change with time. George was beginning to settle down at university and was unsure of what he should do. He used a Making Choices form to give him more clarity of the problems he was facing.

Making Choices form

State problem or issue: Changing my degree course	
Pros	**Cons**
I would be able transfer over to a more suitable course	I don't know whether I would enjoy it any more than the one I am on already
I may be able to take a gap year and go travelling until next year	I will lose a year and I probably won't get my act together to go travelling
I could choose a university closer to home	If I do this, I may have to stay at home
I will have the opportunity to meet new people on a different course	It will probably be harder now, as people have probably already established their circle of friends
I could choose a more flexible degree which has more variety in the modules I choose	It is unlikely I will get a place on one of these degree courses now. I will probably have to wait until next year.

© Centre for Coaching, 2005

Using the form gives more clarity to the situation and makes you brainstorm all the potential scenarios so you do not rush into something you are not sure of.

Have a go! Making the right decision

Think about all the options that are currently available to you. Use the Making Choices form to gain a greater insight into the advantages and disadvantages of changing your course now.

Making Choices form

State problem or issue:	
PROS	CONS

Chapter summary

This section looked at what you could do if you feel that the course you are on is not right for you. It included a Making Choices form to help you work out how you are going to deal with the situation.

Learning points from the chapter

If you have any thoughts or comments about this chapter, you can write them down in the space provided below.

[...]

Part 2

DEVELOP YOUR PERSONAL SKILLS

5 What Makes a Good Communicator?

NOEL WILLIAMS

Introduction to the chapter

This chapter offers help on assembling and presenting information. The aim is to help you become a better communicator. It starts by outlining some principles of effective communication [3.1], especially in the academic context, and then applies them to specific presentational tasks, covering:

- writing tasks:

    - essays;
    - reports;
    - summaries;
    - references and bibliographies;
    - personal logs and reviews;

- talking and presenting:

    - as an individual;
    - in a group;
    - in a seminar;

- using information and communication technologies for effective presentation.

3.1 Principles of good communication

3.1.1 Think of the audience

'Audience' is fundamental to communication. You can't communicate unless you have someone to communicate with. For a student of culture or communication, there are three senses in which audience research might be important. You might need to know about:

- audience research within particular theoretical perspectives (e.g. in media theory);
- audience in a professional context (e.g. to determine how to construct a radio broadcast for a particular market);
- audiences you'll communicate with in practice as a student.

These three concerns can overlap, of course. The difference between 'communicating as a professional' and 'communicating as a student' is not a great one, especially for any student who wants to do the best possible job. Nor should theoretical ideas of how audiences work be truly separate from actual communications practice if the theories have any value. But these three concerns represent rather different emphases: either you are considering audience in the relatively narrow and specialist context of yourself as student, or in the slightly wider, but entirely applied, context of yourself as professional communicator, or in the much wider, but also theoretically problematic, universe of 'the nature of audiences'.

Effective communication cannot take place without, in some sense, addressing the needs of the audience. If you don't provide the information readers need, or talk in the way listeners expect, or structure your website so that users can find what they want, then you have failed: little effective communication occurs. So, in an entirely practical sense, the more you know about your audience and their needs, in any given context, the more likely you are to be able to address their specific requirements and therefore to communicate effectively.

Some branches of professional communication, such as technical communication, formalize the process of 'audience analysis' quite strictly, with well-defined processes and practices intended to stipulate exactly what audience requirements are being met by a particular communication (see, e.g., Burnett 2000 and Schriver 1997). More often, however, the process is less formal, less clearly structured, more subjective, and more open to difficulty. This is because audiences are tricky beasts, and dealing with all their needs in appropriate ways can be as much an art form as a professional skill.

Understanding audiences often helps in understanding the forms and processes of communication. One way of approaching the question of genre for example, is in terms of audience expectations: a genre can be seen as a constrained form of communication where the constraints have been established (usually through a historical process) by a sort of negotiation between audience and a series of originators.

As a practising communicator, one of the best lessons you can learn is that effectiveness depends on satisfying audience needs, which generally also means according with their expectations. Remember, though, that expectations are not necessarily tightly constrained, and can be successfully violated (usually in satisfying some 'higher order' expectation). In certain kinds of communication, it is perfectly possible to be creative, novel or different and thereby be more effective than would have been achieved by merely following the 'rules' which seem to be conventionally defined.

For example, films which merely follow the conventions tend to be mediocre. The film which does something just a little different, exploiting rather than merely satisfying the conventions, often has the most powerful effect. This is because audiences generally go to films to be entertained, and part of contemporary western entertainment is surprise or shock, through novelty and variety.

Compare this with a commercial report, where expectations can be quite limited (even to the point where major organizations establish 'house styles' and templates which every writer is supposed to follow). Violating the expectations here is a much riskier business, because there is no audience requirement for novelty or creativity: the primary audience requirements for a report are that it should contain useful information and that it should provide that information in the most succinct and coherent way. People do not want to read reports, but they have to. So the shorter the report the better; the less work demanded of the reader the better. Originality in the structure or presentation of a report is counter-productive.

Analysing the audience can therefore be critical to any practical work you do. But understanding audience analysis is also very important in the theoretical debates about communication in general. Are the audience merely passive receivers of information? Are they receptors, readily persuaded and influenced by propaganda and advertising? Or do they engage more actively, more critically, in more sophisticated interactions with the messages they are sent?

3.1.2 Address audience expectations

Whatever form of communication you are using, your audience will have certain expectations and assumptions about that communication. These expectations can be of different kinds, namely:

- fundamental;
- training;
- conventional;
- personal;
- contextual.

Fundamental expectations   These are the basic expectations your audience will have about your communication, assuming that it is intended as an effective communication of a particular kind. For example, they will expect that you will make sense, that you will be using the language they speak, that you will follow the conventions of that language, and so on.

Expectations by training   We are all trained to read and hear in particular ways. One fundamental tenet of much media, communication and cultural studies work is that there is no natural communication, but that it is all culturally determined.

We learn, for example, to read bold text as more important than the text surrounding it, to hear differences in intonation across the same sentence as signifying 'statement' or 'question', and to see graphics that are close to each other on the page as linked. The good communicator recognizes the educational and cultural background of the audience, and tailors her or his communication to fit that background.

Expectations by convention   These aren't really separate from the previous ones. Rather it's a different way of looking at expectations. Every communicative form or genre exists partly by virtue of the conventions that it operates. As a simple example, a limerick is a limerick by virtue of the fact that it has five lines, that it has the rhyme scheme AABBA (i.e. lines 1, 2 and 5 rhyme, and lines 3 and 4 rhyme), that it has a humorous generally nonsensical intent, and that it has a particular rhythm (rather too complex to elaborate here). In fact, you only have to say 'There once was a man from Caerphilly' to bring all those expectations to the fore. In a similar way, we expect an index to be at the back of an academic textbook, a headline to summarize the story that follows it, a lecture to begin with a statement of its topic, and so on.

So the good communicator knows the conventions of the genre, and uses them appropriately. Some of these conventions can be learned quite explicitly (such as rules for clear report writing). Others are more subtle, and learned by practise and experiment as much as by explicit lessons in 'rules': essay writing is more like this.

Personal expectations   The first three sets of expectations I've given here are not too difficult to work with. Being a good communicator means knowing the conventions and traditions of the particular forms, and therefore the likely expectations of the audience. By developing your knowledge of these, you develop your communicative skills.

However, all individuals in your audiences will have particular experience of these forms, to a greater and lesser extent, and these experiences may be quite particular, and could affect the value of your communication quite profoundly. At one extreme, there may be members of the audience who are completely unfamiliar with the particular type of communication: quite literally, they do not know what to expect. In general, it's good practice to identify these people before you begin, so you can deal with their particular needs, perhaps separating them from the more experienced members of your audience (e.g. an information brochure may have an introductory section for complete novices on 'how to use this brochure').

At the other extreme, you may have an audience made up of many different kinds of individual with radically different experiences of the form you are using. You can see this, for example, if you try to gather people's opinions of what makes a 'good' website. Everyone's experience of the Internet is very different, often very personal, driven by their particular needs but also by their particular experiences. What they see as 'good' communication through a website will also depend very much on what they have so far experienced as bad communication.

With small audiences, dealing with personal differences in expectation is not too difficult. For example, a presentation to a small seminar group can be designed so that it begins by asking key questions of each member of the audience, or tailors itself so that specific issues known to be of interest to each member are addressed. But with a large audience, if members come from very different backgrounds, it is a major task to communicate effectively with all of them. Too low a level will patronize the experienced. Too high a level will confuse the novice.

The best advice for complex audiences is not to have them! Wherever possible, try to deal with the different subsections of the audience separately – give them what they need in the form which is most appropriate to them. This may mean different documents for different people; or perhaps structuring your talk so that you expect some people to leave half-way through. If you have no opportunity for separating a heterogeneous audience into smaller, more coherent audiences, then you have to include in the communication different elements which will satisfy the expectations of each different sub-group. This means that your communication has multiple structures, containing different information in different forms for different people at different points. In a complex discourse such as a multimedia CD-ROM or a website, this is not too difficult to achieve. In a single written document or a talk, it's much harder.

With a written document, the best way is to provide the different kinds of information in different clearly identified places, and show each kind of sub-audience what the purpose of each of those different places is. For example, you might use boxed text to give 'additional detail for people unused to the topic', or you might have an introductory section at the start of each chapter with a general account for 'people who simply want an overview'. A talk is harder, because every member of the audience experiences all parts of it, no matter what their needs. But you can use visual aids to cover the differences in need, and you might also consider ways in which the differences in the audience can be used as a resource: for example, you might offer moments in the talk in which the experts can offer their expertise to the novice.

Contextualized expectations Within any communicative context, the communication itself can be used to create and satisfy expectations in particular ways. For example, if a document says that it is a 'Reference Guide', the reader will expect that it contains information in separable sections that are not to be read in a linear way from beginning to end. If an essay says 'firstly I will discuss the development of print as mass communication, and then I will contrast this with the development of television', then reader expectations have been created which will lead to confusion or frustration if unsatisfied (see also [3.1.7]).

But if the writer does not use such phrases in the document, the reader may not read it with the correct expectation. So guiding readers may not merely help *them* to understand what you have written, it can also help *you*. It makes the reader more likely to read your document or attend to your talk in the way you want them to. The more guidance you give them on how to read your text, the more likely it will be read in the 'right' way.

By telling readers what to expect, you can alter their expectations.

3.1.3 Prepare for a critical audience

Any audience with an academic purpose is likely to assume a critical attitude to your work. The heart of academic activity is reading (or listening) critically. You can be reasonably certain that *any* audience will be actively considering what you say, no matter why they have your communication. Audiences are not passive receivers of information, even if they often appear to be that way:

- They will be assessing your communication against their own purposes and against any criteria you've set up (such as: 'is what he's saying relevant to what he said he would talk about?').
- They will skip some parts of your writing if it seems familiar, redundant, uninteresting or irrelevant.
- They will slide down the attention curve no matter what your presentation offers.

Good communicators know that their audience will engage in variable ways with their communication. So they learn as much as they can about the following:

- communication processes which may apply (e.g. that offering a structure to readers can reduce confusion by guiding them through your document);
- reader psychology (e.g. recognizing that variety raises attention);
- document conventions and rules (e.g. knowing which features of a document readers will expect to see, and which can be dropped).

Audiences may vary in many ways. The trick is to recognize the variations which might matter, and ignore those which won't. Market research often records demographic information, such as age, occupation, educational background, socio-economic group or class. These can be relevant variables. For example, you must pitch your communication to the educational level of your audience, and, if it varies, find ways of communicating with people who have different kinds of understanding of your material.

However, other variables may turn out to be more important. Attitudinal variables, such as the beliefs, values and ideologies of the audience, may seriously affect how they interpret your messages. For example, very few political speeches are heard in a neutral or objective way: they are heard by someone with a particular political background as spoken by someone with a different political background. Some audiences go to some speakers only to hear messages they want to hear (few unconverted people go to religious rallies); others go only to object to the opinions of a speaker.

In the same way, people's attitudes to the position you are taking in your writing may affect how they read it. If you are writing an essay for a tutor who you know strongly believes in Marxist approaches to cultural theory, and you begin by asserting that Marx was clearly mistaken, you have probably started on the wrong foot. If you want to argue that Marxism has serious defects, then, for this audience, you will have to work up to it carefully, and assemble a gradual and extremely watertight case, and you will probably want to argue that 'Marxism may exhibit some weaknesses', a rather gentler case, than boldly assert that the reader's beliefs are wrong!

Environmental factors can also be important. These are external factors which might affect the way a reader reads. In the case of an examiner marking assignments, for example, the time that the marker has, and the other work he or she has marked on the same subject, will affect how your work is read. So bear the marker's situation in mind when writing if you want to get the best marks you can. If you've done the same as the other students (used roughly the same sources, not checked the grammar, roughly reproduced the lecture on the topic), and that marker has only twenty minutes to mark your five-page essay, your essay will be marked much like the other twenty.

For this reason, anything you can do to make the marker's task easier is likely to reward you and get slightly better marks. The better your presentation, the more readable it is, the better disposed will the harassed marker feel towards it. The more you set yourself apart from the average student essay, the more likely yours will be seen as better. For example, if you have not simply reproduced the information from the lecture; if you have sought out sources others have not used; if you have taken a slightly different slant on the topic; if you have organized your material in a novel way – all these can pay off in positive marks.

3.1.4 Research the audience

All the factors discussed above suggest that the better your information on the audience, the better your communication is likely to be. So part of your task as a communicator is to find out as much as you can about that audience. As a student, this is often quite easy: you know exactly who is going to read your work, your subject tutor. But are you certain of this? In my university, for example, usually the subject tutor is the marker but a sample of assignments are second marked by another tutor. Any problematic assignments may also be seen by an external examiner, a member of another university, responsible for checking the quality of the course.

And, of course, your assignment may be to write for an audience other than your tutor, for a hypothetical audience of some kind (e.g. if you are asked to write a business report, or create a curriculum vitae for future job hunting). In these cases you are supposed to be acting as a professional communicator, so information on your supposed audience may be essential for success. Indeed, finding out about, and responding to, the needs of that hypothetical audience may be a key strand of the assignment. Yet, at the same time, you are still being assessed by your academic audience. So here you would be writing for two distinct audiences, one of which is assessing the way you are writing for the other.

All of this suggests that you need some system for approaching the 'typical' writing task. Here are some key questions to ask yourself early in a writing task, to help clarify what you need to do:

- Do I have one dear audience, or several, with different needs or requirements?
- What does my audience want from my document?
- What does my audience already know, what do they need to know, and, therefore, what do I need to tell them?
- What are the benefits my audience will get from reading my document (compared with not reading it, and compared with reading other competing documents)?
- What problems, if any, can I solve for the reader in the way that I write?

The basic rule? Try to design all your communications to give the audience the information they need in a way that best meets their needs and objectives.

3.1.5 Be clear about the purpose

Any communication addresses a purpose. Usually there are several. Try to make sure that you are as clear as possible about all the purposes of your document or talk, and that you address all of them in the way you design your communication. Recognize that there are three people, or groups of people, whose purposes your communication might be addressing:

- your own purposes;
- the person who commissioned the document or talk;
- the people who will receive the document or talk.

For a typical student essay, your purpose is generally to get good marks, the 'commissioner' is your tutor, and the person receiving the document is probably also the tutor. Your tutor's purpose will primarily be to assess your knowledge of the topic and your associated academic skills, but there might also be other purposes, such as 'make the assignment easy to mark' or 'experiment with a new form of assessment'. You also may have purposes other than getting the marks: you might want seriously to learn about the topic; or it may be relevant to some practical aspect of your non-academic life (e.g. you want to get a job in public relations, so you choose an essay on that topic).

In a professional communications context, 'your own purposes' may include those of the group you belong to, such as the organization you represent or the work team you are in. The 'commissioner' will be a client or customer, and again may be either a particular individual, or a group or organization of some kind. Clients often commission documents for other people (e.g. manufacturers commission advertisers to communicate with consumers).

In all these cases, be as clear as you can about what you are trying to do through the document. Recognize also that the purposes of different interested parties may conflict. For example, your tutor's purpose may be to give you a really difficult testing assignment, but your purpose may be to spend as little time on it as possible (not good practice if you want a 2:1!). Or, professionally, a government department may commission you to report positively on consultation you feel was actually negative. Such conflicts raise ethical issues beyond the scope of this book. They will occur.

You do not have to put these observations in the piece itself (although often it helps if the introduction outlines what the communication is supposed to achieve). In some cases, you definitely do not want to make some purposes clear to other people: for example, if your purpose is to do the minimum amount of work, or to prove to your boss that you are a good employee. But it can be a useful exercise for you to write out clearly, for yourself, what you are expecting to achieve through the communication, and to use this private statement as a checklist during writing, to see how well you are doing what you set out to do.

Think about what you are trying to do in your document, that is, how you are going about the task of getting your marks. What, precisely, do you want to show in your document? What skills and knowledge do you wish to exhibit? Are you trying to:

- show how knowledgeable you are about the topic?
- prove that you have done a lot of relevant reading?
- produce a professional looking document of the highest visual quality?
- impress with your skills in argument?
- show that you are an adept writer with a good turn of phrase?

Positive answers to any of these questions would require you to do quite particular things in your work.

3.1.6 Use good information

To communicate well, you need to abstract and summarize from all the sources available to you, being selective and analytical in the information fragments you choose to include. Good information has as many of the following properties as possible:

- relevant to the topic in general;
- relevant to the specific point being made;
- appropriate to audience expectations and needs;
- drawn from an authoritative source;
- objective, or drawn from objective data;

- up to date;
- precise and unambiguous;
- clearly and succinctly expressed;
- clearly connected to other points in the discussion.

3.1.7 Structure your information appropriately

Any study of communication shows that there are many different ways that information can be structured. As a practical communicator you need to decide why you might use a particular structure. Broadly speaking, there are three dimensions of choice:

- to address a writer's purpose;
- to address the reader's purpose;
- to fit with expectations (e.g. to fit the norms for a particular genre).

Obviously this means you need to know three things when deciding how to structure your information, and we can summarize these needs as principles of good document design.

- Know what your document is for. (What do you want to achieve in the document?)

  - Are you promoting, persuading, informing, requesting?
  - Are you aiming for everyone, or people with particular interests?

- Think of the reader's purpose. (What do the readers want to get out of it?)

  - Why do they have your document?
  - Why will they want your information?

- Design for different tasks. (What are the normal expectations for this kind of writing? Will different readers have different expectations?)

  - Help readers find what they might want.
  - Offer different routes for different needs.
  - Address the *particular* aim(s).

When you create a structure for your document, the building blocks of your structure are not sentences, or paragraphs, but something more like 'information fragments' or 'chunks of information'. The sentences and paragraphs that you produce are representations of these fragments in some sort of coherent order. The pieces of information that you have gathered through your sensitive and detailed research should be turned into 'bite-sized' chunks, where each chunk is a single idea or piece of information that can be understood in one go. What counts as a single chunk of information obviously depends on your audience. If you are writing about perception for five year olds, then a sentence of four words might be a single chunk. The same topic for postgraduate researchers might be a paragraph or a page.

When you have a series of meaningful chunks, your job is to take them all and weave them together into something which can stand as a unified, coherent document. So as well as the information pieces you are presenting, you need to 'link elements' that effectively join things together. Linguists refer to such elements as devices for 'coherence' and 'cohesion'. You achieve 'coherence' by making sure your writing connects properly, consistently and reliably to the outside world. If you cite a fact, make sure it is true. If you give a reference, make sure it is correct. If you report an opinion, make sure it is accredited and accurately reported.

You achieve 'cohesion' by fastening the different parts of your argument together sequentially in a logical way, often by using 'clue words', such as connectives. Weak student writers realize that they have to use such words, but do not always understand how to use them. Strong students realize not only that they have to use them well, but also that they are creating 'signposts' for the reader by using such words. These are contextual clues which set up expectations about structure which, as I've just suggested above, guide the reader on how to read the information you are presenting. Table 5.1 gives a few simple hints on use of some of them, but there are many other phrases you may use in your writing which serve to connect different parts of the writing together. Effectively they 'point', like a signpost, to some parts of the writing, or some relationship between those parts. If you use these phrases, as you should, check each time that you have used them appropriately. Examples include:

- 'Firstly': Writers sometimes forget to give a 'secondly'.
- 'In conclusion': Make sure it really is a conclusion, not a new argument or observation, and not followed by other new material.
- 'As I've said above/below': Make sure you really have said it, and not removed it in editing, or said something else. Also, preferably refer to the explicit page or section where it was said.
- 'To summarize': Make sure the following text briefly restates what preceded it.

More generally, you can also help readers through a document by telling them explicitly how it is constructed. For example:

- Show them the value of information.
- Explain why the information will be useful.
- Show them what the benefits might be.
- Tell them how the document works:
  - what it contains;
  - how it is organized;
  - how to use it.

Table 5.1   *Clue words and connectives*

Clue word or connective	Explanation	Example
and	This is a 'weak' connection. The more you use 'and', the more your writing seems like a list rather than a progression. Only use it if you really have nothing better to offer.	Weak: Gaze is a natural form of communication and everyone uses gaze. Better: Everyone uses gaze because it is a natural form of communication.
because	States causality, so make sure there is a causal relationship between the two linked statements. As we saw in Chapter 2, use of words like 'because' does not necessarily lead to logical connection. Make sure the reasoning is clear.	Weak: Myth tells us much about culture because myths are stories. Better: Myth tells us much about culture because myths are stories created and maintained by social groups, not by individuals.
Therefore, consequently, so	States that the current clause or sentence follows *necessarily* from the previous one. The reader's automatic reaction is 'does this really follow?' If the connection is not self-evident, then there may be a case for an additional explanatory statement.	Weak: Chomsky's theories focused on grammatical models. Therefore, they were little use in real social situations. Better: Chomsky's theories focused on grammatical models, with no consideration of social context. Therefore, they were little use in real social situations.
However	Indicates a contrast or opposition between two statements. Make sure they actually are opposed or clearly contrasted.	Weak: Email offers versatile communication. However, phones are also versatile. Better: Email offers versatile communication. However, phones are not as versatile.
On the other hand, whereas, nevertheless, however	Indicates a contrast or opposition between two statements, but the opposition between them may be more to do with the way the writer is presenting them (to make a point) than with any inherent opposition. So, make sure that it is clear to the reader how you think they contrast, what your rationale is.	Weak: On the one hand, Peirce invented semiotics. On the other hand, it was Barthes. Better: On the one hand, Peirce could be said to have invented semiotics, because of his account of different kinds of signs. On the other hand, Barthes could also be said to be semiotics' inventor, because he showed how semiotic analysis could be applied in a wide range of different situations.

Table 5.1 *(Continued)*

Clue word or connective	Explanation	Example
also, moreover, in addition	Introduces additional points which are similar to that just made, probably reinforcing it.	Weak: Fairclough uses Hallidayan linguistics. Also, Fairclough's work is very influential.
		Stronger: Fairclough uses Hallidayan linguistics. Also, Fairclough's work draws on other linguists.

3.1.8 Answer questions through your structure

There are many possible ways that you can structure a presentation, whether spoken or written. However, if no obvious structure suggests itself, a useful way of thinking is in terms of a 'question and answer' approach.

Because communication is essentially two-way, even when it appears to be only one-way thinking in terms of the two sides of the communication can be a useful way of getting a handle on the way to do it. Effectively you are thinking of your communication as a dialogue: the reader asks questions and you provide the answers. By recognizing that your readers will be *actively* interrogating your document and taking a critical attitude to it [3.1.3], and by anticipating the kinds of critiques and questions they will ask, you can build a structure designed to forestall their queries, and deal with them.

Questions can be used in different ways in your writing. A direct method is to question the reader, which you can find most obviously in documents like advertisements of the 'Do you suffer from dandruff?' kind. Such a question lets the audience define itself: only those who answer 'yes' will bother to read the rest of the advert.

More subtle versions incorporate a persuasive element, such as 'Do you want to look younger?' too which few people will answer 'no'. Politicians use this approach as a rhetorical device for controlling interviews or directing the audience in political rallies, for example 'Do we want a country where gun crime increases every year?' The answer to the question, of course, is generally the product, service or political party you are trying to advocate. If you need to write a persuasive document of some kind, this can be a useful technique.

More often, as a student, you will be providing informative rather than persuasive documents. Questions can still be used as a structuring method. In an explicitly informative document, such as a brochure or report, which seeks to answer the readers' questions, you can do this quite explicitly by using those questions as headings, and the body text as answers. For example, in an investigative report:

What was the problem?
How was it tackled?
What were the outcomes?

However, for the bulk of student writing, and for much of the subtler kind of professional writing, keeping the questions implicit can work just as well, and make structured writing a relatively simple task. In a book called *The Pyramid Principle,* Barbara Minto expands this idea into a complete method for report writing. In essence, she advocates a six-stage approach, which can work for essays and other kinds of writing as well as reports (Minto 1991).

Stage 1. Create your 'thesis statement'. This is the key point your essay or report is going to make, the 'thesis' it is advancing. It should be a single sentence that summarizes the key thrust of your argument, such as:

> The account of discourse analysis given by psychologists cannot be reconciled with Foucault's account of discourse.

Stage 2. Consider what the readers' questions might be in response to such a statement. For example:

- What is the psychologists' account of discourse analysis?
- What is Foucault's account of discourse?
- Why can the two accounts not be reconciled?

Stage 3. For each of these questions, write an answer. For example:

Psychologists use the term 'discourse analysis' to mean the analysis of conversation. Foucault sees all human activity as discourses.
Conversation analysis only works for one kind of communication, but Foucault wants an approach which works for all kinds.

Stage 4. Anticipate the reader's questions for each of the answers you have provided, such as:

- Don't psychologists use 'discourse' in other ways?
- Aren't there activities that Foucault does not regard as discourse?
- Why does Foucault see all activity as discourse?
- Why does Foucault want an approach that works for all kinds of communication?

Stage 5. Continue in this way, generating answers to these questions, and then guessing the audience's response to these, until you have a 'complete' outline of your essay.
It might be difficult to know when it is complete, but indications will be as follows:

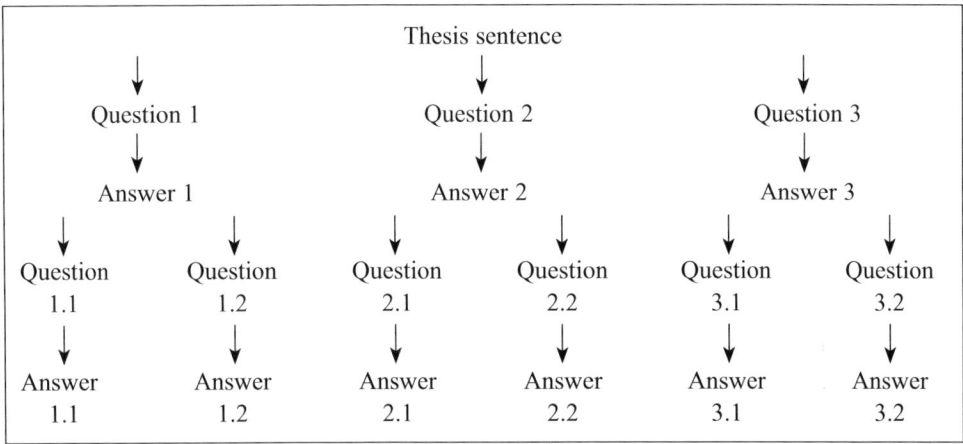

Figure 5.1   *Hierarchical structure created by questions and answers*

- You can't think of any more questions readers might have.
- Your audience probably already know the answers that you are generating.
- The kinds of questions and answers you are generating seem likely to be patronizing to the audience that you've identified.
- There's 'enough' material.

What you should produce by this method is a pyramid structure, something like Figure 5.1.

Stage 6. Rewrite the outline as proper prose. This generally is not too difficult if your sequence of questions and answers makes sense, because you simply trace the argument through the text you write. For example:

> In this essay I am going to argue that the account of discourse analysis given by psychologists cannot be reconciled with Foucault's account of discourse. Psychologists generally use the term 'discourse analysis' to mean the analysis of conversation, although more recent work has extended the use of the term somewhat. But in Foucault's account, all human activity, all communication, is seen as discourse. So no single approach to analysis will work.

You can perhaps see in this brief example not only how the outline can be turned into prose, but also how much of this happens by translating the structural relationships in the outline (the pyramid) into connective clue words of the kind discussed in [3.1.7]. The questions and answers are related to one another through words like 'although', 'but' and 'so', which represent the links between different parts of the structure.

In other words, the question and answer approach uses the needs of the audience to devise an argument structure, and as a result it creates prose which should use clue words appropriately, and thereby stand up to the tests of critical analysis.

3.1.9 Make appropriate stylistic choices

Stylistics is a branch of linguistics, which you may study as part of your degree. It looks at language variation, the conscious and unconscious choices we make when using language for different purposes, different audiences and different situations.

When you write or talk you are always making choices: there is *always* another way to say what you want to say. If there is not another word with the meaning you want, there'll be a phrase. If there isn't a phrase, you can construct a variant sentence. The choices you select should be appropriate to the audience and purpose, as you've identified them [3.1.4], and those choices usually mean you will be aiming to write or talk within a particular genre or style of communication. You want to make sure that all the choices fit that overall style, and that all those choices are consistent with each other.

However, there are also general principles that you can seek to apply in choosing language, to get clear communication. These principles are generally grouped together under the heading 'Plain English' (see Collisons et al. 1992, Cutts and Maher 1986).

Usually, by 'Plain English', people mean something like 'language which can be understood easily by most people, using words and structures that the average speaker of English would be familiar with'. In other words, you shouldn't need any special education in order to be able to understand it. It does not necessarily mean informal or chatty language, as these can also have their own weaknesses and restrictions. For example, consider chatty text messages whose conventions are by no means 'plain', in using weird spellings like 'nel' for 'anyone' and odd abbreviations like 'CWOT' for 'complete waste of time'.

Most people's writing can be improved by applying some of the principles of Plain English. To highlight these principles, consider first the following example paragraph. It's not a real quotation, but it is based very closely on an actual document I came across. Read it for meaning, then read it again, critically, thinking about how it might be improved with clarity and the audience in mind.

As an exciting new innovation within the University, it has been decided that selection of degree programme will be made by full-time and part-time students at the culmination of Level 1, thereby enabling deferral of informed choice, creating improved flexibility of provision and facilitating more effective employment of available resources.

You might try re-writing it to see what kinds of changes you can make which would improve it. Each of the changes you propose is a *choice,* a selection of one form of language over another. The writer of this document chose one form. You are identifying other possibilities. This is how you should always look at your own writing and speech. Ask: Is there a clearer way to say this? Is there a way of presenting which is more helpful to my readers? Is there a choice which fits the tone better? Could the writing be simpler, without patronizing people?

Before outlining some principles, let me suggest a possible way of re-writing the example paragraph which produces plainer, clearer English; language which is easier to understand:

> The University has decided that students will choose their degree programmes at the end of Level 1. This lets:
>
> - students wait to choose a degree
> - the University offer more choices
> - departments use resources more effectively

What kinds of things have I done here? Obvious ones are as follows:

- Reduce the overall number of words.
- Use words which are more familiar to the reader.
- Remove repetition and redundancy.
- Reduce the complexity of sentence structure.
- Organize the text on the page so the structure is clearer.
- Use shorter words.
- Use shorter sentences.

All of these choices made separately might improve a text, and they tend to go hand in hand. In particular, if you just apply the last two principles, you are likely to improve writing, because shorter words tend to be more familiar, and shorter sentences tend to be more straightforward. However, if you apply any of the principles mechanically, you can still end up with poor writing. After all, the shortest words in the shortest sentences would be 'I.A.', but this makes no kind of sense. Familiarity is sometimes more important than length: which would you find easiest to define, *television* or *id?*

Slightly less obvious choices, which perhaps require a little knowledge of language to recognize, are:

- Reduce the number of abstract words.
- Change the passive voice to the active voice.
- Remove nominalizations.

These three bullets use linguists' jargon (i.e. they are not Plain English!) to name three things which are easiest to understand by example. So here goes.

Most of the time we communicate in the active voice: it's the most direct form. We find it most familiar, and easiest to understand. A sentence like:

Janet phoned Julian.

is simple, childlike, unproblematic. We know who was doing something, what they were doing, and who (or what) they were doing it to.

But we can turn such a sentence into an equivalent passive:

Julian was phoned by Janet.

The same information is here, but it has been transformed. The sentence is longer, with two extra words, and the relationship between Janet and Julian in the sentence has changed so that Julian comes first, making him seem more important in the sentence.

Noam Chomsky suggested that passive sentences are 'transformations' of underlying active sentences, that is, that people somehow 'translate' passive sentences into underlying active ones to make sense of them. This means that understanding passive sentences takes more work: we have to do the translation. Some work by cognitive psychologists suggests that this is actually the case: it takes us longer to process a passive sentence than the equivalent active sentence. And this makes sense, because passives generally seem less intuitive and contain more words.

But passives also allow two things: agent deletion and increased abstraction. 'Agent deletion' means 'getting rid of the agent, the person who performed the action'. We can get rid of Janet from the passive, and it still makes sense, but we can't do that for the active equivalent:

Julian was phoned.

– that makes sense,

phoned Julian.

– that doesn't make sense.

This use of the passive, where the agent is deleted, is typical of writing that wants to appear objective, such as scientific, military and government writing, which effectively hides the agent, suggesting that the person doing the thing is unimportant. 'The bunsen burner was lit and a test tube was placed over it and there was an explosion.' This sounds as if nobody was responsible. The positive aspect of agent deletion is that it focuses entirely on the process, and ignores the agent (so scientists can argue that science is true no matter who held the test tube: the positivist view).

The negative aspect is obvious. By hiding the agent, you construct actions without people in them, and raise questions which can't be answered in the sentence, about responsibility. For example:

Communications were carried out and it was decided that all students would now pay double fees.

Whom do we protest to? The people who 'communicated' and 'decided' are hidden behind their passive sentence.

Passive sentences are often more abstract, therefore a bit vaguer, because they omit the agent, or because they obscure the relationship between agent and action, or because they lead to a *nominalization*. A nominalization occurs when a word for an action (a verb) is turned into a noun, such as turning 'separate' into 'separation' or 'communicate' into 'communication'. You'll notice that nominalizing lengthens the word, and it usually adds '-ion', making the concept more abstract.

Communication was held with Julian.

The rule of thumb is: 'if you find a nominalization, turn it back into the underlying verb'. Doing this usually makes you consider the active version of the sentence, and the agent, and whether there is a simpler way of expressing their relationship, such as:

Janet talked to Julian.

Table 5.2 below gives some things to look for in choosing clearer language, with a checklist question you can ask yourself as you review your own writing. And here are some guidelines which are likely to produce better writing:

- Choose language with the readers in mind. Avoid jargon. If you have to use technical terms, make sure your readers understand them, so give definitions or a glossary if needed.
- Be simple and direct. Avoid complexity.
- Remove unnecessary or redundant words.
- Be as specific as possible, avoid abstraction.
- Remove any emotive or imprecise words.
- Avoid abbreviations and acronyms that the readers will be unfamiliar with. Give unusual abbreviations in full on the first occasion of use, and explain them if necessary.
- Avoid ambiguous expressions and images (such as icons, which are hard to understand).

Table 5.2 *Clues to difficult language*

Long words	Are there any shorter, or more familiar words that would do the same job?
Long sentences	Can any words be cut out of the sentence? Could it be turned into two equivalent but shorter sentences?
Words ending in '-ion'	These are often verbs turned into nouns (nominalizations). Write a more direct sentence by turning it back to a verb.
Consider who is doing what	Can you tell who carried out each action? Or are they 'hidden' from you? If hidden, then consider more direct language.

 # Cultivating Organisational Skills

DAVID MCILROY

KEY CONCEPTS

● ORGANISATION ● PLANNING ● AUGMENTING ABILITY ● CONSCIENTIOUS BEHAVIOUR ● METHODICAL PRACTICE ● CAREER TRAINING ● TIME-MANAGEMENT ● DIVISION OF LABOUR ● TROUBLESHOOTING ● DIAGNOSTIC TOOLS ● FILING SYSTEMS ● PAST PAPERS ● STRATEGIES FOR DIFFICULT MATERIAL ● TIME FOR LIVING ● MANAGING PRESSURE

Achievements require organisation and planning

A WIDE DIVERSITY OF EVIDENCE

In all spheres of life there is evidence of planning, for it is clear that little that is worthwhile can be accomplished without it. Archaeologists have unearthed masses of evidence that ancient civilisations were adept in planning and building their well-structured and efficiently functioning cities. Whether the enterprise is for the family's weekly menu or for the holiday next summer, planning always figures in the process. Sports teams plan for the new season but may be flexible enough to vary their tactics according to the opposition on a given occasion. The news media plan how they will arrange and present the news each day and those who control air traffic have to plan for arrival times, departure times, delays, diversions etc. for each runway.

Planning is of course of little avail unless the plans are carried out – there must be organisation and implementation, but planning is an essential starting point. Some people prefer to document their plans in a diary or notebook, but others opt to conceive and conceal their plans within their own minds. If individuals are likely to lose track of their plans, they would be best advised to keep a diary, and students can easily let plans lapse because of the multiple pressures within limited time frames. The purpose of a diary is defeated unless it is checked every day. Students who have arrived at college or university must have proved their planning and organising capabilities to some extent. However, fresh and renewed thought is likely to be needed in order to raise these qualities to the level where maximum benefit is returned for effort invested. Researchers have claimed that factors such as planning, organisation and motivation are the kinds of qualities that make the difference between good and poor students (Bouffard, Boisvert, Vezeau & Larouche, 1995).

Organisation saves frustration

Example

Some people regularly spend a lot of time looking for their keys before they leave their house! This problem can be simply remedied by choosing a place to hang the keys as soon as the individual enters the house. In that way time is not wasted and frustration is eliminated (both for the individuals concerned and those who may have to wait on them). It can be so easy to misplace a watch, a pen, a ring, a purse, a wallet etc. When this is happening regularly it is time to take measures to prevent it! At university students can save themselves a lot of time, frustration, waste and inefficiency by developing simple and regular habits. For example, a good filing system that keeps all relevant notes together in a logical order within one folder for each module will save endless exasperation. Or a little note enclosed in a textbook to remind a student of the page number, paragraph number and relevance of a particular passage may later prove priceless. If a student is working in the library and stumbles across an article that he or she knows will later be useful, then a careful note should be made about the title, author, reference and relevance of the article. This practice will be especially useful if the note is made in a notebook that is used for the module to which the article is relevant. Students may later waste precious revision time because they have lost track of an article that they desperately need. Moreover, a failure to 'fill in the blanks' from notes taken in a lecture at some point soon after the lecture may lead to the intent behind the shorthand being 'evaporated'. A key to success at university is applying the truth of the adage that 'A stitch in time saves nine'.

Some students may fear being perceived by others as a drudge or 'nerd' or robot. This image projection can be avoided by taking some time to socialise, to enjoy some fun with others and by being supportive of other students in their studies. In reality the person who plans well and is sufficiently organised to carry out their plans, can find time to do things to supplement their academic life. However, this is all a matter of prioritising – it is necessary to resolve to be applied to academic work, and then to have fun in the time left over (not vice-versa). Too many late nights and too much over-indulgence too often may throw the whole body clock out of rhythm. Grades may suffer and career ambitions may not be realised if students are unable to regulate their lives.

On the other hand it is important to take breaks and to factor these into the planned scheme for each new week. A car will not continue to run efficiently unless it is given a regular service. No student will function to their potential unless they break from their studies, have times of relaxation and engage in pursuits that will take their mind away from their academic work. These times serve to 'recharge the battery' and then the student can return to study feeling fresh and reinvigorated. Students should ensure that they have a good break at holiday time, at weekends and some short breaks in between study periods. They can learn to alternate smoothly between study and rest, work and fun. Many contemporary students find it necessary to have part-time work, and although this has some disadvantages, it has the clear advantage of diverting the mind from academic pressures.

A lesson from the four seasons

In recent years there has been much discussion about the alleged effects of global warming on climate changes and the overlap in seasonal patterns. However, in spite of the alleged change to extremes in temperature, rainfall etc., it is still possible to observe the characteristic differences between the seasons. There are regular times in the year when the flowers start budding, the birds start nesting or when birds migrate or animals go into hibernation. Each season – autumn, winter, spring and summer – serves its purpose for the growth, renewal, decline and rejuvenation of nature. The animal kingdom knows how to adapt behaviours according to the season of the year. Likewise humankind also adapts according to the season in terms of dress, food, sport, leisure, work (for example, construction), holidays etc.

In a similar kind of way, various 'seasons' come and go in the academic calendar at university. First, there is the season of initiation when the student learns to get adjusted to the new world of academia, then there is the season of preparation for assignments when it seems that the student's whole life is preoccupied with beating deadlines. There are also shorter periods within the academic semester when practical/lab or field studies run or when tutorials and seminars are operational. Moreover, there is the all round 'run-of-the-mill' season when students are engrossed in listening, reading, learning, writing, accumulating and compiling information. Finally there is the season of exams (or tests) when all lectures have come to an end and the period of intense revision begins, culminating in the exams themselves. Students have to adapt and adjust their behaviours according to the particular 'season' they find themselves in. Each new phase comes and goes very rapidly. However, in spite of the changes in academic activity during each semester, it is necessary to keep a number of commitments running in parallel with each other. Just as nature benefits from the fluctuations in the seasons (buds, blossoms, blooms), so students can capitalise from using the opportunities that come and go to add usefully to their repertoire of knowledge.

MORE TO ACADEMIC ACHIEVEMENT THAN ABILITY

Researchers believe that students' academic achievement is a combination of ability, thinking styles, behavioural patterns, planning, discipline, motivation, organisation and self-concept (Purdie & Hattie, 1995). Students who obtained a good standard before entering university cannot afford to 'rest on their laurels', and students who were in the lower echelons of achievement prior to university entrance should not imagine that they are doomed to stay there. Some researchers have argued that the most capable students do not always turn out to be the best students, simply because there is more to achievement than ability, and these students do not always fulfil their potential. Given that students have enough ability to satisfy the university or college's entrance requirements, there is room to use and develop the kernel of ability that is there. Therefore it would be short-sighted to envisage future performance as entirely commensurate with past attainment.

Checklist

Are you an organised person? Insert a number in the space provided after each question according to the following code — 1 = Always 2 = Almost Always 3 = Frequently   4 = In-between   5 = Occasionally   6 = Seldom   7 = Never

1. Do you have to rush out each morning at the last minute? ....
2. Are you late for your scheduled appointments? ....
3. Do you plan your meals for each new day? ....
4. Do you leave your meetings with friends to chance? ....
5. Are you caught out with nothing clean to wear for scheduled events? ....
6. Can you account for how much you spend on any given week? ....
7. Do you know roughly how many hours that you will watch TV on any given week? ....
8. Can you make a list of the range of foods you eat in any given week? ....
9. Do important events (birthdays, anniversaries) overtake you before you are aware of them? ....
10. Do you lose time through misplacing items such as keys, watch, pen ? ....

Total score ....

Scoring key — Any score over 40 means that you are reasonably organised (the higher the score, the more organised you are). Any score below 40 means that you are less organised (the lower the score the less organised you are). The above questionnaire was designed for the present study guide.

Role of conscientiousness

IMPORTANT IN PERSONALITY AND EDUCATION

In the study of personality there are a number of theories that present different perspectives, but almost all have a central role for conscientiousness, although it may not always be explicitly labelled as such (Wolfe & Johnson, 1995). Personality theorists such as Cattell, Eber and Tatsuoka (1985), and Costa & McCrae (1992), distinctly label one of the factors in their system as 'conscientiousness.' Other theorists such as Eysenck do not have a factor in their system labelled as conscientiousness, but the content of their system contains the same concept within larger factors. Questionnaires associated with these perspectives have been designed to assess responses to each personality trait including conscientiousness. A trait implies that there is a stable underlying disposition in a person that gives rise to consistent behaviours over time and across situations. As one of these central traits in personality, conscientiousness is manifest in behaviours that are planned, acted on promptly, follow rules, show evidence of industry, discipline and organisation. This does not imply that every individual is at either one end or the other of two dichotomous poles of conscientiousness. It is better to think of conscientiousness as a continuum where few people are at either extreme and most are at some point on either side but not too far away from the centre. Moreover, people may be more conscientious in some behaviours than in others. Nevertheless, conscientiousness has emerged as an important trait in human personality that serves well in explaining individual differences in people's behaviours.

It comes as no surprise therefore that the role of conscientiousness has been assessed in relation to educational achievement, and it has been found to be one of the important variables in predicting students' performance. In other words when students' conscientious behaviours are assessed, the results are likely to be good indicators of those who will perform best and worst in exams and course work. Empirical studies have demonstrated that this is indeed the case (for example, Wolfe & Johnson, 1995; Colquitt & Simmering, 1998). Some researchers have assessed a form of general conscientiousness that encompasses the full spectrum of life and have then used these scores to predict academic performance. Others prefer to assess conscientious behaviours that are exclusively and specifically related to academic settings. Students should certainly aim to cultivate behaviours that are characteristic of conscientiousness within the academic context.

REFLECTED IN OVERT BEHAVIOURS

In a university-based study we constructed a simple questionnaire that can be completed in about one or two minutes. The total score for each student's response to this measure can then be used to indicate where each student lies on the continuum of academic conscientiousness. In constructing the measure we first examined what personality theorists said about the construct of conscientiousness and all the features that represent it. We attempted to incorporate their range of indicators including planning, organisation, regularity, rules, industry etc. Second, we took these principles and applied them to students' application to study, lectures, assignments and exams. Third, we explored what students and lecturers thought were the important behaviours in optimising academic performance. In the fourth place we carefully worded the items (questions) so that there would be no ambiguities for respondents. Finally, we ran the study and analysed students' responses both in themselves and in relation to their subsequent academic performance. We found that each item elicited a range of differences in students' self-reported responses. We also found that students who reported higher levels of conscientiousness were more likely to achieve a higher standard in both course work and examinations. If you have had some experience in third level education, you may find it helpful to complete the following questionnaire (or complete it based on what you think you would do with reference to your past experience). You can then score yourself based on the guidelines given in order to ascertain where you currently lie on the continuum of academic conscientiousness. Moreover, you will be able to see particular weaknesses and be better equipped to address these.

Academic conscientiousness scale

Directions: The following are the kinds of statements students sometimes use to describe themselves. Read each one carefully and respond to all items by encircling the number which best describes you according to the following code (try to avoid using Neutral if possible):

1 = Strongly Agree   2 = Agree   3 = Slightly Agree   4 = Neutral   5 = Slightly Disagree   6 = Disagree   7 = Strongly Disgree

1. I go to work on my assignments immediately after
    learning what the [essay] titles are.   .... *
2. I always plan my study time as a top priority.   .... *
3. I never lag behind other students in my application
    to study.   .... *
4. I have a well-established pattern of regular and
    consistent study.   .... *
5. No matter how good my intentions are, I usually
    end up leaving revision until near exam [test] time.   ....

6. I normally try to consolidate what I have learned as
    soon as possible after lectures.   ....   *
7. If I miss out on my study time, I immediately apply
    myself to making up for the lost time.   ....   *
8. I seldom work as hard at my studies as I intend to.   ....
9. I can clearly see vast room for improvement in
    my application to academic study.   ....
10. I make every effort to attend all scheduled academic
    sessions at university.   ....   *

Total Score ....

* Denotes items to be reversed in scoring. The code for reversing is as follows:
$1 = 7, 2 = 6, 3 = 5, 4 = 4, 5 = 3, 6 = 2$ and $7 = 1$. First reverse score all the items
with an asterisk, and then add up your total score. If you have a score above 40
then you are on the 'right' end of the academic conscientiousness continuum. If
however your score is below 40 then your are on balance toward the lower end
of the continuum. The further away from the midpoint (that is, 40) of the scale
you are then the closer you are to the extreme points of the continuum. The low-
est possible score is 10 and the highest possible score is 70 (provided all
questions were completed).

A methodical approach to study

In the 18th century the movement known as 'Methodism' had its origins under
the leadership of John and Charles Wesley. These founding members and others
combined as students at Oxford University to form what was called 'The Holy
Club'. This was comprised of a small number of students who resolved to meet
regularly and to discipline their lives for holy living. Among the practices they
committed themselves to were prayer, fasting, study, meditation, acts of charity,
prison visits, visits to the sick etc. It is alleged that other students who observed
their behaviours nicknamed them, 'Methodists', because their lives were so
methodical. Later the movement was to spread rapidly throughout the British
Isles and over to America. The fruits of John Wesley's efforts are still evident
today whereas other pioneering names of the same era are largely forgotten.

It is claimed that the secret of John Wesley's effectiveness was his personal discipline and his great ability to organise. For instance, he was able to capitalise on all the enthusiasm of the new converts by organising them into small lay groups and by mobilising lay people into active participation in religious services. He did this in spite of not having all the facilities of the established churches such as buildings and an ordained ministry.

The lesson from the story of Methodism is that lasting achievements can only be attained by planned, systematic effort and by a disciplined, organised, methodical approach to given tasks. No student is likely to be successful within the sphere of academia unless there is a concerted attempt to address study on a continual basis. An occasional binge on a study spree when the mood dictates is definitely not the pathway to success at university. Study may not always be full of joy and excitement but the end result will bring much satisfaction and the passport to a professional career. Moreover students will be able to acquire skills that will be of much use to them in their later career.

Illustration

It is reported that Queen Victoria once complimented the great violinist, Paganini, as a genius. His response was that he may have been a genius, but he was also a drudge. It is no surprise that he said this, given that he was alleged to have practised each bar of music 50 times over! The result of his drudgery was the beautiful melody that allowed him to play before a queen. It is reassuring to know that the times of drudgery at university will rapidly come to an end and that they are leading the student toward a definite goal.

TRAINING FOR YOUR FUTURE CAREER

Many students are prone to complain about the multiple pressures they have to endure and the looming deadlines they have to negotiate. However, students should also realise that life will not necessarily become a lot easier after graduation. The media frequently highlight the stress many professions such as nurses, doctors, teachers, civil servants etc.

are under. In many ways therefore university is about much more than acquiring a degree or diploma – the road to attaining a professional qualification helps develop the qualities that will enable efficient functioning within a professional environment.

Example

Take as a typical example the responsibilities entailed in managing a clothes shop. This is a very extensive role and entails co-ordinating a range of tasks combined with the careful management of personnel. Managers may be responsible for completing tasks themselves or ensuring that they are done. The following list is not necessarily exhaustive:

1. Monitoring stocks and ensuring a steady flow of supplies.
2. Observing stock that moves and stock that is static.
3. Dealing with customer complaints.
4. Keeping an eye on the competition.
5. Trying to accommodate staff requests – sickness, leave, holidays etc.
6. Always at the ready for 'drop-in' inspections from higher management.
7. Keeping abreast of security issues, theft etc.
8. Dealing with disciplinary problems such as staff who do not shoulder their responsibility.
9. Endeavouring to ensure that staff morale is kept high.
10. Keeping accounts up-to-date and presenting reports of progress to management.
11. Conducting interviews and making decisions based on fair employment legislation.
12. Preparing for the rigours of special sales days and extra opening hours.

When a graduate has spent a few years in a role such as the one described above, the pressures they were under at university may not look quite so bad! Remember that university will help to prepare you for the world of professional practice, but you will still be expected to continue to develop. A similar scenario to the above might be written for hotel management, computer sales, car sales, book sales, medical work, teaching etc.

Exercise — Matching current skills to future career

A. Write down about three occupations that would be your first preferred professions.
B. Make a list of the essential qualities for each job — think of the multiple roles you would have to play.
C. Make a list of the ways in which your university experience will help prepare you for these roles.
D. List how your 'failure' experiences at university may be beneficial to your future career experience.

Balancing your budget of time

PARALLELS WITH THE CHANCELLOR'S BUDGET

Illustration

The UK chancellor presents a budget each year in the month of March. This speech essentially consists of a parliamentary address that is both retrospective and prospective. The chancellor trumpets the achievements of his government since they took power and particularly over the previous year, and also maps out the course for future fiscal policy. Tough decisions have to be made that sometimes include increasing taxes directly or indirectly. Overall the aim is ostensibly to enable the nation to be more prosperous and for each family to improve their lot.

Every student should at various stages engage in a parallel exercise such as a periodic review. It is always good to do this at the end of the first semester after exam results are available. For example, you may need to look at why you have done so well in two subjects but poorly in another. Try to do some 'troubleshooting' to see if you can locate where the problem (s) is (are). Perhaps you have done well in exams but not in course work or vice-versa. At the end of the full academic year you will be able to compare your performance across two semesters. There is an adage that says that 'if it isn't broke, don't fix it'. If strategies are working for you, then stay with them, but some retrospective analysis may help you rectify debilitating weaknesses.

Exercise — Periodic review

Below is a simple graph that plots out fictitious course work marks and exam results for an undergraduate student in semesters 1 and 2 of year one. Subjects are labelled A,B,C (semester 1) and D,E,F (semester 2). Marks achieved were in the range of 38 to 85.

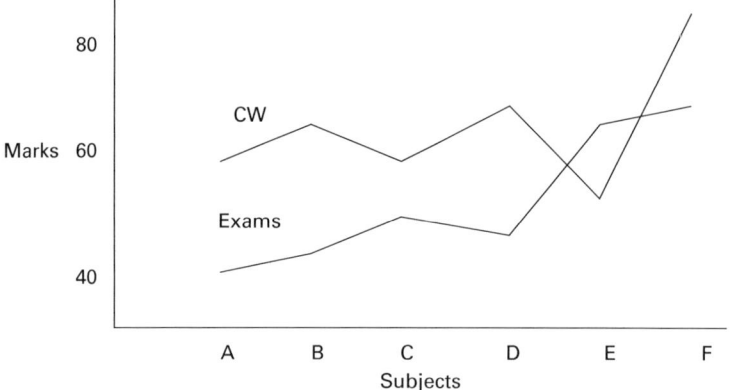

Figure 6.1   LINE GRAPH SHOWING EXAM AND COURSE WORK PERFORMANCE (CW) FOR 6 SUBJECTS OVER TWO SEMESTERS: ABC = SEMESTER 1. DEF = SEMESTER 2.

Questions:

- ◆ Is the student better at course work or exams?
- ◆ Has the student improved from semester 1 to semester 2?

+ Should the slump in performance on course work at point E be a great cause for concern?
+ How would you summarise the detailed trends overall in comparing within and between the two semesters with reference to both indexes of achievement?

LIMITED TIME TO EACH SEMESTER

Much activity is compressed into each academic semester, so there is no room for procrastination (which is said to be the thief of time). At the end of the academic year the student can enjoy a long break, and that will always come soon enough. An academic semester may only run over three months for teaching and one month for revision and exams. In each semester students may be expected to complete three full modules, each comprised of one or two items of course work and one test or examination. If there are six modules in an academic year this amounts to 18 pieces of work that are assessed (12 assignments and 6 exams). Since all these have to be completed within about an eight month period (this and the number of assignments and exams may vary from university to university), students need to learn to 'make hay while the sun is shining'. The opportunity to achieve goes as quickly as it comes. A two-edged sword of concerted effort and sound strategy should be applied. Some students always need to 'work harder' and others need to learn to 'work smarter' (a former advertising slogan). All students should be aware that they are battling against time. However, the strategies advocated throughout the book will help to keep anxiety under control and channel motivation into successful achievement.

THE DIVISION OF LABOUR

Self-perception theory claims that once individuals appropriate beliefs about them-selves, they feel an unpleasant mental/emotional state of dissonance unless they act in a manner congruent with their beliefs (Aronson, Wilson & Akert, 1994). The up-side of this self-perception is that it can work in our favour if our self-beliefs are construc-tive and adaptive. For example, if students believe they can attain a good academic standard, then they will act accordingly. The down-side is that if students have nega-tive self-perceptions they may entertain doubts about investing effort. They may, for instance, get fixated on the belief that they are good at course work but poor in exams or tests. Low expectation may lead to diminished investment of effort. Students should not therefore allow themselves to become fixated on such negative perceptions but should work toward developing all round abilities and skills. Labour needs to be divided between a whole range of academic activities including reading, listening, note-taking, consolidation, revision, interacting, computing, practical studies, maths/statistics and presentations. A key to success at university is to ensure that none of the range of required skills is left undeveloped but that every skill has been nurtured with care. Each student should give due attention to what they know is 'the weakest link' in their repertoire of skills.

TAKING TIME FOR LIVING

According to the late psychologist, Hans Eysenck (1998), extraverts love to party, to socialise, to be talkative and to be near others, even when they are studying. On the other hand, introverts prefer their own company and may spend much time in isolation with their books. He argues that a minority of people are at these two extremes but most of us are a mixture (that is, ambiverts) who are toward one side of the centre or the other between the two extremes. Either extreme in the continuum is not healthy for a student. This chapter has advocated the need for conscientiousness, industry, organisation, planning etc. However, when students leave university they should also be equipped with social and communication skills and with a settled awareness that they need friendships, breaks, fun and relaxation. Therefore it is vital that these provisions are factored into any disciplined regime.

Exercise and thought

It would be useful, at the end of each weekday, to take a moment to write a rough plan for the next day. Try to do this for a typical day at college, drafting out a plan that includes a lecture, lunch, library search, private study, rendezvous with friends, computing practice and some physical activity. For the evening you might want to plan time for preparing and eating a meal, relaxing with some music, recapping and revamping summary material that you have learned on the day and finishing with watching a video. This does not mean that each day necessarily has to be strictly regimented to the last minute, but on the other hand if you aim at nothing you have a good chance of hitting it! Planning can easily become a natural part of your daily behavioural repertoire.

Ways of Handling Stress and Anxiety
(or, what can I do about the stuff that life is throwing at me?)

GORDON RUGG, SUE GERRARD AND SUSIE HOOPER

Emergency help for immediate stress. General methods for handling stress. Ways of preventing stress. Ways of achieving well-being.

This chapter begins with emergency help for immediate, urgent stressors. The following sections then give suggestions for getting less urgent stressors under control. After that, we deal with ways of preventing or reducing common stressors; finally, we discuss ways of achieving positive well-being, and moving your life towards where you want to be. There are further techniques, tips and exercises in the appendices, which you might find useful if you're in the middle of a stressful situation.

EMERGENCY HELP FOR IMMEDIATE STRESSES

The following sections give quick stopgap support for the following problems:

- panic attacks
- serious injury or crime
- serious bad news
- feeling that your life has fallen apart.

The sections after these give more in-depth information and techniques for handling stressors when the situation is less urgent.

Are you having a panic attack – feeling terrified, faint, with shallow breathing and clammy skin?
If so:

- sit down – if there's no chair, sit on the floor
- breathe in slowly, counting slowly to four

- hold your breath, counting slowly to four
- breathe out slowly, counting slowly to four
- hold your breath, counting slowly to four
- repeat.

This should get your carbon dioxide levels back to normal within a minute or thereabouts, and clear away the feeling of panic. Panic attacks feel horrible when they strike, but there are effective ways of handling them, such as the one above. Sitting down is helpful in terms of blood pressure, but is also useful because it reduces the risk of damage through bumping your head if you do faint. Some sufferers worry about whether or not they'll die during an attack. What actually happens is that if you faint your brain stops thinking about whatever was making you panic in the first place and then normal physiology takes over; you'll wake up again in a few seconds.

How does this strategy work? The usual way to handle panic attacks is to get your physiology stabilised, in particular your blood pressure and your carbon dioxide levels. During panic attacks, people hyperventilate, which drives down their carbon dioxide levels and gives rise to the light-headed feeling. One simple way of fixing this is to breathe into a paper bag (or your cupped hands if you don't have a bag); the bag will store the carbon dioxide from your exhalation, and after a few breaths your carbon dioxide levels will be back to normal. Another simple way of handling panic attacks is to use breathing exercises, such as the one above. These exercises do two things: they (a) occupy the brain with something other than the thing it was panicking about and (b) get your physiology into a more normal state as regards blood pressure and carbon dioxide levels.

Once you've stopped the panic attack, you should talk to a supportive friend or counsellor about it. If it was triggered by an underlying anxiety or phobia, then your life will be improved by fixing the underlying cause. Most people find reasons to avoid doing this, because of an understandable worry that the treatment will be almost as bad as the panic attack; in fact, the treatments usually involve calm relaxation, and can be actively pleasant.

Is there blood involved?
This is a vivid, memorable figure of speech referring to whether or not physical injury has occurred. If either you or someone else has been injured, raped, or otherwise traumatised, then:

- Stabilise the immediate situation (get yourself or the person involved into a safe place and stop any serious bleeding).
- If you're starting to panic, breathe slowly and deeply, counting slowly to four on each breath, and pausing for a few seconds between breaths.

- Call for proper help – if in doubt, call 999 and explain the situation to the operator.
- If you are feeling physically shocked (cold, shaky, faint, dizzy or can't think clearly) keep yourself warm, eat or drink something sweet to raise your blood sugar levels, and find someone to be with you.

Err on the side of safety; the 999 operators are trained to deal with stressed callers, and will advise you on which service is needed. For instance, if a friend has had a fall, and is dazed and bleeding from the ears, then you might not be sure whether to call for an ambulance or to drive them to A&E (Accident and Emergency) at the local hospital. Other useful emergency contacts include NHS Direct, the local police station and your university 24-hour counselling service. There are other contacts you may find helpful, and we have provided a list for you to complete in Appendix 2. Their numbers are easily found via directory enquiries, but since most of these numbers are local, it's not possible for us to list them here. If in doubt, it's always better to err on the side of calling 999 than to risk having someone die because you were afraid to bother the emergency services.

[…]

Have you had serious bad news?
If so:

- Take some slow, deep breaths to help you stay calm and sensible.
- Decide whether you have to do anything immediately (like in the next two minutes). Usually you don't – generally another five minutes won't make any difference to the bad news, but will give you more time to think about what's best to do.
- If you do have to do something immediately, then do it. If it's not immediately obvious what requires doing, then your best option is to take a few minutes to think through the situation calmly and clearly.
- Call a capable friend and ask them to be available for backup – emotional support, notifying the department and feeding the cat if you need to go home suddenly, and so on.
- If the bad news involves yourself, such as bad exam results, then read the section below about when your life feels as if it's falling apart.

Sometimes people get delayed shock after bad news – they're numbed at the time, and it's only hours or days later that the full emotional impact hits them. If this happens, and you find yourself panicking, treat it as a panic attack (see first section above). If it strikes while you are driving (for example, on your way to a sick relative after hearing the news), then pull over in the first safe place and wait until you're sure you've sorted out the panic before even thinking about going anywhere. If you realise you're not in a fit state to drive, then you can try calling the AA/RAC/a friend/a taxi to get you to somewhere safe.

It's also quite normal after hearing bad news to become obsessively focused on some minor issue, such as whether you'll inherit that nice vase of Aunt Kate's if she dies. This can leave you wondering afterwards whether you're a callous monster deep down, but that isn't the case; what happens is that the mind often tries to block out unwelcome major issues by focusing on minor ones instead. The minor issue often involves something practical, like arrangements for getting an essay handed in. It's very helpful to have an efficient friend around at such times, to steer you gently away from the minor issues and to help you do what's needed for the major ones.

Are you feeling that your life has fallen apart, and you don't know how to start fixing it?

- If you're feeling distraught and unstable, with nobody to turn to, then call the university's 24-hour counselling service.
- Don't make any impulsive decisions that you might regret later, such as withdrawing from your course.
- If you can't face calling the 24-hour counselling service, then take some slow, deep breaths, and read the more detailed section on page xx, about handling feelings of being out of control.

HANDLING STRESS

This section goes into more detail about techniques for handling stress, and about how these techniques work.

Relaxation and centring techniques

One set of techniques deals with feelings of panic and anxiety; these are usually referred to as relaxation or centring techniques. The term 'centring' is a reference to the image of getting yourself back into balance, centred around the real inner you, as opposed to focused on ephemeral external issues. Centring techniques are usually based around a core of shared features. One feature is removing external distractors – being somewhere quiet, without passers-by or ringing phones. Another is slow, regular breathing, which helps induce the relaxation response, a physiological state where the pulse rate slows, blood pressure drops and the brainwaves shift into the characteristic patterns of relaxation; it usually takes about five to twenty minutes to reach this state. A third is the use of music, soothing sounds or mental images to focus the mind on something other than the preoccupations and hassles of daily life. We've included a variety of these techniques in the appendices. They're closely related to meditation, though that is often linked to a set of beliefs, rather than being based solely on physiology.

You can use these techniques as part of your daily life; twenty minutes of relaxation each day can be very effective for keeping things in perspective, and helping you to feel balanced and well. You can also use them when occasion arises, such as if you're experiencing exam nerves (with the obvious proviso that you shouldn't use them in contexts like driving a car, where you need to be fully alert). The same techniques are widely used to tackle various aspects of stress, including phobias, anxiety, exam nerves, obsessive and intrusive thoughts, and feeling generally out of control. A widely used way of tackling these problems is to use a relaxation technique until you're feeling completely calm, and then to imagine a very mild form of whatever you're worried about – for instance, child's drawing of a very small spider, in the distance, if you're phobic about spiders (see Chapter 1). You keep using the relaxation technique while you imagine this, and thereby learn to associate the image with a feeling of calm. Once you're completely comfortable with the very mild image, you can then move on to the next stage, and so on until you're comfortable with the whole range. It's best to do this with a professional, who'll help you to stay calm and relaxed. It's usually fast (two or three one-hour sessions) and very comfortable.

Case study, from Susie: Joe's fear of lifts was a real pain to him. Merely thinking about getting into one set off a train of unhelpful, panicky feelings. First, he learned to deeply and quickly relax. Then he constructed a hierarchy of possible situations concerning lifts, from watching people going in and out of lifts, to being stuck in a lift, between floors. Whilst he was very relaxed, he was asked to imagine each situation in turn, until, several sessions later, he could imagine even the most stressful without feeling anxious. The next step was to test his new confidence out in reality. We went into shops with large lifts, watched people using them, got in and rode up first one floor, then two and so on. All the time he was reminded to practise relaxation. After about an hour of lifts, we

(Continued)

> *(Continued)*
>
> progressed to a tiny lift in a tower block. Part of the therapy was to make going in lifts a boring, dull pastime rather than something to be feared. Joe also agreed that being stuck in a lift was a low probability event that he need not concern himself with thoughts of. Now he was so good at relaxing that he knew he would cope with that situation if it ever arose.

These techniques are very effective for relieving the immediate feelings of stress. For the underlying causes of those feelings, there are other techniques and approaches. These range from the very practical (for example, life-planning using lists and prioritised goals) to the intangible (for example, psychotherapy); within a single approach, different professionals may vary widely in their favoured methods. Which is best? That's a reasonable question; the answer will depend on what you are like, what your problems are like, and what the professional is like. Often, the immediate problem is actually a side-effect of a very different underlying problem, which only becomes apparent when you've been working with a professional for a while.

There are other issues to take into account. One is where the line should be drawn between personal choice and a problem needing to be fixed. For instance, some people with bipolar disorder (formerly known as manic depressives) are extremely creative when in the manic phase, and view the bleak horrors of the depressive phase as being a price they're willing to pay for the creativity; for such people, their condition is a gift with a price attached, not a straightforward problem to be fixed. It's easy to make the judgement for cases at each end of the spectrum, but cases in the middle are not so easy. A related issue is that counselling and psychotherapy are like swimming across a pond – the swimming can stir up a lot of mud that's been lying beneath the surface, and there's a decision to make about whether the journey across the pond is worth the stirring up of the mud. Sometimes the answer is yes; a wise psychotherapist can help you work through unresolved problems that might otherwise have cast a blighting shadow across the rest of your life. Other times the answer is no; there's considerable debate among professionals about when it's best to let minor issues lie undisturbed to wither away with time, rather than turning them into a major issue by bringing them to the forefront of your mind. It's a difficult, grey area. As a very rough rule of thumb, if you feel uneasy about a counsellor, or you feel that they're pushing a personal agenda, particularly one that involves fostering negative feelings towards an individual or a group of individuals, then you should consider changing to someone else.

Case study, from Susie: Clare came to see me once a week throughout her academic course. The sessions always took the same form. She would arrive carrying two bags of shopping. This was dumped on the floor and she stood between the bags and started to talk. She never sat down and never stopped talking. For fifty minutes. At the end of the time she would ask, 'Is the same time next week OK?' I would say 'Yes. See you then,' and she would leave. I had barely spoken for the whole of the time but I understood, from what she was saying, that she was sorting out her life. By chance, I was introduced to her father. 'So glad to meet you,' he said. 'My daughter Clare thinks you are wonderful!' Sometimes, a sympathetic listener can act as a safety valve, reduce pressure and help you to resolve the issues that are making you stressed, just by listening.

If you feel that you are faced with problems or feelings that you cannot deal with alone, we strongly advise that you seek professional help from a qualified counsellor or psychotherapist. That said, you may feel that you are in a position to address some of the feelings of stress yourself. So, what can you do about the underlying causes of stress? A lot of these involve feeling that your life is unstructured, out of control, unpredictable, unpleasant and generally a mess, so we've approached this area from the viewpoint of getting your life back under control.

Handling addictive behaviour

We usually associate addictive behaviour with dangerous or illegal activities, such as gambling, alcoholism or drug abuse. But all sorts of behaviour can become addictive, and any addiction is going to raise your stress levels because, by definition, you are not going to be in control of your life. When we are feeling stressed, depressed or anxious, it's a signal to the brain that something is wrong; and the brain will look for a quick fix to get its physiology back to normal. The quick fix may be in the form of sex, drugs or rock 'n' roll, or nicotine, alcohol, eating, shopping, computer gaming, weight-lifting or all-night clubbing. What happens is that the quick fix will give you a high which makes you feel better for a while – and then you come down from the high, find your problems haven't gone away, and that the quick fix may itself have made things worse. You address this by going for another quick fix, which makes the situation even more difficult and so on. Strategies that make your situation worse are known as *maladaptive strategies* and are best avoided if you want to stay in control of your life and away from addiction. There are a couple of ways to do this. One is to recognise that if you're feeling low, your brain needs a 'high' to balance itself. The art is in choosing a 'high' that has positive benefits, or at least no serious downside. This is why some people are such strident advocates of sport and exercise, which can give you a great feeling of well-being, and keep you fit into the bargain. The problem is that even activities which do you good – like sport – or no harm – like playing computer games – can themselves turn into a damaging addiction, with high costs in terms of time, money and stress levels. One way to avoid this happening is to have a range of strategies available for when you need a quick fix to make you feel better, not just one or two. Use them in turn. So Monday's quick fix might be a brisk walk, Tuesday's lying down with your eyes closed listening to a favourite album, Wednesday's playing squash, Thursday's watching a DVD, Friday's going out for a drink, and so on.

Another strategy is to employ *delayed gratification*. Babies find delayed gratification impossible because of their immature brains. They want something, and they want it now. You will doubtless be able to think of some adult acquaintances who have the same problem. Let's say you are struggling with your academic course, avoid tackling the problems and make yourself feel better by having a few pints in the union bar each evening. You do not have a 'drink problem' as such, but your expenditure on alcohol is escalating, your assignments are stacking up, you feel permanently sluggish and you are putting on weight. If you decide to deal with the problem by never darkening the doors of the union bar again, you will simply make yourself feel worse. A more effective solution would be to decide to stay in on a Monday evening, say, and get some work done. The following week, stay in on a Monday and Tuesday. The week after, make it Monday, Tuesday and Thursday. If this seems too drastic, try delaying your visit to the bar for an hour, then two hours, then three, to cut down on available drinking time. If you are still finding this difficult, you may have a drink problem, or at least a self-control problem, so seek professional help. The advice you get on controlling one form of addictive behaviour will probably prove very useful if you overcome one kind of addiction only to develop another as soon as you find the stress levels rising.

Handling the feeling of being out of control

Panic attacks are what the medical profession calls 'acute' as opposed to 'chronic.' These terms are used differently in the medical world from in everyday life, which is a fine source of potential confusion when medics interact with non-medics. 'Acute' in medical language means that something happens at a particular point in time; 'chronic' in medical language means that it goes on for an extended length of time. Stress often arises out of a situation that appears set to go on for a long time or for the foreseeable future – that's generally what makes the situation stressful, if you aren't sure that you can keep going till the end, or aren't sure if there even is an end to it. That in turn is usually bound up closely with a feeling of being out of control. As a general principle, anything that helps you feel you're getting your life under control is likely to help reduce stress. Fortunately, there are usually plenty of things you can do to help yourself with this. Three useful starting points are:

- look at the bigger picture
- have a temporary working plan
- start small and work up.

Looking at the bigger picture

A striking feature of stress and related concepts is that they involve a lot of obsessive thoughts, typically miserable ones, which usually lead to getting things completely out of proportion. Here are some examples.

Embarrassment: a !angled web

The great Joe Haldeman wrote a science fiction story called *A !angled Web*, about an alien species called the !ang (the exclamation mark stands for a clicking sound, but that's another story). They had a richly formalised way of handling embarrassment. The embarrassed person would begin by saying 'I am embarrassed.' They would then elaborate on the extent and the consequences of the embarrassment, with the phrasing being different every time – for instance, 'My cheeks grow hot with embarrassment. They grow so hot that the sea dries up. They grow so hot that the land dries up. The fish die, the plants die, the animals die.' They would then conclude by saying 'All die. I am embarrassed.' Embarrassment isn't much fun, but if fear of embarrassment is holding you back from doing something, then it's worth considering whether you're weaving a !angled web for yourself and getting things just a bit out of proportion.

Brooding fantasies of failure; the dog on the string

When worried, it's traditional to brood about the problem and spin elaborate fantasies of gloom and despair. For instance, you might find yourself imagining a disastrous failure in your next exam, dragging down your degree to a level where nobody is willing to employ you, so you end up begging in the street, with a dog on a string, and eventually die of hypothermia, abandoned by the dog and miserable and starving. Well, yes, it could conceivably happen, but it's not the usual outcome of a bad mark in an exam by any stretch of the imagination. Planning for reasonable worst-case scenarios is sensible; weaving elaborate fantasies of failure isn't. The time spent on a miserable fantasy can be spent instead on one about being happy; better for you, and more pleasant.

HEAL – assessing thoughts, so you can replace bad ones with good ones

You can assess a thought in terms of its:

Helpfulness – is it helping you in any way?
Evidence – is there good evidence to support it?
Accuracy – does it correspond reasonably well to reality?
Logic – does it make sense?

So, for instance, the thought 'I'm going to fail this exam' is unlikely to be helping you. If you've passed all your previous exams, and this exam isn't significantly different from them, then the thought isn't based on good evidence. Sometimes a thought does have some evidence behind it, but doesn't match well with reality – for instance, the thought 'those lecturers stopped talking when I went past, so they must have been talking about me' has some evidence (if they really did stop talking) but is unlikely to be accurate; it's much more likely that they stopped talking for some other reason, like having reached a break in the conversation. The dividing line between evidence, accuracy and logic can be fuzzy, but that's not terribly important; what matters is the concept of checking whether a particular thought is doing you good and is related reasonably closely to reality.

When you're stressed, thoughts tend to go round in your head like a hyperactive hamster in an over-oiled wheel. Simply trying to throw a thought out isn't usually effective; the very action of trying to throw it out involves thinking about it, which gets you back to where you started from. What works much better is replacing that thought with something else, particularly something that is going somewhere. A prominent feature of stress is the feeling of no escape – going round a set of thoughts endlessly because you can't see a way out of them. The more you go round, the more of your attention they take up; it's a vicious cycle. One handy metaphor is that a vicious cycle of this sort is like a runaway riderless motorbike on a wall of death circuit; it's going round in circles, and you may not be able to stop it right now, but that doesn't mean that you need to jump on top of it and try to bring it to a halt. What you can do instead is leave it to run out of petrol and grind to a halt, while you get on with something completely different, in the form of positive thoughts.

The positive thoughts you choose should be helpful, rational and reasonably close to reality. For example, if you're worried about just getting through the exams, you can remind yourself that they won't go on for ever, and that you're going to treat yourself to a really enjoyable day out to reward yourself for doing them all, regardless of how well you did. You can imagine the taste of that rich chocolate biscuit as you sit watching people go by, and the smell of the freshly made coffee in its white china cup on the table in front of you. It's helpful, because it's moving you into a positive cycle, and it's rational and reasonably close to reality, because all it requires is the cost of a coffee and biscuit. It's also giving you positive reinforcement about your ability to get through the exams.

If you're going through testing times, you're likely to feel physically tense, probably without realising it. The physical tension will tire you, so it's a good idea to do some muscle-relaxing exercises periodically. The one below has the added advantage of being good for when you've spent too long at the keyboard or hunched over a book – common problems for students. (It's more productive, and ergonomically sound, to take a ten minute break every hour when studying.)

If you're feeling tense and sore around the shoulders:

- Straighten up in your chair and close your eyes.
- Take several deep breaths and concentrate on your breathing.
- Breathe in and lift your shoulders as high as you can.
- Hold your shoulders high while you take three slow breaths.
- Breathe gently out while you drop your shoulders as low as possible.
- Keep your shoulders dropped for one breath.

Repeat the exercise three times.

Having a temporary working plan

If you're feeling that your life is out of control, then having a plan will get some of it under control. A temporary plan will buy you enough time to put together something more sophisticated and far-reaching. Here's an example of a temporary working plan, with explanations for each part.

- Get to bed by 11.00 pm as elsewhere and up by 7.30 am throughout this week. (Lack of sleep causes stress, and makes small stressors appear much bigger than they really are.)
- Spend twenty minutes on Tuesday and Thursday evening doing centring exercises. (These will help you stay calm.)
- Arrange a meeting with an approachable lecturer to discuss ways forward with your academic work. (This will help you identify possible solutions that you hadn't known about before. It can also help you find out about other support services, such as support with essay-writing technique.)
- Have an evening out with friends on Wednesday. (This is fun, and helps maintain your social support.)
- Spend twenty minutes on Friday morning planning the weekend and what you'll do next week. (This saves you from a potentially bleak unstructured weekend, and helps you move on to a better plan.)

This isn't the world's most sophisticated strategy, but it's a start. You'll probably have already spotted some obvious gaps in it; this is a good sign, because it means that you're starting to move forward and work out better ways of getting things done.

Starting small, and working up

Another easy but effective approach to tackling stress is to develop small, safe routines – things that you do at the same time each day or each week, or in the same way. For instance, you might start your day by having a cup of coffee while you get your working materials into place, easing yourself gently into working mode. Similarly, you can do your shopping at the same time every week, and have a standard set of favourite meals for some days of the week, or a standard 'emergency meal' for when you can't face making another decision about what to eat. Each of these routines means one less thing that you have to make decisions about. End-of-day routines are at least as important as start-of-day ones; they help you to approach sleep with calm, positive feelings, so that you're more likely to wake up refreshed the next day. Don't allow routines or rituals to dominate your life. Having a 'lucky T-shirt' that you wear to exams is fine; wearing it every day and refusing to wash it, in case you wash away the luck, is obsessive (and smelly). The routines should be helpful servants, not dominating masters.

A related strategy is to tackle small manageable tasks. You can keep a list of these pinned up somewhere visible, or in a frequently used folder. They're things like tidying up your desktop, mucking out a bag, or cleaning the sink. Being small and manageable, these tasks don't take long, they're useful, they'll make your life a bit better, they're evidence that you have control over some of your world, and they also help break you out of cycles of negative thoughts. Small manageable tasks make excellent displacement activities – the things you do when you're putting off something that you find unpleasant. For instance, if you're putting off writing a difficult letter, then instead of displacing by watching television, you could displace by tidying your desk – it gives you the opportunity to gear yourself up to facing the difficult task, time to think about it, and gives you a tidy desk.

A variant on this theme is to have small manageable goals, either as goals in their own right, or as part of some longer-term strategy. For example, if you're saving money to pay off a debt, or to fund your holiday in the Bahamas, you can choose to stay in and read a book one evening rather than going out, and squirrel away the amount of money that you'd otherwise have spent on nightlife. This makes staying at home into a positive choice, and you can schedule in a reward for yourself, such as a sticky bun and cocoa mid-evening. The goals need to be clear and achievable – 'clean the kitchen windowsill' is better than 'do some cleaning.' This leads into the next section, which describes ways of preventing stressors from arising in the first place, and ways of preparing for any stresses that can't be prevented.

PREVENTION AND PREPARATION

An effective strategy is to prevent the bad things that you can reasonably prevent, and to prepare for those that you can't. It's wise to get the balance right – you'll eventually reach the *point of diminishing returns*, after which any extra effort doesn't make much more difference. Spending some of your time preventing bad things is sensible; spending all of your time making contingency plans for increasingly remote possibilities is not good for you, and is not a good use of time.

Getting started

Getting started can be the hardest part, especially with tasks that look unpleasant, boring and/or threatening. However, unwelcoming tasks seldom curl up and die if left alone, so it's better to get going with them. Three good ways of getting started are the salami technique, the Mars bar technique and the BANJO technique, described below.

The salami technique involves the difference between trying to eat a whole salami in one go, which is not advisable, and trying to eat the same salami cut into thin slices, presented in several different ways in several meals, which is much more appealing. If you have a large chunk of work that you are putting off, divide it into small ten to twenty minute sections and do one at a time. It then appears much less off-putting and when you do one section, you may find it is easy to do a second immediately after it. Even doing one section at a time will soon build up to a sizeable chunk of the project, making it easier to tackle as the deadline draws near. (This approach is sometimes phrased as a joke: 'Q: How would you eat an elephant? A: One bite at a time.')

The Mars bar technique involves actual food rather than allegorical food. It consists of delaying any sort of reward until you have actually done a chunk of work. Sit down, start, continue working, no coffee, no chat, no TV, complete the planned chunk of work, and then give yourself the Mars bar (or equivalent). Only good behaviour gets the reward. This does need self-discipline initially, but it's very productive once you get into the habit.

The BANJO technique is named after the acronym for 'Bang A Nasty Job Off.' Undone nasty jobs are like the monster in the cupboard in horror movies; they don't go away, and the more you think about them, the worse they seem. When you get them out of the cupboard, though, they soon start looking like someone in a rubber suit. It's the same with festering undone jobs; the sooner you do them, the sooner they stop haunting you and making you feel bad. If you have a nasty job to do, do it as soon as possible: many BANJO players do their unpleasant jobs first thing in the working day, so that the rest of the day feels horror-free and enjoyable. If it was a particularly important task, you could give yourself a reward as a further pat on your back.

Lifestyle and well-being

One of the tricky features about giving advice is that the advice may be helpful, but so well established that it can sound like a self-evident cliché – for example, that people should get plenty of exercise and sleep. In such instances, we've borrowed the semi-ironic term 'a Good Thing' from the humorous history book *1066 and All That* as an indication that the advice is sound, but also as an indication that we can sympathise with readers who had heard the same advice more than often enough before opening this book.

A lot of stress-related bad feelings involve the interaction between the body and the mind. When you're stressed, anxious or depressed, it's easy to neglect your body, which leads to physiological reactions that make you feel even worse. Some simple ways to counter this are described below.

Exercise is a Good Thing; it stimulates the body to release endorphins, which make you feel better, as well as having assorted other positive effects. The exercise doesn't need to involve jogging outfits or gyms occupied by scarily muscled people; twenty minutes of walking per day is enough to make a difference. In the winter, it's a good idea to get some daylight, and a brisk walk at a bright time of day will help you feel better and sleep better. If this sounds a bit boring to you, then you can set yourself a small manageable goal of making the exercise fun in some way and fitting it into your schedule.

Getting enough sleep is a Good Thing. People usually sleep best by having a regular bedtime, a regular bedtime routine, and a calm sleeping environment. The bed should be reserved for getting to sleep (reading, or thinking calm thoughts), for sleeping and for sex – not for eating, watching TV, arguing, writing essays, or the like. The bed needs to have associations of calm, of post-coital snuggling, and of sleep.

Watch the caffeine levels. Due to some lamentable fault in the design of the universe, caffeine doesn't help you sleep well, and is found in tea, coffee, many fizzy drinks and chocolate (to add insult to injury, the better the chocolate, the higher the caffeine dose). If you're having trouble sleeping, then try not having caffeine during the hours before bedtime.

Watch the alcohol levels. Alcohol in moderate doses can take the edge off your worries, and social drinking can be very enjoyable, but in large doses alcohol will add more worries, while leaving the original worries still in place when you sober up. Alcohol plays a large part in student life, and many students feel that if they don't drink heavily then they'll look bad in front of their mates. It's worth turning that problem round, and asking yourself whether it's really a good idea to hang around with people who want you to do something that's bad for you.

Healthy diet is another Good Thing. This is not the same as living on lettuce and broccoli, nor is it the same as spending hours at the stove. There are plenty of good cookbooks from which you can learn to produce fast, cheap, meals; we have a section on the essentials of eating elsewhere in this book.

Have a life. Friends and a support network are important, and so is having another facet or two in your life apart from studying and the Student Union. Having several strands in your life will help keep each strand in perspective, so you don't get so worked up about things. As usual, you need to keep a sense of perspective – having several varied activities in your life is good, but having dozens will over-stretch you and cause more problems. The different activities don't need to be anything major, like international competitive hockey; just going to the cinema once a month with some friends can be enough to keep you in touch with other people, and give you something to think about apart from exams.

Handling uncertainty and decision-making

A common feature in stress is uncertainty. This can often be handled by simply getting the relevant information; it can also be reduced by having a plan for each of the outcomes that may emerge. It's particularly useful to have a worst-case plan which is positive, rather than involving sitting miserably in a corner waiting for death. For instance, if the worst case is that you end up unemployed for a year, you can develop a plan for using that time to do things that you wouldn't otherwise have time to do, like practising your calligraphy or learning a new skill or making new friends. One common source of uncertainty involves agonising about whether or not you've made the right decision; we talk about handling obsessive thoughts in a later section. Meanwhile, here are some useful ways of handling decisions.

Work backwards from where you want to be

This includes wanting to be somewhere that keeps your options open. People often become obsessed by an intermediate goal, such as getting a highly paid job, which has all sorts of associated problems. When you look at your higher-level goals, you often see a much better way of getting to them than the problematic intermediate goal. For instance, if you want a highly paid job so that you can afford to travel, then you might instead consider simply getting a job that involves a lot of travel.

Identify the possible options and relevant factors

What are the possible options, and what are the preconditions for each option? There are usually more options than you realise; it's worth doing some background research if the decision is an important one.

Check the question

If you can't answer a question, this may be because you're asking the wrong question; subtly changing it could make a lot of difference. One way is to imagine the possible answers to the question; if they're either silly or impossible to know, then it's not the most useful of questions. For example, asking 'Will I be happy at Fenlands University?' doesn't do too well by this criterion, since that's impossible to know in advance; asking 'Would going to Fenlands University be easily compatible with my love of rock climbing?' performs much better.

Remove irrelevant distractors

This simply involves crossing out any options that are out of the question for whatever reason, and identifying the options that are definite contenders.

Choose the best contender

What does 'best' mean? That depends. Think about one of the worst contenders. What makes it bad? That tells you at least one criterion that you can flip around to assess what constitutes a good option. Other things worth considering are whether an option is irreversible (it's usually better to go for reversible ones if possible) and what the payoffs look like. The payoffs in this context are the possible outcomes from an option; some options may pay off spectacularly if all goes well, but have disastrous consequences if things go wrong, whereas others won't pay off so spectacularly in a best case, but won't cause significant problems in a worst case.

Flip a coin

If you can't decide between two options, then this probably means that they're both equally good, so choose one at random and get on with your life.

TIMETABLING AND PLANNING

Timetabling and planning are very effective ways of getting pleasure and calm into your life; something as simple as scheduling Wednesday 2–3 pm for relaxation will give you an hour that's there just for that purpose. They also help you to spend your time more effectively. There's an effect called a *Pareto distribution*, in which 20 per cent of one thing gives you 80 per cent of another thing. For instance, 20 per cent of the time you spend on an essay will typically produce 80 per cent of the text – the remaining 20 per cent of the text will be fiddly bits that take 80 per cent of the time. If you're stressed because of lack of time, then it's a good idea to look critically at the most time-consuming activities in your life, and to see whether you're spending time on them beyond the point of diminishing returns. Instead of jumping straight into the essay and working for ten frenzied hours, for instance, you'll usually be better off spending half an hour planning the essay, then working in a more focused way for five or six hours. That gives you as good a mark, but with a lot less stress and a lot more free time to spend on other things. What other things should you spend your time on? It's your life, so it's your choice. Things that make you happy, as long as they're not damaging someone else, are usually a good choice.

How to decide how you spend your time

An important starting point is to clarify your goals. If you have a clear idea of what you want out of life, your goals are obvious. People who have clearly worked-out goals can withstand a lot of stress because they keep the goal in sight. Suppose you want to pursue your interest in mazes (or motor racing, or whatever else your hobby may be). That is too vague to be a goal. You need to refine it so that it is SMART: Specific, Measurable, Achievable, Realistic and Time-limited. Making it *Specific* could be 'To visit the most interesting mazes in Europe'; *Measurable* would be identifying which those were, and listing them. To make sure this was *Achievable* you'd need to work out whether there were any practical blockers, such as one of those mazes being in the middle of a long-running war zone. *Realistic* involves assessing whether it's actually sensible and worth trying, as opposed to possible in theory. You might in principle be able to visit each of them by travelling non-stop through a weekend, but it would be more realistic to visit them in a specified vacation, or after you graduate. You also need a specific *Time-limitation*, such as 'Next year' or 'By the time I'm 30.' This will help ensure that you actually get round to doing it, and will also help you set intermediate goals, such as applying for a passport or booking a ticket for the relevant date. Having clear goals lets you work out what is important to you. Anything that moves you closer to your goals is something that counts as important. If one of your goals is to laugh a lot, then watching comedy on TV becomes more important and watching the news becomes less important. Spend time on things that are important to you, and you will be less stressed. It also helps to work out what you would do if you met obstacles along the way to your goal. You can brainstorm possible setbacks, then think about how you would get round them. You will then be prepared for most eventualities and have plan B (and C) in place. If you wait until there is a crisis, you will have to decide what to do whilst under pressure, which is seldom fun and which rarely leads to good decisions. It's better to make the contingency plans in advance, when you are calm and have plenty of time.

Using reminders and lists

It's a good idea to write reminders to yourself to nudge you back into positive thoughts if you drift out of them. You can write a big version to put in your personal space, to remind you of just what the good thought was; you can then use something associated with this in shared space, to spare you potential embarrassment if you're shy. For example, if you're in a shared house you can put a little blue sticky dot next to the kettle and another on the bathroom mirror, and tell your housemates that it's to remind you about exam preparation; each time you see one of those dots, it's actually a reminder to you about your positive thought. Lists are indispensable, but not just any old list will do. Prioritise everything on the list and do the most important things first. Only move on to the less important things when you have made real progress on the top priority tasks. Or, if a top priority job gets too hard or too boring, use a low priority task as a 'filler.' Avoid doing several low priority, trivial tasks and letting them fill a morning. You may feel smug at having crossed six things off your list, but you won't have achieved anything worthwhile. When you have crossed all the things you have done off your list, you will be left with a rather depressing list of the things you didn't do. Making a list of things you *have* done is a good way to realise that you have achieved lots and will boost your mood.

Getting on with your life – forget the fart, and put down the supermodel

Most people worry occasionally about the risk of doing something silly which will haunt them for the rest of their lives. There's a classic story, often re-told, of a noble at the court of Elizabeth I who, when bowing to the great queen, accidentally let fly with a very loud fart. He fled the court in embarrassment, and lived quietly in the provinces for twenty years, eventually returning to the court just after the defeat of the Spanish armada, when he thought that recent events would have driven memories of his *faux pas* far from everyone's mind. The queen greeted him warmly, with the immortal line 'How pleased we are to see you again; we had quite forgotten the fart.' A good story, but an almost identical one is also told about a noble at the court of one of the great Islamic caliphs, raising the suspicion that it might be no more than a richly documented urban legend.

So what do you do about it? There's a Zen story about two monks who meet a beautiful woman at a flooded river; she can't wade across without spoiling her expensive clothes. One monk offers to carry her across; she accepts, he does so, and they go their separate ways. After a couple of miles in monastic silence the second monk says to the first monk, 'That's outrageous! We're not even supposed to talk to women, but you carried that one right across the river!' The first monk replies, 'Are you still carrying the woman? I set her down two miles ago.' (All right, so she wasn't a supermodel, but why spoil a memorable and useful good principle for the sake of pedantry?) We all make mistakes sometimes; we need to learn from them, then set down the supermodel and move on.

WELL-BEING

Fixing stress is a Good Thing, but there's more to life than that. The next section is about strategies that can help to make your life positively enjoyable and about achieving well-being.

Working backwards

When you're working out where you want to go with your life, it's tempting to focus on what's immediately in front of you, usually in the form of the option that is most familiar/easy/unthreatening. That's understandable, but it tends to nudge you gently into a gradually deeper rut, until one day you realise that there's hardly anything in your life that you like. That's a bit like choosing your holiday destination by going to the local bus station, because it's the easiest place to start, and then choosing the bus that leaves the soonest, because it involves least waiting. There's a chance that it will take you somewhere nice, but the likelihood of ending up in Corfu or Hawaii or somewhere similar is pretty slight. A better approach is to work out where you want to be, and then work backwards from that end point; if you have decided that you want to go to Hawaii, then you can start choosing the dates, flights and accommodation which will get you to that goal. It's the same with other things in your life, such as what sort of job you want, where you want to work, what you want to do with your life, and so on. This doesn't mean that your life has to be a relentless pursuit of achievements; exactly the same principle applies if you decide to lead a life of quiet monastic contemplation (in which case you'd need to find out about how to become a monk or nun, and where you can lead the said life of quiet contemplation, and so forth).

The closing scene

There's a nice scene at the end of the film *Death Becomes Her* involving the funeral eulogy for the main character. The mourners remember him fondly, as a man who gave generously to good causes and was humble despite his amazing achievements, a loyal and caring friend, a great person to talk to, and all sorts of other wonderful things. One simple but effective exercise is to think about what you would like to hear in your own eulogy – whether it would include something about what an interesting life you'd had, or what a nice person you were, or what a great parent you were, and so on. A similar exercise is to imagine yourself in old age, looking back on your life, and thinking 'I'm glad I did that.' What would the things be that you'd want to look back on? Once you've identified some of these things, you can do something about making them happen. Most of them are much more accessible than people think, particularly if they involve things that are under your control, rather than things that involve chance (such as going wreck-diving in the Bahamas, as opposed to finding a lost treasure galleon). For instance, if you want to go wreck-diving in the Bahamas, you need to do three things: save up money, sign up for a scuba diving course and book a wreck-diving holiday.

You can also do a smaller-scale version of this for events that you're concerned about. For instance, you can try imagining the interview panel for your first job reminiscing about what a wonderful interview you gave. This is a gentle way into thinking about just what would constitute a wonderful interview anyway, which will help motivate you to do some research about interview technique and about preparations for the next phase of your life. The more vivid and detailed the image, the better; you might imagine the twinkly-eyed, grey-haired woman with the glasses telling you how rare it was to meet a candidate who had done some proper background research about the organisation before applying, or the tall man saying how well you kept your cool when one of the panel members mistook you for another candidate.

Assertiveness

Many things that can cause pressure will grow if you neglect them. Putting up with a flatmate's irritating habit for months will drive you to distraction and eventually lead you to asking them to stop in an inappropriate way. If your unhygienic mate has left his smelly socks on the sofa seventeen times before you suddenly threaten to kill him if he does it again, you may get the justifiable response 'But I didn't think you minded. I've been doing it for months and you never said anything.' The time to speak up is when they have done it twice. The first time could be just a one-off, but twice is becoming a trend. (And three times is definitely enemy action.) So speak up and say it in an assertive way. Say what happened, say why that is a bad thing and request a new behaviour: 'You left your socks on the couch twice this week, and I'm upset because they make the room smell. Please keep your dirty clothes in your own room.' The last bit is important because often people can't think of anything to do to solve a problem and if you don't tell them, they will just revert to old patterns. Also, if you start a sentence with the word 'Please' it frames your request in an assertive way. If you ask assertively, and the unhelpful stuff continues, ask again. And again. And again. Each time refuse to be side-tracked, or put off. Stay calm and polite and persistent. When a flat-sharer owed rent to one of us, he wrote out the cheque seven times before he got it right. Staying calm and persistent eventually extracted the money, without lasting harm to the relationship.

Saying 'no' is sometimes difficult, especially if you don't feel you have a socially acceptable excuse. 'I don't want to' somehow seems not good enough. It helps if you offer an alternative. 'No, not tonight; how about

Wednesday?' is easier to say, and to hear. Again, be firm or you will spend your time doing things you don't want to do instead of doing the things you do want to do.

Handling criticism

Criticism can cause strain, especially if you don't know how to handle it. There are two types of criticism and you need to recognise the difference. The first is legitimate feedback that is intended to help you improve your skills. For instance, if you take a long time to come to the point in an essay and a tutor highlights a passage as irrelevant, this is constructive criticism, even though you may not feel pleased about it at the time. The other sort of criticism aims to manipulate you and make you feel bad. This type of criticism is based on a grain of truth, or the possibility – or fear – of a grain of truth.

One common response is to think that the criticism may be horribly right; another common response is to rise to the provocation by making an angry retort which shows just how much the criticism has struck home. There are much more effective ways of responding. The key principle is to refuse the emotional double-bind of either getting into an argument or of leaving the criticism unchallenged and rankling. One way of doing this is via a calmly worded response which makes it clear that you're not going to rise to the bait, but which doesn't give the critic any easy way to respond – for instance, saying 'Maybe you are right' or 'Oh, really, thanks for telling me.' The sub-text is clearly that you're confident enough not to be bothered by their opinion, and there's not much they can say to that without looking either silly or obviously aggressive. (One obvious proviso is that you shouldn't use this in response to a criticism that contradicts your basic beliefs, such as someone saying that you're a Nazi.)

Another strategy is to ask a factual question which forces the critic to come up with something tangible, such as: 'What exactly don't you like about my clothes?' This will usually either make it clear that the criticism is just a matter of subjective opinion, or, more rarely but more usefully, give you some factual information about an area where you actually could benefit from changing your ways. If you're dealing with someone who typically stores up piles of grudges, looking for an excuse to trot them out, then go for the first strategy so they don't get a chance to wheel out their list of specific complaints; if you're dealing with someone who typically says whatever comes into their head, without any thought behind it, then go for the second, so they have to back off because they don't have any specific objections to your behaviour. The best thing about this tactic is that you no longer behave like a victim, and it is such an unexpected response that it often throws your critic off balance. You may need to persist, but usually the critic just goes away and picks on someone else.

Aiming to fail often enough

If you aim to succeed in everything you do, without ever making a mistake, then that is setting you up for neurosis. If you aim to fail in everything you do, then that's setting yourself up for misery. Somewhere inbetween is healthy; what's it to be for you? If you set a sensible failure rate, then that gives you a reasonable benchmark for assessing that your overall goals are realistic. For instance, when you apply for jobs, a rejection rate of 100 per cent suggests that you're either doing something wrong or aiming too high, but an invitation-to-interview rate of 100 per cent suggests that you're aiming too low, and could go for something better. Also, aiming for a realistic achievement rate reduces the risk of becoming neurotic about success, and the risk of being guilt-racked and miserable if things don't always go as intended. You're human; every human being makes mistakes and has things go wrong sometimes; it's good to forgive others who have made mistakes and are genuinely sorry about them, so you should also forgive your-self for not being utterly perfect all the time.

SUMMARY

There are simple, effective techniques for handling the stress response; these usually involve deliberate breathing and deliberate mental imagery. There are also simple, effective techniques for sorting out your life and planning the future that you want, as part of moving on from stress towards well-being. Key themes in this include working backwards from where you want to end up; setting clear, achievable goals; re-assessing your plan at intervals, to take account of developments since the plan was made; and learning to view criticism and your own human fallibility in a positive light. This chapter dealt with general stressors. The next chapter deals with specific stressors relating to the move from school and home to university.

BIBLIOGRAPHY AND SUGGESTED FURTHER RESOURCES

Handling immediate stress

There are numerous good books on this topic; here are a few examples:

Philip Banyard's book *Applying Psychology to Health* (Hodder, 1999) is an entertaining introduction to many of the issues raised here and treats specific topics like Post-Traumatic Stress Disorder (PTSD) in more detail.

For a self-help programme to overcome PTSD, *The Trauma Trap* by David Muss (Doubleday, 1991) is a very useful practical guide.

William Dement's book *The Promise of Sleep* (Dell, 1999) is a very comprehensive cover-age of the way we spend about one-third of our lives. It includes practical advice to combat failure to sleep.

The Origin of Everyday Moods by Robert Thayer (Oxford University Press, 1996) focuses on managing energy levels as well as tension and stress.

We also recommend Stafford Whiteaker's book *The Little Book of Inner Space: Your Guide to Finding Personal Peace* (Rider, 1998). This contains a lot of useful, bite-sized pieces of good advice. It's small enough to fit easily into a handbag or pocket, so if you want something calming you can carry round with you, you may find this one useful. Another good book in the same series is *The Little Book of Calm*, by P. Wilson (Penguin, 1999), which featured in the TV comedy series *Black Books*; it really does exist. If you're looking through the Little Books series, then be aware that *The Little Book of Stress* is not what it might appear from the title; it's a darkly humorous book whose front cover proclaims 'Calm is for wimps. Get real. Get stressed.'

Achieving your potential

There are many books, videos, DVDs and courses on this topic, as well as a philosophical/spiritual movement known as the Human Potential Movement.

A good, straightforward introduction to the rational-emotive approach to tackling behaviours and achieving your potential is *Peak Performance* by Windy Dryden and Jack Gordon (Management Books 2000 Ltd, 1993).

Susan Jeffers's *Feel the Fear and Do It Anyway* (Arrow Books, London, 1991 edition), is a classic book about helping yourself to make the most of your life and to achieve your dreams. It's both inspirational and realistic, as well as being very readable – the sort of book you can keep somewhere near to hand, and dip into when you need some positive thoughts, or some ideas about what you can tackle next.

Habits and behaviours

There's lots of material about curing yourself of bad habits, and getting yourself into good habits. Some of this is about low-level, specific habits such as smoking, drinking and addictive behaviour. Some is about broader issues such as your beliefs about life as a whole, and the patterns of behaviour that you use. We've listed a few books of each type.

Eric Berne's *Games People Play: The Psychology of Human Relationships* (Penguin, 1968 edition) is one of the classic books about patterns of behaviour that people use, and about how these form part of people's world-views. The mention of 'games' in the title is in some ways unfortunate, since this has connotations of leisure pastimes – Berne made the choice quite deliberately, and for good reason, but it does deter some people from reading the book. The book is clearly written, and contains numerous case studies. The main strength of the book is the identification of behaviour patterns – for instance, the 'ain't it awful?' pattern, where the person has a pattern of looking for something to complain about, and if necessary making bad things happen so that there is something about which they can complain. If you want to look at the bigger picture of how you're tackling life, then this is well worth reading.

8 Relaxation Skills

STEPHEN PALMER AND ANGELA PURI

What this chapter covers

This chapter addresses two methods of dealing with stress. Section 1 covers imagery, which is a proactive technique that addresses the visual images individuals may have about a stressful or anxiety-provoking situation which is yet to occur or which is currently impacting on you. The four main types of imagery covered in this section include: coping imagery, time projection imagery, motivation imagery and relaxation imagery.

In section 2, we explore how relaxation can assist in reducing your stress levels. The techniques outlined in the section include: diaphragmatic breathing, meditation and easy-to-use, stress-busting techniques.

Section 1: Imagery

Imagery is a powerful method of stress reduction, especially if you visualise your thoughts and feelings about situations in pictures and mental images inside your head. When you are stressed or worried about a situation you are more likely to conjure up negative mental images of the event or situation going wrong. These images are likely to increase your anxiety and stress levels.

'I had a lecturer who would go through your work during the lecture in front of everyone else. It was mortifying! I dreaded going to her lectures — I'd always imagine her as being this big giant, glaring down at me, waiting for me to make that one mistake, so she could enjoy her moment of glory. I would picture her picking me up in her big hand and showing me to the rest of the class as being an example of stupidity! A bit extreme I know, but she really did intimidate me that much!'

Michael, 22 years, Aberdeen

As Michael's images illustrate, the mental picture does not have to be realistic, but it can still provoke anxiety. Michael found the lecturer so intimidating that he soon conjured up negative images of her and how she dealt with him. Having negative images can be very stressful, and as time goes on they are likely to make it harder for you to handle the problem effectively. In fact you may choose to avoid the situation completely.

Have a go! Imagery

Think of the last time you were really stressed or worried about a future event. Picture the event in your head. Do your negative images invoke greater feelings of stress or do they calm you down?

Fortunately, there are a number of imagery exercises that have been designed to alleviate some of the stress you may encounter by negative images. This section will focus on a number of imagery exercises that have been found to be beneficial in reducing the negative images you may sometimes experience under stressful circumstances. These include:

- Coping imagery
- Time projection imagery
- Motivation imagery
- Relaxation imagery

Coping imagery

This technique enables you to edit the image in your mind by replacing the negative and stressful scenario with a more helpful yet realistic interpretation of a situation.

Notice that this type of imagery is called *coping* and not *mastering* imagery. This is because if you are concerned about your ability to handle a situation it is unlikely that you will be comfortable imagining yourself handling a situation perfectly – as it will probably feel unrealistic. Coping imagery helps an individual to accept that they may not be able to give the perfect presentation or be the life and soul of a party but if things go wrong, they are equipped with the skills to deal with the problem.

The technique consists of four simple steps:

Step 1 – Think of a future situation that you are stressed about.

Step 2 – Note down the aspects of the situation that you are most stressed about.

Step 3 – Develop ways to deal with these difficulties.

Step 4 – Practise the new approaches to dealing with the difficult situations

Practise step 4 daily, especially when you become stressed about the forthcoming event.

This simple approach can be used for a wide range of problems. For example, if you are stressed about being asked difficult questions after giving a presentation, then you need to focus on how you would deal with this situation if it did actually occur. Don't pretend that it might not happen. Perhaps you might decide the best strategy would be to inform the audience that you are unsure of the answer to that particular question but will get back to that person after the presentation. This strategy would then become the key aspect of the visualisation that would be practised in step 4.

Case study **Coping imagery**

Bob is an 18 year-old student. He has wanted to ask Stacey from his tutor group out on a date. He has been told that she is going to be at the Student Union on Friday night. Although Bob is very eager to ask her out, he is very anxious that she will say no and he'll look stupid in front of his friends.

Bob keeps imagining Stacey saying no and sometimes visualises her laughing in his face. But his worst fear is his friends watching him when Stacey tells him that she is not interested.

Bob developed a new picture to deal with this potentially stressful scenario – Stacey rejecting him. Instead of standing around awkwardly and getting embarrassed, which was his current mental image, he imagined himself casually walking away from Stacey towards his friends and shrugging his shoulders. This was much more acceptable and less anxiety- provoking than his previous image, as he felt he still maintained a level of dignity in the process.

Bob practised the new image every day. Although the picture varied sometimes from him shrugging his shoulders and walking away, to him shrugging his shoulders and saying to his mates *'Oh well, it was worth a go! You win some, you lose some!'*

The anxiety of asking Stacey out was reduced as he had learnt a new way of dealing with the worst possible outcome he could imagine!

Although this may appear to be a simple technique, many people get stuck at step 3, as they are unable to develop ways to deal with the situation. In these cases, it may help to discuss the problem with a colleague or friend. Remember, the idea is to deal with your worst fears and not to pretend that they simply may not happen. This method helps to prevent negative images becoming self-fulfilling prophecies, by challenging and addressing negative thoughts and images.

Time projection imagery

So often, people lose their perspective when they are faced with stressful situations such as failing an exam or breaking up with a partner. Time projection imagery helps you to keep stressful situations in perspective by assisting you to realise that the problem or situation may not be *that bad*.

Method

Step 1 – Think of a problem or situation that you are stressed about.

Step 2 – Picture yourself three months in the future. Will the current problem be as stressful as it is now?

Step 3 – Picture yourself six months in the future. Will the problem be as stressful or as important as it is now? Can you see yourself getting on with your life?

Step 4 – Picture yourself 12 months in the future. Will the current problem be as stressful or as important as it is now? Can you see yourself getting on with your life?

Step 5 – Picture yourself two years in the future. Will the current problem be as stressful or as important as it is now? Will you laugh at your problem when you look back on it? Can you see yourself having fun again?

Are you getting the idea? The technique is all about taking a step back and looking at the problem afresh.

Case study Time Projection imagery

Lisa received her exam results for a module that she had been struggling with all year. She had failed the exam by 5 per cent and was devastated. Lisa had persevered with the course even though she found it difficult. Failing the course made her question her ability and she felt that all her hard work had gone to waste.

Lisa used time projection imagery to help her put the examination result into perspective.

She pictured herself in three months time. Was the result still stressful? Lisa felt it wouldn't be as intense as it was now, but it would still be a worry for her. She would need to decide whether she was going to retake the module or just accept her mark which would impact on her pass mark for the year.

Lisa then imagined herself thinking about the exam result in six months time. Was it still as important and stressful? Lisa felt that she wouldn't be as worried after such a long duration. She would have decided whether to retake the module or not by then, and would probably be taking a course of action to rectify the situation. However, she thought she would still question her abilities to a certain extent.

Lisa pictured herself 12 months into the future. She imagined that she would have moved on by then. She would be into her next year at university and this mark would have no relevance to her anymore. She believed that she would take on board the lessons learnt from this experience but it would not impact on the way she lived her life in any other way!

By doing the time projection imagery, Lisa was able to establish how much relevance and importance to place on the exam result. Although she had to deal with the problems it raised in the immediate future, its long-term implications appeared to be minimal.

Motivation imagery

This technique is used to motivate people into action and can be applied to any given situation or problem (Palmer and Neenan, 1998). The technique highlights the impact of doing nothing compared to seeing your goals through.

Have a go! Motivation imagery

Think about an area of your life that you need to do something about. Until now you may have avoided thinking about it or have found you are too busy to change the situation. For example, starting a piece of course work or finishing a relationship that is no longer working out.

Now imagine you do not do it. What impact is this likely to have on you? Would you have any regrets if the situation stays the same? How do you feel about it? Happy or sad? How do you think the people around you may react?

(Continued)

(Continued)

Now imagine making the change (i.e. starting the course work or splitting up with your partner). What would be the short-term, medium-term and long-term benefits that the change would make in your life?

Finally consider how you are now going to make that change. Put your thoughts into action.

Please note that the order of the exercise should stay the same, beginning with imagining that you do **not** change the situation and then imagining that you do act and change the situation. Only then can it aid your motivation to carry out the task. Doing it in the reverse order can be demotivating!

Relaxation imagery

When you are feeling stressed out, imagery is a fantastic tool to unwind, releasing all the tensions of the day. The aim of relaxation imagery is to help you to imagine yourself relaxing in a place which gives you comfort and or that you enjoy being in. This then leads to you actually feeling more calm and relaxed. This technique has been found to be very useful for people who suffer from sleeping problems. To use this imagery, just follow the nine simple steps outlined below (Palmer and Strickland, 1996):

1. Find a place where there is as little noise as possible, and where you will not be disturbed.
2. Either lie or sit in a comfortable position.
3. Close your eyes and picture your favourite relaxing place.
4. Concentrate on the colours in this place.
5. Concentrate on one particular colour.
6. Concentrate on the sounds in your place. It may even be complete silence.
7. Imagine touching something in your place.
8. Concentrate on the smells and aromas in your favourite relaxing place.
9. When you are ready, open your eyes.

You may find it easier to record your voice or have someone read this out to you for the first few times. After a while you will find that you automatically follow the steps and will be able to reach a relaxed state quickly and without much effort. You can make it last only a few minutes or extend the exercise for up to 20 minutes.

Section 2: Relaxation techniques

There are a number of different ways to relax and you are the best judge of what works best for you. Relaxation can range from painting, listening to music to meditation and positive relaxation imagery. The aim of relaxation is to re-energise yourself by giving your body and mind time to wind down and forget about the day-to-day issues it has to deal with. By clearing your mind of tensions whilst you relax, you are likely to find that when you re-visit a problem at a later stage, you will be able to deal with it more efficiently.

In this section, we will introduce you to a few different methods of relaxation, including deep breathing, meditation and easy and quick relaxation tips to use when you are on the go!

Breathing

Our chest is full of muscles which pull our ribs up and down as we inhale and exhale. This is what enables us to breathe. We need oxygen to work our muscles and so the air we inhale is passed through our lungs and into our bloodstream, from where the oxygen is passed around the body. How we breathe is a great indicator of how we are feeling. When we are nervous or anxious, our breath is shallow and fast, whereas when we are relaxed our breath tends to be slower and more controlled. There are many breathing techniques which assist in relaxation by slowing down our breath. In this section we will concentrate on diaphragmatic breathing.

Diaphragmatic breathing

Although this is not the natural way we breathe everyday, it is great for energising or relaxing our body and mind. Diaphragmatic breathing allows more oxygen into the body, by taking longer and deeper breaths. The technique is outlined below.

Step 1 – Gently fill your lungs up with air (your chest will naturally rise up and your stomach may come out slightly).

Step 2 – Gently breathe out through the nose (your chest will drop) and squeeze your stomach in to dispel all the carbon dioxide from the lungs.

Step 3 – Repeat the exercise two or three times, or until you feel less stressed and calmer.

This breathing technique gently massages the abdominal organs and makes you aware of how you breathe.

Please note: People who suffer from asthma, anxiety attacks or have smokers cough may have some problems with deep breathing. You may experience dizziness. Please do the breathing exercises gradually and only breathe in and out at a level which is comfortable for you.

Laughter

It may seem like just another cliché but we all know how great we feel once we have had a good laugh. It has been suggested that one minute of extensive laughter can provide up to 45 minutes of relaxation. Laughter is great for the body as it releases tension and stimulates the immune system. It is also said to create a feel-good factor by releasing endorphins into the blood.

A simple smile can have an impact on the way we feel. A smile is the universal expression of happiness, and apparently the most frequently used facial expression. Supposedly, even if you fake a smile, it can make you feel better!

In addition, people who are more relaxed are said to live longer, healthier lives and are better to cope able with pain. They are also meant to be able to handle difficult people more effectively too!

Massage

Massage is a brilliant way to relieve the tension and stresses of the day! The basic goal of massage is to help the body heal itself and to increase health and well-being.

Many practitioners learn specific techniques, in which they use their sense of touch to determine the right amount of pressure to apply to each person and also to locate where the areas of tension are.

When we are stressed, our muscles can become very tense and overworked. This produces waste products which can cause soreness, stiffness and even muscle spasms. By improving circulation, which increases blood flow and brings fresh oxygen to body tissues, massage assists in eliminating waste products from the body.

Therapeutic massage can be used to promote general well-being and enhance self-esteem, as well as boosting the circulatory and immune systems to benefit blood pressure, circulation, muscle tone, digestion, and skin tone. Massage is found in many different forms (such as Swedish massage, shiatsu or Indian head massage), so it is worth finding out what is available before embarking on a course of treatment. Also, self-massage can be a useful skill to learn as you do not need to rely on others.

Relaxation methods

Relaxation methods are techniques to progressively relax your body and calm your mind. Three relaxation methods are included in this handbook:

- Guided light meditation
- The Benson Relaxation Technique
- Self-hypnosis

The self-hypnosis method is available in Appendix 1 of this handbook. You may find that one strategy works better than the other so give them a go and see which one you prefer.

These relaxation methods are written out as scripts below. You may find it useful to ask a friend to read them out to you or record your own voice reading them and play it back whenever required. During the relaxation exercises you may experience tingling or a warm sensation. This is quite normal. However, if you do not like it, gently open your eyes and the sensation will stop.

Guided light meditation

Guided light meditation uses more imagery than other types of meditation. The aim is to imagine moving the light from a candle to different parts of your body. Whilst you do this, you automatically become more relaxed. However, if you find it hard to visualise the light, you may find the mantra meditation more suitable (the Benson Relaxation Technique).

This exercise requires you to light a candle and place it carefully in a safe place, at a sensible distance away from the body (a few metres away from the body). The candle should be placed at your eye level. Sit comfortably on the floor or on a chair. (The script is to be spoken out loud.)

Gently lower your shoulders and relax the body. Forget about all the things you have been doing today, and all the things you still have to do. Be present, in this room, now *(pause for 5 seconds)*

Feel the air in the room gently brush against your face …

(Continued)

(Continued)

Listen to the noises inside the room *(pause for 5 seconds)* … now take your hearing outside this room, take it as far as it can go *(pause for 5 seconds)*

Now bring your hearing back into the room … and look at the candle flame in front of you.

Look carefully at the flame – notice its colours and the aura around it *(pause for 10 seconds)*

Gently close your eyes and **imagine** taking the light from the candle flame to your forehead, between your eyebrows … and into your head. Let your head fill up with light from the candle *(pause for 10 seconds)*

Now imagine moving the light behind the eyes and let the eyes be filled with light *(pause for 5 seconds)*

Now imagine the warmth and light of the flame move into you ears … now move it to your mouth and tongue *(pause for 5 seconds)*

Now imagine the light gently travelling down your arms … to the hands … right down to the fingertips … and let the light permeate them *(pause for 5 seconds)*

Allow the light to gently move down through the body … imagine it slowly moving down the legs … to the feet and right down to the toes *(pause for 10 seconds)*

Now gently bring the light back to the head *(pause for 5 seconds)*

Expand the light … let it become brighter and brighter *(pause for 5 seconds)*

As the light fills your body … let it then radiate the room … let the light fill the room with brightness *(pause for 10 seconds)*

Now staying with that calmness, bring your thoughts back into the room you are sitting in *(pause for 5 seconds)*

Become aware of your feet and body … notice the air gently brush against your cheeks … hear the noises in the room *(pause for 5 seconds)*

Remember what you still have to do today … and remember throughout the week that if you want to relax all you have to do is fall still, as you have done so now.

Slowly count to 10 … and when you feel ready, gently open your eyes.

The main difference between the Benson Relaxation Technique (Benson, 1976) and the guided light meditation is that one visualises light going through your body and the other concentrates on repeating the number 'one' or another number of your choice. It is down to personal preference as to which one you find easier to do.

Find a comfortable position in a place where you will not be disturbed. (The script is to be said out loud.)

Close your eyes

Relax your muscles in groups, starting at your face and progressing down to your toes *(pause for 10 seconds)*

Now focus on your breathing. Breathe naturally through your nose. Imagine that your breathing is coming from your stomach; do not let your shoulders rise *(pause for 5 seconds)*

In your mind, say the number 'one' every time you breathe out

(continue this for 5–20 minutes – finish when you feel ready, but keep still for a few minutes before opening your eyes)

Self-hypnosis

Self-hypnosis works by aiding you to relax and as you relax you become more receptive to positive or helpful statements made. Please note that self-hypnosis is not a form of controlling another person's senses or mind.

Fitting relaxation into your life

When life gets hectic, we often find that our well-intentioned plans get left behind, as daily pressures build up. Time to *fit in* relaxation is less likely to happen if it is not planned, so you need to make the time for relaxation.

Have a go! Relaxation

Think about the scheduled activities that you have to do this week, including lectures, meeting family or friends, personal study time and so on. Based on the commitments you already have planned for the week, when can you fit in time for relaxation? It is easy to think of relaxation as being a bit self-indulgent, but if you want to be more efficient and effective in other aspects of your life, looking after your body and mind will help to keep those stress levels down!

[...]

Chapter summary

This chapter was broken down into two sections. Section 1 explored how imagery can help you deal with negative images that you may have visualised in your mind's eye, especially when you are under uncomfortable levels of pressure. Four types of imagery were discussed:

✓   Coping imagery: editing a negative image and replacing it with a more helpful and less stressful scenario

✓   Time projection imagery: taking a step back from the problem and putting it into perspective

✓   Motivation imagery: highlighting the impact of not changing a situation or problem compared to taking action, and addressing the issue at hand

✓   Relaxation imagery: imagining yourself in a familiar and comfortable place, which helps to relax your mind and release your tensions

Section 2 of this chapter concentrated on relaxation skills to assist in alleviating stress and tension from your body and mind. Techniques included:

✓   Breathing: exercises to help energise or relax your body and mind

✓   Laughter: how laughter releases tension in the body and stimulates the immune system, promoting relaxation

✓   Massage: the effects of massage on the immune system and your feeling of well-being

✓ Relaxation scripts: methods of progressive relaxation which gently relax the body and still the mind

✓ Fitting relaxation into your life: the need to make time for relaxation and quick tips on instant relaxation!

Learning points from the chapter

Use the space below to write down any techniques or comments that you have from reading this chapter.

Helpful resources

***30 Scripts for Relaxation, Imagery and Inner Healing*. Julie T. Lusk (1992). Duluth, MN: Whole Person Associates.**
The book incorporates scripts for relaxation, ranging from five minutes to 30 minutes. Each script states at the beginning how long it should take and gives a brief description as to what to expect from the practice.

***Stress Relief and Relaxation Techniques*. Lazarus, Judith (2000). Chicago, IL: Keats Publishing Inc.**
This guide helps readers dissolve stress, gain clarity and cultivate a more peaceful existence with relaxation and stress relief therapies, ranging from meditation to massage, biofeedback and journal-writing.

9 Anger Management

STEPHEN PALMER AND ANGELA PURI

What this chapter covers

This chapter is divided into two sections. Section 1 looks at assertion techniques whilst section 2 looks at how to manage your anger levels.

In section 1, we will cover the four main behavioural styles that we use when dealing with situations (aggressive, passive, indirect and assertive). There is also a questionnaire to help you identify how assertive you are. A number of assertion techniques are also outlined to assist you in being more effective when dealing with confrontational or stressful situations.

Section 2 will look at the reasons why you get angry. It will concentrate on challenging the anger response, so you can deal with confrontational or stressful situations in a rational way, which is less damaging to your health. In addition, an anger de-activating exercise is included. This will help you to increase your awareness of what your anger triggers are, and how you can learn to address them.

Section 1: Being assertive

Acting assertively is a fantastic way of managing your stress levels. It enables you to express your needs directly and calmly without causing conflict or misunderstanding. It helps you to stand your ground and prevent others from wasting your valuable time.

How do you behave?

Researchers have identified four types of behaviour that people display: aggressive behaviour, passive behaviour, passive-aggressive behaviour (or indirect behaviour) and assertive behaviour. The main characteristics of the four behaviour types are outlined below, along with their effectiveness in stressful or pressurised situations.

Aggressive behaviour

Aggressive individuals tend to react to stressful situations with hostility or anger, regardless of whether or not they are provoked by others. Their bursts of anger may even make them feel temporarily in control or even superior to others around them. In addition, aggressive individuals believe that they are being assertive, but the way they stand up for their rights often violates the rights of others. Eventually this behaviour may cause conflict with others as they become resentful of the aggressive individual's behaviour.

The main problem with aggression as a behaviour style is that it can belittle and insult other people. It may also anger others or intimidate them. Typical aggressive behaviour is characterised by feelings of anger, power or agitation. Aggressive people tend to be *bullies*, with behaviours ranging from pointing, shouting, thumping fists, to picking on other people's vulnerabilities to make them feel more powerful and superior. Their language is characterised by phrases such as *'You should be/you must / don't act dumb / this is all your fault!'*

In the long term, if an aggressive style of behaviour is consistently used, an individual is likely to upset friends and colleagues, and may find that they are unable to influence others, leading to feelings of isolation and rejection. They may also lose the respect of others, which can impact on their own levels of self-esteem. All of these potential outcomes will increase levels of stress.

Passive behaviour (Unassertive behaviour)

Unassertive people are often denoted as being the *mug* or *push over* in a given situation. Individuals who display this type of behaviour are likely to allow others to walk all over them. This behaviour is particularly unhelpful because these individuals end up doing things for others or accepting situations that they are uncomfortable with. So, they may end up regretting doing the favour or resenting others for *putting them in it* (blaming others). The type of language used by passive individuals includes phrases such as *'Could I? … Would it be okay if I …? It's not important … It doesn't matter … Never mind … Sorry to bother you.'*

Passive behaviour is often characterised by feelings of guilt – people are unable to gratify the wishes of others. This occurs alongside suppressed anger for being taken advantage of. Their behaviour tends to be apologetic and they avoid confrontation at any cost. Passive individuals lack self-confidence and this is displayed in their physical behaviour, for example through downcast eyes, shrugs or hand wringing. Unassertive individuals tend to play the role of the victim. They usually blame or whinge about a particular situation without taking responsibility for themselves (i.e. they forget that they *do* have a choice!). Unfortunately this behaviour may also lower one's self-esteem, as the passive individual is more likely to view themselves as powerless and helpless with regards to their circumstances. They are likely to have a high external locus of control as they view circumstances as happening to them, and are more likely to see themselves as being too helpless to deal with the situation. These feelings and perceptions of themselves are likely to increase stress and anxiety levels.

Passive-aggressive behaviour (or indirectly aggressive behaviour)

Individuals who fall into this category tend to display a mixture of both aggressive and passive behaviour. They are likely to be more manipulative with their requests and can be more defensive in their approach to situations. Individuals who display passive-aggressive behaviour tend to be more moody, more controlling of other people and may use emotional bribery to get their desired response.

Initially, passive-aggressive individuals can be quite influential. However, over time, other people become wary or confused by their behaviour because of the mixed signals they receive from them. Passive-aggressive individuals use these techniques to protect themselves by avoiding confrontation, as they fear they may be undermined. However, this behaviour also leads to a reduction in self-esteem and self-confidence.

Assertive behaviour

Assertive people avoid misunderstandings and actively reduce the possibility of being exploited. It is a useful behaviour pattern because it deals with interpersonal difficulties in a straightforward and constructive manner, which reduces resentment. An assertive person uses co-operative statements such as *we could*, or *I feel*. Assertive individuals are adaptable and collaborative in style and approach. They tend to be good communicators, both verbally and behaviourally. Physical behaviours include good eye contact and being both relaxed and confident. They make others feel valued, respected and listened to, whilst remaining confident themselves, and possess an inner sense of power.

The benefits of assertive behaviour are that it gets quicker results and the individual is in a good position to seize opportunities when they arise. Assertive individuals are also more likely to develop honest relationships that are based on mutual respect. An assertive individual is also more likely to be confident and have higher self-esteem. They suffer less stress as they are calmer and perceive themselves as having more control over their problems.

How assertive are you?

Fill in the following questionnaire to see whether you display assertive behaviour in the situations outlined below. Circle the response which best describes how you would respond in each of the following scenarios.

CAN YOU:	Yes	No	Sometimes
Say no when a colleague or friend makes an unreasonable demand?	Y	N	S
Accept compliments easily?	Y	N	S
Admit easily to mistakes?	Y	N	S
Apologise when it is your fault?	Y	N	S
Ask for help from others?	Y	N	S
Listen to criticism about yourself?	Y	N	S
Speak up for yourself?	Y	N	S
Express your feelings appropriately?	Y	N	S
Avoid being exploited by others?	Y	N	S
DO YOU:			
Take responsibility for your behaviour?	Y	N	S
Accept the consequences of your decisions?	Y	N	S
Tell friends your true opinion?	Y	N	S
Tell your lecturer if you are dissatisfied with your assignment?	Y	N	S
Readily ask for clarification if you do not understand something?	Y	N	S

Add up all the circles in the Yes column.

If you have 12 or more responses in this column you display assertive behaviour on a regular basis.

If you circle between 8 and 12 in the Yes column you are reasonably assertive and may just need to focus on a few areas.

If you have less than 8-circled responses in the Yes column you are likely to exhibit aggressive, passive-aggressive or passive behaviours that may need more attention.

As mentioned earlier, the less assertive you are, the more likely it is that some of your stress is a direct result of your lack of assertion. For example, it is very difficult being a good time manager if you are unassertive!

Getting assertive

Acting assertively helps you to maintain your rights and gives you the confidence to do what is right for you. Below are a few techniques on how to get a message across assertively.

The three-step model

The three-step model can be applied in any situation, but especially if you are feeling intimidated or under pressure to comply with other people's demands. Using this model, you can make your point in an assertive manner without offending, becoming emotional and, more importantly, without drifting off the point you are making.

The three-step model begins by clarifying what the issues are and repeating back the points mentioned. This conveys that you have been listening to the other person and also avoids any misunderstandings.

Step 1 – Actively listen to what the other person is saying and repeat it back to demonstrate that you have heard and understood what they have said.

The second step consists of stating your opinions about the situation. It is at this stage that you explain your own thoughts and feelings.

Step 2 – Say what you think and feel (a good linking word to use between steps 1 and 2 is 'however').

In the final step of the model, you explain what you want the outcome of the situation to be. This needs to be clearly stated to avoid any misunderstandings.

Step 3 – Say what you want to happen (a good linking word to use between steps 2 and 3 is 'and').

For example:

Step 1 – *I know I said I would come home this weekend,*

Step 2 – ***However**, I have an assignment due in on Tuesday and I think it would be a good idea to work on it over the weekend*

Step 3 – ***And** I will be coming home next weekend instead.*

Broken record technique

This requires you to keep on stating your own opinion – and to keep on expressing your viewpoint in a consistent manner until your message is not ignored. The words do not have to be the same; it is the essence of the statement or belief which is important. This is a particularly useful technique when others are putting pressure on you to do something that you do not want to do or do not have time for.

Friend: *Come out tonight, you have the whole day to revise tomorrow!*
You: *I know that, but if I have a late night today I won't be able to concentrate.*
Friend: *Yeah, but we are all going out – c'mon! It's only one night. It won't make that much of a difference!*
You: *I wish! It will be to me. Have a great night and cheers for asking!*

De-fogging

This is when you find a person manipulating a situation and possibly using irrelevant facts to get the outcome they want. You need to clarify what the discussion is about and keep irrelevancies out of the dialogue.

Flat mate: *You always leave your dishes in the sink and it's not fair for the rest of us to keep tidying up after you!*

You: *During this term it's the second time I have left the dishes in the sink, and I'm sorry for doing that.*

Inquiry

This really puts the onus on the others to come up with a good explanation or reason for their negative statements about you. It encourages constructive and helpful feedback.

Lecturer: *Your essay missed the point.*

You: *In what way did it miss the point?*

Workable compromise

With this approach an agreement is reached in such a way that your self-respect is not affected.

Girlfriend: *You promised me that we'd go out to eat tonight.*

You: *I didn't realise that the football was on. How about we get a take away tonight and I'll take you out for dinner tomorrow? Would that be okay?*

Section 2: Managing your anger

Anger is an instinctive response to stress and danger, but as the dangers we face today are generally not life threatening, we usually do not require the aggressive behaviour that anger can trigger.

We all feel angry sometimes. It is a normal, usually healthy human emotion. Anger only becomes a problem when it starts getting out of control or is the first emotion we use to deal with any given situation. So, in itself, anger is not a bad thing, but problems arise if it is not managed in the right way.

Most people do not realise the long-term effects of ongoing anger. Anger can lead to a number of physical illnesses, notably coronary heart disease. But in addition, it has a large number of other side-effects – it consumes mental and physical energy, ruins your peace of mind, can negatively impact on relationships and can undermine your self-esteem. In extreme circumstances, anger can be an all-consuming emotion, clouding your mind of reasonable judgement. All of these effects have a major impact on your stress levels.

Understanding your anger

If you find that your anger is out of control and affecting your quality of life, you may benefit from looking at the way you handle your feelings when you are angry.

Anger is the emotion you experience when situations or circumstances in your world are not going according to *your* plans! It can be an adaptive response to threats to the way your world should operate. Anger can be a very powerful emotion as it allows you to fight and defend yourself when you are attacked. Aggression is another behavioural reaction to stress. When you get angry, your heart rate and blood pressure go up, as do the levels of the hormones adrenaline and, in particular, noradrenaline in your body.

To stay in control of excessive anger you need to learn how to express your feelings in a healthier way, so your annoyance or frustration is a more controlled response to the situation you are presented with. There are several techniques to handle your anger, many of which have been covered in the thinking skills and imagery chapters of the handbook. These techniques have been adapted below to be more specific to anger management.

Challenge your beliefs

As mentioned previously, your thoughts are very powerful and play a very large role in the way you react to events. When you are feeling angry, find out what it is about the particular situation or person that is causing it. What are the thoughts that go through your head once you are aware that you are getting angry (the triggers)? Do you see an image of them which upsets or annoys you? Or do you have a particular belief that keeps going through your mind?

Once you are able to identify the thinking errors or negative images you can begin to concentrate on creating new, more constructive ways of approaching the problem, which will lower your levels of stress and anger.

Case study **Anger management**

Rick found that he was losing his patience with his girlfriend every few days, and that usually the anger he displayed was unwarranted. Rick decided to write down the thoughts that went through his head every time he felt his anger manifesting and noted down why he was getting angry.

Rick soon noticed a pattern. Every time they tidied up the flat, he would find that he couldn't find some of his personal belongings. Rick couldn't stand anyone touching his possessions and he would get furious at the thought that his girlfriend may have misplaced his important documents or his CDs.

Rick wrote down a list of more helpful beliefs he could say to himself to counter-attack the negative thoughts and images that would wind him up and eventually get him angry.

Anger activating	Anger de-activating
Why does she have to touch my things?	She wouldn't have to if I put them away myself.
She has no respect for what I say!	Although I think it is wrong that she touches my belongings, does she really disrespect me? She is only trying to keep the place clean.
I bet she is looking really smug now that I can't find anything!	Imagine her feeling a bit concerned about how upset I am.
I told her I would move it myself!	That was last week. Maybe she did not think I would do it.
She always misplaces my stuff!	Am I exaggerating the truth? If she moves my stuff she normally puts it in one place, and she usually finds things I've misplaced!
I told her to leave my papers alone!	She warned me that if they were sprawled across the breakfast table, she would move them, and I didn't listen.

(Continued)

(Continued)

Anger activating	Anger de-activating
Does she do it just to irritate me?	Maybe she feels that I keep my belongings out just to irritate her.
The place is already tidy – I don't know what her problem is!	She knows she can be a bit over the top. I will tell her that she is being a bit unreasonable when I have calmed down.
I can't stand it when people touch my things!	Maybe it would be less stressful to think that *'I'd prefer it if she didn't touch my stuff. However, when she does I don't like it but I can stand it.'*

Have a go! Anger management

Think of a situation or person (or both!) which you feel angry about. Note down the negative thoughts and/or images that you have, and then challenge them by creating constructive ways of dealing with the situation or person which is not so anger-provoking.

Anger activating	Anger de-activating

Other issues to consider when dealing with anger

- **Is it worth it?**   Even if you are right to be *justifiably* angry and someone or something has done wrong by you, does it make you feel happy? You are consuming a lot of energy which could be used elsewhere in a more enjoyable way! After the situation has been rectified or the problem discussed, remaining angry is usually pointless, because it doesn't change your circumstances. You are not able to change the way another person thinks and behaves and, generally speaking, you do not have the right to. Sometimes it may be better to '*live and let live*'.
- **Use logic!**   Being logical defeats anger, because if anger is unjustified, it quickly becomes irrational. Remind yourself that this isn't the *worst day of your life* and that the day just didn't go according to plan! If you attempt to rationalise your thinking and use logic each time you feel angry, you will probably get a more balanced perspective of the problem. This is the approach most people tend to take once they decide to calm down. However, using logic earlier can save a lot of time!
- **Maintain communication.**   When anger consumes you, you're more likely to make assumptions and jump to conclusions without fully understanding the whole situation. Nothing is more unproductive than two people arguing about two completely different issues without realising it! If you find yourself in a heated discussion, take a deep breath, slow down and think before you speak! Remember to listen to the other person, as everyone has the right to his or her own opinion.
- **Stay calm.**   We realise that this may be easier said than done, but taking a few deep breaths or leaving the room for a quick walk can give you enough time to collect your thoughts and put the situation back into perspective.
- **Get fit.**   If you find that you are feeling very tense on a regular basis, exercise is a great way of reducing the tension and it also gives you some time away from everyday stresses. Relaxation exercises such as yoga, relaxation imagery and meditation can also help to release the build-up of tension in a controlled and healthy way.

Chapter summary

The aim of this chapter was to equip you with skills that would help you deal with confrontational or anger-provoking situations in a more effective manner. The two skill sets used were:

✓ Assertion skills – including a variety of thinking skills and imagery to help you become more effective when dealing with conflict

✓ Anger management – highlighting techniques to help you deal with your anger by exploring what triggers your anger response

The techniques mentioned in this chapter are generic and can be used in almost any context. However, the rest of the handbook focuses on how to deal with stress within the context of life at university.

Learning points from the chapter

Use the space provided below to write down any thoughts or comments you have about this chapter. Are the techniques helpful in reducing your stress levels?

Helpful resources

British Association of Anger Management
Tel: 0845 1300 286
Email: info@angermanage.co.uk
Website: www.baam.co.uk
Professional body of consultants, counsellors and trainers who offer individual support, workshops, seminars and bespoke packages to assist with anger management

British Association of Behavioural and Cognitive Psychotherapies
The Globe Centre, PO Box 9, Accrington BB5 0BX
Tel: 01254 875277
Fax: 01254 239114

Email: babcp@babcp.com
Website: www.babcp.org

Provides a list of accredited therapists who deal with stress, anxiety, phobias, panic attacks and depression using cognitive-behaviour therapies.

***Asserting Your Self*. Birch, C. (1999). Oxford: How to Books**

The book offers a variety of techniques to help transform unhelpful defensive behaviours into productive and assertive ways of being.

10 Asserting Yourself

BOB SMALE AND JULIE FOWLIE

What is assertiveness and why is it important?

Are you saying what you really want to say? Do you sometimes fear saying what you mean to say or fear the reaction of others?

From our prehistoric ancestors we have retained two basic responses to trouble, namely **fight** and **flight**:

- **Fight = aggression**, which is evidenced by violent language or behaviours.
- **Flight = avoidance**, in which we avoid and 'bottle up' problems and are diminished in the process.

Both responses lead to unwanted physiological changes in our body chemistry through increased adrenaline, causing short-term and long-term symptoms. The alternative approach is for us to learn to be assertive.

Every incidence of failure to assert requires two players, a manipulator and a 'nice guy'. For example, consider the following scenario:

> You kindly give me a lift to the supermarket every Friday after work, then one week I say, 'Look I am feeling really tired tonight, and also there is something on the television I want to see. If I give you some money and a list, can you get my shopping for me and drop it round later? After all, I am on your way home.'

If you are such a nice guy that you get my shopping for me, have you allowed me to manipulate you? What would be the implication of you refusing to get the shopping?

Activity: How assertive am I?

Assess how assertive you are by taking the following test. Circle the letter for the response that, in your opinion, best answers each of the following questions.

1. You are in a long line to pay for your lunch. Someone walks up and moves into the line in front of you. The assertive thing to do is:

(Continued)

(Continued)

a. to complain to others around you in a loud voice.
b. to ask the person to go to the end of the line.

2. Which of the following is a reason to be assertive?

a. to achieve your goals.
b. to show who is right.

3. The definition of assertiveness usually includes the following:

a. 'deny the rights of others'.
b. 'ask for what you want'.

4. A non-assertive person may respond to a situation with non-verbal cues such as:

a. a whiny voice.
b. direct eye contact.

5. Aggressive words from others violate your right to courtesy and respect. Which of the following is an aggressive comment?

a. 'Don't be such a fool.'
b. 'Would you mind very much if we skip the formalities?'

6. Which of the following is an appropriate assertive response?

a. keeping your opinions to yourself when you are angry with your boss.
b. asking your boss for a meeting in which you can express your point of view.

The correct answers are: 1: b   2: a   3: b   4: a   5: a   6: b

Learning some assertiveness techniques

Assertiveness techniques help us to express our needs in a way that is polite and generally acceptable to others. Most of the time people are cooperative and thoughtful, but when conflict arises people respond in different ways. Some act aggressively, some passively, and some assertively. In order to become more assertive, here are some techniques that can help:

- Remember that no one can manipulate you, unless you allow him or her to do so.

- Avoid *knee jerk* reactions. In a busy life it is easy to feel that we have to respond to every situation immediately.

- Give yourself thinking time. Take stock and think what you should say or do. It could be nothing!

- Learn to say no, when it is appropriate to do so.

- Learn how to say no, avoiding 'I can't' which is negative and diminishing in favour of 'I won't', which is your positive choice.

- Learn to say yes when you *want* to and not because you think you *ought* to.

- Be persistent when necessary. Smith (1975: 73–87) talks about the **broken record**: 'I won't, no I won't', etc. Eventually they will get the message.

If faced with a threat of violence it may be better not to act assertively, but rather **non-assertively**. If you are being held at knifepoint or a car is speeding towards you, an assertion will be of little use. Flight and/or fight are still appropriate responses in dangerous situations, which is what 'Mother Nature' designed them for.

[…]

Influencing others

Achieving your goals often involves influencing those around you, in order for you to develop and progress. However, people don't like to feel they are being used or manipulated and it is easy to make enemies in the process. The good news is that most people seem to like being helpful, if they are approached in the right way, and so it is important to win people over to your cause. Cooperation will be a key word.

There is no one way to influence people around you, but here are some ideas to work through.

- **Goals** – being clear on your goals and what you want to achieve is a good starting point. Your goals can become a focus for everything else you do. Try practising what you learnt in Chapter 2, reminding yourself regularly of your goals and visualising your success.

- **Interpersonal skills** – improving these involves developing the skills covered in this chapter. This will help you to achieve your goals by improving the interactions you have with others. This development will include your interview skills, understanding emotions, non-verbal communication, and being able to assert yourself when required.

- **Networking** – is an active process in which you commit yourself to building your network of contacts with others. You never know when a contact will become useful, so it is always worth asking for a phone number and giving them yours.

- **Relationship building** – is also an active process, not this time involving casual contacts but rather those who will help and encourage you. In higher education this will include both your friends and friendly tutors. It is good to work out who is going to be important to you and to give them your attention.

- **Leadership** – some situations require you to put yourself out front, for example when completing a group assignment. Someone will have to take the lead and they will most probably have the biggest influence on the final result, so, why not make sure it's you? See also Chapter 5, Completing group assignments successfully.

- **Confidence** – people will be much more likely to react positively to someone who displays confidence in what they are doing. Try to act as if you count, even if you are not sure whether you do. It's amazing how confidence grows when you start to do this and people start to take you seriously. However, avoid arrogance as that will tend to alienate those you need to help you. There is a fine line between confidence and arrogance – and it's very important to recognise it.

[...]

In terms of influencing and persuading, it is essential to consider how you approach people. It's not just a question of what you say and how you say it, but also to whom, when and where.

Letters tend to get filed or – worse still – binned and emails overlooked or deleted, so face-to-face or telephone communications are always preferable. If you do have to write, make sure you call first to get a name, address and position. If you don't get a reply you can always back this up with a phone call, politely asking if the named recipient received your letter.

A student told us...

A student told us that he had telephoned a major corporation (which will remain nameless) for help with a research project and that they had been very unhelpful. When asked how many people he had spoken to he replied, 'One'. He was then informed that the corporation currently had in the region of 160,000 employees and that he might just have been unlucky. He tried again, and got the help he needed.

When calling an organisation, it is often best to explain who you are and what you want, and then to ask who could help you. It doesn't matter how many times you get transferred, if you get to the right person in the end.

When you are referred from one person to another, try to get the name of the person referring you as well as the person you are passed on to. You can then introduce yourself by saying, 'Mr/Ms X suggested I talk to you'. It helps to break the ice.

If someone works in a busy office, can you set up a time to take him or her for a coffee, in order to sit down quietly and have chat? Alternatively, can you make an appointment to see them?

Activity: Developing your influencing skills

- Consider who you need to influence in order to achieve your goals.
- Consider how you might best approach them, what to say, when and how – i.e. the best way, best time, best place.
- Activate your plans, review how they are going and be prepared to change your approach if it is not working.

Giving and receiving feedback

We all learn about the world through feedback but the quality of feedback we receive, how we receive it and how we use it is highly variable. We all give and receive feedback quite naturally, even without speaking we use body language, including eye contact – or the lack of it! See also the discussion above on recognising non-verbal communications.

Imagine taking a draft of your report or essay – over which you have worked long and hard – to your tutor for some feedback. Which of the following responses would be the most useful:

- It's rubbish!

- It's brilliant!

- You make some very good points here, however there are a couple of other things that you should say which I have noted in the margin. You use a good variety of sources, but I notice that one, which I have underlined, does not trace to your bibliography. The presentation is generally good, but you should start a new page for your bibliography.

The first two examples are highly **subjective** and use what we can call **emotive language**. They actually tell us nothing about what is right or wrong, or indeed good or bad, about the work because they reflect only the emotions of the reader. In contrast the third example appears to give a more **objective** commentary on the work. It also uses the **sandwich technique**, which is often used to deliver the bad news more kindly and within a more objective context.

As a student, you will need to get regular feedback in order to progress. This may come in many forms, but if you find yourself in a feedback vacuum, don't be afraid to ask, 'How am I doing?'.

Much of your feedback may be in written form, in particular when you get assignment work returned to you by your tutors. The next time this happens, notice how many other students just look at the grade and ignore the written comments. To get the most out of your written feedback we suggest that you:

- Read everything carefully, including cover sheets notes on the work and any other documents used, such as assessment grids.

- Ask questions of your tutor if there is anything you don't understand or simply can't read. If he or she is too busy at the time, ask for an appointment.

- Think about what has been written, what you can learn from it and what you might need to do differently in the future.

The feedback we give impacts upon others just as much as the feedback we receive does. You may well also be in the position of giving feedback to others and this might include:

- when working in teams or on group assignments.

- as a mentor to other students as part of a mentoring programme.

- when reviewing another student's work informally or as part of a formal peer assessment programme.

- when completing feedback documentation on your course and / or modules.

There are some clear guidelines for giving feedback effectively (adapted from video material, Davis, 1999) and these include that feedback should be:

- objective rather than subjective or emotive.

- based upon identified criteria. With assignment work, the objectives should be clearly stated in the brief. If they are not, ask your tutor for them, preferably before you start on the work.

- specific rather than generalised, in order to tell you what is actually right and wrong.

- descriptive, so as to provide a useful level of detail. 'Could do better' is not acceptable in this day and age!

- structured, so as to cover everything point by point.

- essential, in that the feedback should stick to what you **need to know** rather than what is merely **nice to know** – in other words, it avoids waffle.

- constructive rather than destructive, because the aim should always be to help you to develop.

- non-evaluative, because giving feedback on your work is not the same as judging you.

With regard to the process:

- Fixing a convenient time and finding a suitable place is important. Being rushed or uncomfortable will naturally detract from the process and for feedback, the **corridor meeting** – although much loved in universities – is not acceptable.

- Feedback can often usefully start by asking the other person how they felt the activity went. Often we are our own sternest critics, and the role of the person giving feedback can then become to put our own thoughts into perspective.

- There should always be time for a two-way discussion and for the person receiving the feedback to ask questions.

- The process should end by making a plan for future action and perhaps making a date to meet again, if this is appropriate.

When we receive feedback we have to be prepared to listen and take it on board. Goleman (1998: 263) suggests that

> **Feedback can be a priceless tool for self-examination and for cultivating change and growth.**

Baddeley (1990) suggests that when we look at a particular situation, we see it through the lens provided by the mental models we have built up through past experience, education or training. We approach situations we encounter with a mindset, a recipe we have acquired from the past, and we use that to understand what is happening and to decide what response/action to take. The mental models we create may or may not be the most appropriate given the situation, or we have not had enough experiences, education or training to develop the most appropriate response to a given situation.

Activity: How good am I at receiving feedback?

This self-assessment will help you measure your current skills in receiving feedback. For each of the statements, tick the 'rarely', 'sometimes', or 'often' box to indicate how consistently you use the described behaviour.

	Rarely	Sometimes	Often
1. I truly listen to what feedback givers are saying.			
2. I keep feedback in perspective and do not overreact.			
3. I try to learn from all feedback, even if it is poorly given.			
4. I am willing to admit to and learn from questions about my performance or behaviour.			
5. Rather than avoiding feedback, I attempt to turn every feedback session into a useful encounter.			
6. I accept redirections, reinforcing rather than denying them.			
7. I accept responsibility for my role in achieving individual, team and organisational goals.			
8. I accept responsibility for searching for solutions to performance and behavioural problems that threaten goals.			
9. I accept responsibility for keeping my emotions in check during feedback discussions.			
10. I am committed to listening and learning from all feedback sessions.			

In general when receiving feedback we suggest that you:

- Listen! It is so easy to go into **private circuits**, especially if you are still thinking about the last point when the next one comes up.

- Try to confirm what has been said by using reflective questions (see the section in this chapter on questioning and listening skills), e.g. 'Could you explain that?' or 'I'm not sure but did you say…?'.

- Take notes, because you won't remember everything that is said.

- Conclude positively, thanking the person for their comments – whether negative or positive, and whether you agree with them or not.

- Consider what has been said and be open-minded. It's all too easy to be defensive about criticism or even praise if you underestimate yourself.

Activity: How am I doing?

- Consider the question: How do I know how well I am doing?
- Review the feedback you have received to date.
- Ask for additional feedback if necessary.
- Consider what all this tells you about how you are doing and what you need to do as a result.

Finally, we ask you to not be afraid to ask for feedback from your tutors, your peers and anyone else who can help. Ensure that you are clear about assessment requirements and don't wait until you get a bad mark before asking for help. Try to be open to the feedback process and learn as you go. Too many students fear the process, especially when they are struggling, and so avoid it and then fail.

Follow-up activities

TIME FOR ACTION – CHECKLIST

Have you:

- practised your interpersonal skills by asking closed, open and reflective questions?
- learnt to recognise both your own emotional responses and those of others?
- considered how you can use your knowledge of non-verbal communications?
- thought about how you might use alternative strategies to resolve conflict?
- asserted yourself when you had the need to do it?
- considered when and where you need to use persuasion techniques?
- asked for feedback on how you are doing?

Further reading

Berne, E. (1968) *The Games People Play*. London: Penguin.

Berne, E. (1975) *What Do You Say After You Say Hello*? London: Corgi.

Cameron, S. (2008) *The Business Student's Handbook*, 4th edition. Harlow: Pearson.

Goleman, D. (2003) *Destructive Emotions and How We Can Overcome Them*. London: Bloomsbury.

Guirdham, M. (2002) *Interpersonal Skills at Work,* 3rd edition. Harlow: Pearson.

Hunsaker, P. L. (2005) *Management – A Skills Approach,* 2nd edition. Upper Saddle River, NJ: Pearson.

Lee-Davies, L. (2007) *Developing Work and Study Skills*. London: Thomson.

Mehrabian, A. (1971) *Silent Messages*. Belmont, CA: Wadsworth.

Moon, J. (1999) *Reflection in Learning and Professional Development*. London: Kogan Page.

Moon, J. (2006) *Learning Journals: A Handbook of Reflective Practice and Professional Development*, 2nd edition. Abingdon: Routledge.

O'Connor, J. (2002) *The NLP Workbook: A Practical Guide to Achieving the Results You Want*. London: Element.

Pease, A. (1984) *Body Language*. London: Sheldon Press.

Russell, T. (1994) *Effective Feedback Skills.* London: Kogan Page.

Smith, M. J. (1975) *When I Say No I Feel Guilty*. New York: Bantam.

Stewart, I. and Joines, V. (1987) *TA Today*. Nottingham: Lifespace.

Websites to look up

- For general help with people skills / interpersonal communications:

http://www.ezinearticles.com/?People-Skills:-Eight-Essential-People-Skills&id=12294

- For further information on transactional analysis:

http://www.itaa-net.org/ta/keyideas.htm
http://www.changingminds.org/explanations/behaviors/ta.htm

- For more information on body language / non-verbal communication:

http://www.peaseinternational.com/
http://www.mybodylanguage.co.uk/more_on_body_language.htm

http://www.changingminds.org/techniques/body/body_language.htm

- For information on assertiveness:

http://www.assertiveness.org.uk/
http://www.bbc.co.uk/dna/h2g2/A2998551

- For information on conflict resolution:

http://www.mindtools.com/pages/article/newLDR_81.htm

- For information on influencing styles:

http://www.ezinearticles.com/?Understanding-The-Different-Influencing-Styles&id=340096

 # Time for review and reflection

This is your space to log your reflections on this chapter, to think about what you have learnt, how you will use it and what else you need to find out.

Part 3

LOOKING AFTER YOURSELF

11 Staying Healthy

STEPHEN PALMER AND ANGELA PURI

What this chapter covers
This chapter concentrates on your health and well-being whilst at university. Although nutritional food and exercise may not necessarily be on the top of your list of priorities, the chapter highlights the importance of staying healthy to combat stress and maintain a positive outlook. A health questionnaire is also included for you to assess how healthy your current lifestyle is.

Food for thought

Life as a student is busy and nutritional food does not tend to be high on the list of priorities. However, the take-away curries, the coffee, the biscuits and chocolate, along with the large amount of alcohol that is often associated with the student lifestyle, plays havoc with the body. Fatty foods with little nutritional value cause various heart conditions and physical impairments in older age although this is less of a problem with younger people. However, reports of early onset diabetes among the young are increasing so good nutrition is important for everybody. Individuals who are overweight are more likely to suffer from stress and depression and have lower self-esteem due to their weight.

Here are a few tips which may help you to balance your diet:

1. Eat at regular intervals – this prevents snacking.
2. Ensure your diet contains a proportion of starchy food such as bread, pasta and rice. It's cheap and has good nutritional value.
3. Eat protein such as fish when you need to get your brain in gear (i.e. when revising or taking exams). Keep the pasta for when you want to relax!
4. Eat five pieces of fruit or vegetables a day. Stick to fresh food. Not only is it cheaper than processed food, it does not contain as many additives.
5. Cut down on the fat in you diet – eat lean meat, grill rather than fry food. Low-fat cheese is preferable.
6. Reduce your sugar intake – control the amount of chocolate and sweets you eat.
7. Drink plenty of water – the recommended amount is two litres a day. Water is excellent at keeping you hydrated and healthy, which in turn makes you feel more alert. Another useful tip is to drink water whenever you feel peckish – many of us mistake the thirst signal for hunger.

By making a few small changes to your diet, within a month you will notice a change in the way you feel. What have you got to lose? Give it a go!

Eating food on the cheap

Money on food or money on entertainment? It is not always easy to make the right decision – from books, to pubs and to the clothes you wear, university can be expensive. However, there are a few practical things you can do to ensure you eat well, without having to burn a hole in your pocket!

To reduce the stress that lack of money can bring, plan a budget. Work out how much you spend on food each week and then factor that into your finances. Attempt to have a balance of fruit and vegetables as well as more traditional student foods, such as pasta and tins!

Take the time to compare prices. Supermarkets' own brands are always cheaper and keep an eye on the offer for the week. Last-minute bargains at supermarkets can be found if you go to the supermarket last thing on a Saturday when the stock is being cleared – you can often pick up quite a bargain if you are lucky!

Learn how to cook a few basic meals. Many people find that cooking is relaxing and can help you unwind after a busy day. Cooking also helps with saving money – as you know, processed meals are not only unhealthy, they are also quite expensive. Once you start cooking you will be surprised at how much cheaper it is the DIY way!

'Once I moved to self-catered accommodation I cooked a lot more! Not just for me, but for my friends too! I had two other friends who lived on campus with me, but in different accommodation. Once a week, one of us would cook, and the other two would bring a bottle. We were so tight with our money we used to have competitions on who could make the cheapest meal and who had got the best bargain on their bottle of wine! I'm sure I wouldn't touch the stuff now, but it tasted great at the time!'

Justine, 24 years, Reading

Exercise and sports

Exercise is a great reliever of stress. Over time, exercise improves both your physical and mental health. It builds up stamina, lessens fatigue (if you don't over do it), assists in anger and weight control and can reduce feelings of depression in an individual.

Here are a few tips to consider when exercising:

1. Exercise can be enjoyable! If you do not like going to the gym or aerobic classes, add an element of fun to your exercise. Your student union may run a number of classes that you can attend, from self-defence to belly dancing! So you can choose an exercise, which is a lot more interactive, entertaining, and sociable!
2. Be flexible with your exercise regime. Aim to have some exercises or sports which are not dependent on good weather conditions – the British weather is too unpredictable!
3. Integrate exercise into your daily routine. Walk instead of taking the bus to university, or take the stairs rather than using the lift.
4. Choose an activity which is fairly easy to get to from where you live. For example, traipsing across town to get to your *'one hour of power'* aerobics class or to reach the closest sports centre which does rock climbing, may end up being a de-motivator.
5. Don't give up! Sometimes, for reasons out of your control, you may stop your exercise routine. Stay focused and remind yourself of the reasons why you started exercising in the first place!

Exercise should be pleasurable so aim to enjoy it. Attempt not to place too many demands on yourself, such as reaching a certain target at the gym or making that ideal weight an obsession. It really isn't worth stressing yourself about it. Exercise helps you to relax and let go of all the day's tensions, so keep it simple.

How healthy are you?

To assess whether or not you lead a healthy lifestyle, fill in the following questionnaire.

How healthy are you?

Against each question below circle the answer that applies to you, where seldom is denoted by 'S', occasionally is denoted by 'O' and frequently is denoted by 'F'

Exercise scale

1.	Do you undertake physical exercise, such as jogging or cycling?	S	O	F
2.	Do you take part in sports activities that involve physical exertion?	S	O	F
3.	Do you integrate exercise into your daily routine?	S	O	F
4.	Do you feel exhausted after little physical exertion?	S	O	F

Nutrition scale

5.	Do you drink more than five cups of coffee a day?	S	O	F
6.	Do you drink more than eight cups of tea a day?	S	O	F

(Continued)

(Continued)

7.	Do you eat three meals a day?	S	O	F
8.	Do you eat between meals?	S	O	F
9.	Do you eat fruit and vegetables?	S	O	F
10.	Do you binge-drink alcohol?	S	O	F
11.	Do you eat foods high in saturated fats?	S	O	F

Relaxation scale

12.	Do you use relaxation techniques such as meditation?	S	O	F
13.	Do you use imagery exercises to help you relax?	S	O	F
14.	Do you feel physically tense?	S	O	F
15.	Do you suffer from migraines, backaches or headaches?	S	O	F

Miscellaneous

16.	Are you under-or overweight?	Yes	No
17.	Do you drink in excess of the weekly guidelines for alcohol (14 units for women, 21 units for men*)	Yes	No
18.	Do you smoke?	Yes	No

Healthy answers

1 F	7 F	13 O or F
2 O or F	8 S	14 S
3 F	9 F	15 S
4 S (If O or F check with your GP)	10 S	16 No
5 S	11 S	17 No
6 S	12 O or F	18 S

If you answer any question with an undesirable response, you may want to consider changing that aspect of your behaviour or lifestyle, to become more healthier.

*These guidelines for alcohol consumption are recommended by many health professionals. The UK government recommends slightly higher amounts.
Source: Cooper and Palmer (2000)

Chapter summary

This chapter contained advice and tips on how to lead a healthy lifestyle at university. The main areas of discussion included:

✓ Food for thought: advice on how to eat a well-balanced diet with good nutritional value

✓ Eating on the cheap: how to eat good-value food and pick up last-minute bargains

✓ Exercise and sport: how to keep a healthy body to reduce your levels of stress and tension. It included tips on how to stay motivated to stick to your exercise routine

✓ How healthy are you?: a questionnaire to assess how healthy your lifestyle is

Learning points from the chapter

If you have any thoughts or comments that you would like to remember about this chapter, you can write them down in the space provided below.

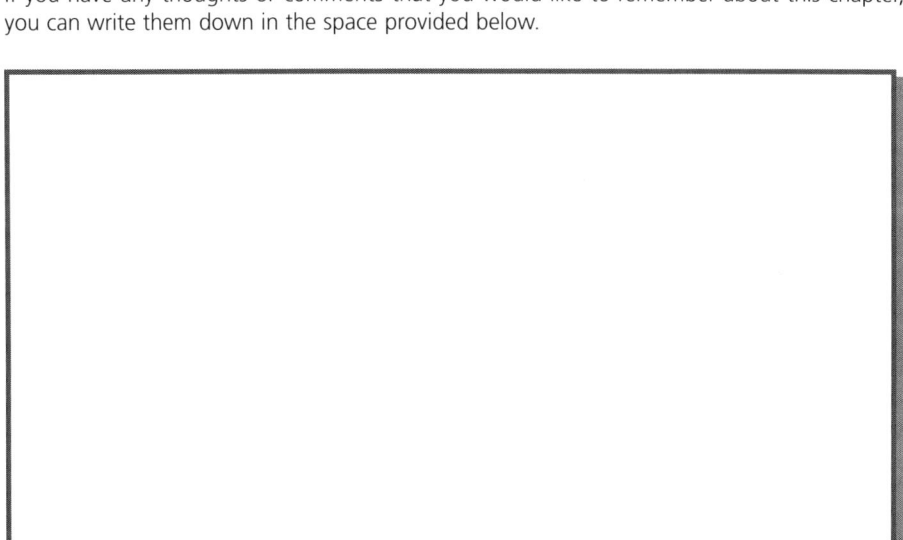

Helpful resources

British Nutrition Foundation

High Holborn House, 52–54 High Holborn, London WC1V 6RQ

Tel: 020 7404 6504

Website: www.nutrition.org.uk

Vegetarian Society

Parkdale, Denham Road, Altrincham, Cheshire WA14 4QG

Tel: 0161 925 2000 (Monday–Friday 8.30am–5pm)

Website: www.vegsoc.org

The Vegetarian Society is an educational charity promoting understanding and respect for vegetarian lifestyles.

Foodfitness

Website: www.foodfitness.org.uk

The Food and Drink Federation's website offers healthy lifestyle tips and a self-assessment questionnaire on eating and exercise habits.

Eating Disorders Association

1st Floor, Wensum House, 103 Prince of Wales Road, Norwich NR1 1DW

National helpline: 0845 634 1414 (weekdays 8.30am–8.30pm, Saturdays 1pm–4.30pm)
Helpline email: helpmail@edauk.com
Website: www.edauk.com

Eating Disorders Association is a UK-wide charity providing information, help and support for people affected by eating disorders and, in particular, anorexia and bulimia nervosa. Details of local contacts in your area are freely available to callers ringing the national helpline.

National Centre for Eating Disorders
54 New Road, Esher, Surrey KT10 9NU
Tel: 01372 469493

12 Alcohol and Drugs

STEPHEN PALMER AND ANGELA PURI

What is covered in this chapter

Alcohol and drugs are part and parcel of university life. From Fresher's week all the way to graduation, many an ex-student could spend endless hours reciting stories of alcohol-infused fun and enjoyment. The aim of this chapter is not to lecture on the vices of alcohol and drugs but to highlight potential patterns of behaviour which may lead to alcohol and drugs abuse – when alcohol and drugs are no longer just a 'laugh' or associated with a 'good night out' but are a craving that needs to be fulfilled to get through the day.

The chapter looks at the attraction of drugs and alcohol, their usage levels and the effects of different drugs on your body. It also helps you identify whether you have a drug problem.

Alcohol

The man takes a drink; the drink takes a drink; the drink
takes the man. (Old Chinese proverb)

In Britain drinking is a socially accepted habit with no questions asked once you hit the age of 18. Statistics show that 90 per cent of the UK population over the age of 15 drink alcohol on a regular basis. Studies relating to the student population have shown that 10 per cent of students drink to hazardous levels (more than 50 units a week), whilst a third are within the high-risk category (drinking between 20 and 50 units a week). Although it is still early days, there is also growing concern regarding excessive drinking now that the licensing laws have been relaxed. Whatever the impact will be, it is clear that with alcohol being on tap 24 hours a day, there is a greater need for students to take responsibility for the amount of alcohol they consume.

The main problem with excessive drinking is that it promotes tolerance to alcohol, which allows the drinker to drink more alcohol and yet feel less intoxicated. So although you may be one of those people *'who can handle their drink'*, looks can be deceptive. Despite feeling fine, the physical damage to the brain and liver continues, co-ordination is affected and the withdrawal symptoms increase over time.

Alongside the physical damage of drinking, heavy alcohol consumption affects our mental state of mind, which makes us more susceptible to depression and insomnia. Alcohol is also consumed to a greater extent when we are stressed and under pressure, or when we are bored and need something to do.

Another, yet less obvious, side-effect of drinking is putting on weight. Alcohol has a high number of hidden calories, making it very hard to lose weight if you are a heavy drinker. For example, it has been stated one gin and tonic contains the same amount of calories as a bowl of ice cream. So consistent drinking can lead to very noticeable weight gain!

Alcohol Concern also warns us that young people are twice as likely to have unprotected sex under the influence of alcohol. This can have a number of distressing outcomes such as unplanned pregnancies, HIV and other sexually transmitted diseases.

So drinking can have some serious implications but these can be limited by drinking in moderation* and planning ahead for a big night out!

Drugs

Having a joint with a few drinks hardly seems like a big deal, especially when we take into account the usage and acceptance of them in certain environments. Drugs have always been used to celebrate, relax and escape from everyday life. The only difference is that certain groups of people have used them to different levels and extents, and it is this which shapes our laws and beliefs within society.

You may have come across a number of drugs already, such as tobacco, marijuana and cocaine. If you have not already been offered or taken some of these substances, it is likely that you may in the future. It is worth taking some time to explore what you think and feel about the various drugs before such a situation arises. There is so much information available over the World Wide Web and from your own university that it is fairly easy to find out all there is to know about literally every drug in existence. By being equipped with all the knowledge about what particular drugs do and the effects they may have, you will be in a much better position to make an informed decision on whether you want to take a drug or not.

Drugs are very powerful substances, and one of the greatest concerns with drug taking is the temptation to over-indulge. However, there is no real classification of

---

*The recommended guidelines set by the Department of Health are 3–4 units of alcohol a day for men and 2–3 units of alcohol per day for woman. However, many health professionals still recommend the previous guidelines of a maximum of 21 units a week for men and 14 units a week for women.

what constitutes an unhealthy level of usage. This is because the effect of a drug varies greatly depending on the drug being used, the amount taken and the user's experience with the drug. In addition, the environment in which it is used and the mental state of the user also impacts on the effects. To complicate things even further, an individual can have a different effect from the same drug at a different time of usage. So it is wise to exercise caution as drugs are powerfully addictive, whether the dependence is physical or psychological.

But experimentation is part of life. Research indicates that 41 per cent of students admit to taking some form of illegal drugs, with 39 per cent having taken marijuana, one in ten ecstasy and one in twelve (8 per cent) cocaine (MORI, 2003). However, it is not usually experimentation that creates problems for the individual but it is the repeated use, coupled with the illegality of some drugs that put you at risk.

The attraction of drugs and alcohol

I want to drink poisons, to lose myself in dreams and visions.
(IHCOYC XPICTOC)

People take drugs* for all sorts of reasons. For many it starts off being experimental, and a bit of fun. Peer pressure also appears to be a major factor.

'I remember my first time. We were at a house party when one of my mates took out some tablets (speed). He said it would be a bit of a laugh and keep us going all night. Everyone else took one, so it didn't look like such a risky thing to do'.

John, 18 years, Nottingham

A number of students also believe that drugs and alcohol will make them more relaxed and a bit more confident. Drugs are often taken in a group setting, which can give you a feeling of group belonging and a feeling of commonality with the other users. In addition, different drugs have different effects, which add to the experimental aspects of drug taking. For example, some drugs are taken for their transcendental affects (LSD), whereby they distort reality and can cause hallucinations, whilst other drugs, such as speed or cocaine, can make the user feel very energetic.

---

*For the remainder of the chapter, drugs will refer to both illegal street drugs as well as more mainstream drugs such as alcohol and tobacco.

Yet drugs are not just taken when people are feeling good; drugs are also used when people are feeling low. With many drugs (including alcohol), they are used as a 'pick me up' or to help people forget about their problems. For the time it's being taken, an individual's insecurities may feel as if they disappear, taking the edge off a situation and making it more bearable for them. This is when taking drugs can have the worst outcomes. Drugs start being used to forget or consistently to give an *added extra*. The drugs stops being used for recreational purposes and starts to be a necessity for the individual.

The effects of drugs

There is no one particular way that people will react to drugs, simply because everyone is different and each drug impacts on an individual in different ways. If you do decide to experiment with drugs, remember:

- One person's experience will not necessarily mirror the experience you will have
- No two experiences are necessarily going to be the same even if the same drug is taken

The effect a drug will have on you will depend on your mood, who you are with and the atmosphere of the place you are in. So it is important for you to decide what you want to take. Do not rely on other people's experiences – do your own research.

'I had known this guy for a couple of months and went round to see him one evening. He offered me an acid tab and I thought – why not! They say that if you are in an unfamiliar place or with someone you don't know that well, it can play on your insecurities ... well that's what happened to me. A little while after I took it, I started getting paranoid about my friend's intentions. Soon his face started distorting – and he turned into a lion! I was shit scared. He kept coming over to check on me, which freaked me out even more. I have never touched it since.'

Alfie, 18 years, London

Know your drugs

Alcohol

Found in drinks like beer, lager, Alco pops, cider, wine and spirits.

The effects

- Many people enjoy drinking alcohol and in small amounts it can help people to feel more relaxed and sociable
- Some people can use alcohol to escape from their problems
- The effect depends on the strength of the drink and how fast it is consumed
- The effect also varies according to when a person last ate, what their weight is, their mood and surroundings
- Speech can become slurred, co-ordination is affected and emotions are heightened
- A hangover can leave you feeling ill for a day or so

The risks

- Alcohol is a depressant drug and users can end up feeling very down
- Women get more drunk than men on the same amount of alcohol. They can also develop drink-related health problems earlier in life
- Drinking too much alcohol can lead to a loss of consciousness. Users then risk choking on their own vomit. This can kill
- Overdosing can also cause alcoholic poisoning, which can be fatal
- Long-term overuse can lead to serious liver, heart and stomach problems
- More than 25,000 deaths in the UK each year are alcohol-related
- Mixing alcohol with other drugs is seriously dangerous!

Anabolic steroids

Trade names include: Sustanon 250, Deca-Durabolin, Dianabol, Anavar and Standzolol, some users may refer to them as 'roids'. Anabolic steroids can only be sold lawfully by a pharmacist to someone with a doctor's prescription. Whilst possession is not illegal, even without a prescription, supply is against the law and C penalties apply (14 years in prison and/or a fine).

Anabolic steroids are similar to, and include, the male hormone testosterone. They are used in medicine to treat anaemia and muscle weakness after surgery, they are not the type of steroids used to treat eczema/asthma. It can be swallowed although most of them need to be injected. Some body-builders and athletes use anabolic steroids, as do people who think it will improve their body image. However, its use in sports is prohibited and a positive test for the drug can ruin a sporting career.

The effects

- Users claim steroids make them feel more aggressive and able to train harder
- With exercise, anabolic steroids can help build up muscle. However, there is some debate about whether they improve muscle power and athletic performance
- They help users to recover from strenuous exercise

The risks
- Taking anabolic steroids carries many health risks and can stop young people from growing properly
- The risks for **men** include: erection problems, breast growth, shrinking testicles, reduced sperm and even sterility, acne, an increased a chance of heart attack and liver failure
- The risks for **women** include: growth of facial hair, deepening voice, shrinking breasts, irregular menstrual cycle, spots, possible miscarriage and stillbirth if pregnant
- Some effects, such as the change in breast size, may be irreversible without surgery
- Injecting into veins can be dangerous and injecting into muscle can damage nerves and veins. Sharing needles or syringes puts users at risk of dangerous infections like hepatitis and HIV

Cannabis
Other names that it goes by include marijuana, draw, blow, weed, puff, shit, hash and ganja.

Cannabis is a natural substance and is derived from the 'Cannabis Sativa' plant, commonly called *hemp*. It comes in a solid dark lump known as resin, or as leaves, stalks and seeds called *grass* or sometimes as a sticky oil. It can be rolled with tobacco in a spliff or joint, smoked on its own in a special pipe, or eaten. There are different strengths of cannabis – some, such as skunk, are very strong.

Cannabis is a Class C drug, with the maximum penalty for possession being 2 years in prison and/or a fine and for supply it is 14 years in prison and/or a fine

The effects
- Getting stoned on cannabis makes most users relaxed and talkative
- It heightens the senses, especially when it comes to colours, taste and music
- Cooking and eating hash makes the effects more intense and harder to control
- It can leave people feeling tired and lacking energy
- Hash may bring on cravings for certain foods

The risks
- It affects short-term memory and your ability to concentrate
- Getting stoned affects co-ordination, increasing the risk of accidents
- It impairs driving skills, so it's not advisable to get in the car and drive or be driven by someone who is stoned
- It can make users paranoid and anxious, depending on their mood and situation
- Smoking joints with tobacco can lead to users getting hooked to cigarettes
- Smoking cannabis over a long period of time may increase the risk of respiratory disorders, including lung cancer
- Many users find cannabis hard to quit

Cocaine

Other names used to refer to cocaine include coke, Charlie, snow and C.

Cocaine is a white powder that can be snorted up the nose or injected. It is a class A drug so the maximum penalty for possession is 7 years in prison and/or a fine, whilst supply of cocaine can lead to life imprisonment and/or a fine.

The effects
- Cocaine is a powerful stimulant and the buzz creates a sense of well being, making the users feel alert and confident
- The effects last about 30 minutes
- Users are often left craving for more
- People may also take more to delay the comedown (which includes tiredness and depression)

The risks
- Cocaine can cause heart problems and chest pain
- Heavy use of cocaine can cause convulsions
- Large or frequent doses over a short period of time can leave users restless, confused and paranoid
- Snorting cocaine can permanently damage the inside of the nose
- Users may find their habit expensive and hard to control
- Users have died from overdose

Crack

Alternatively known as rock, wash or stone. Crack is a smokeable form of cocaine and is also a Class A drug, with the same maximum penalty as Cocaine (possession – 7 years in prison and/or a fine; supply – life imprisonment and/or a fine).

The effects
- The effects of smoking crack are similar to snorting cocaine but much more intense
- The high lasts as little as 10 minutes
- Users often *chase* the high by repeating the dose
- Heavy users may take heroin to dull the craving caused by the use of crack

The risks
- Heavy use can lead to potentially fatal heart problems
- Heavy users risk convulsions
- Crack is highly addictive and because the high can be so intense, crack use is difficult to control

- Smoking crack can seriously harm the lungs and cause chest pains
- After the high, feelings of restlessness, nausea and sleeplessness are common
- Large or frequent doses over a short period can leave users restless, confused and paranoid
- Regular users may find their habit very expensive
- Users have died from overdose

Ecstasy

Other common names for it include E, Fantasy, Doves, Mitsubishis, Dolphins, Rolexes. Its chemical name is MDMA.

Ecstasy usually comes in a tablet form of different shapes, size and colour, but is often white. The effect MDMA will have on an individual is often unpredictable, especially as a tablet may not contain MDMA. However, some are sold as MDMA and can have very different effects.

Ecstasy is a class A drug, so carries a maximum of 7 years in prison for possession and/or a fine, and a maximum of life imprisonment and/or a fine for supplying the drug.

The effects
- Users can feel alert and in tune with their surrounding and other people
- Sound, colour and emotions can seem much more intense
- The energy buzz from ecstasy means that users can dance for hours
- The effects can last anything from three to six hours

The risks
- As ecstasy starts working (known as *coming up*), users may feel a tightening of the jaw, nausea, sweating and an increase in heart rate
- The comedown can leave users feeling tired and depressed, often for days
- Use has been linked to liver and kidney problems
- Studies into the effects of ecstasy are still at an early stage. However, research shows that MDMA dramatically affects the brain chemistry of animals
- There have been about 60 ecstasy-related deaths in the UK

Please Note: As ecstasy affects the body's temperature control, dancing for long periods in a hot atmosphere increases the chances of users overheating and dehydrating. These risks can be minimised if users:

- rest at regular intervals
- sip about a pint of non-alcoholic fluid such as fruit juice, isotonic sports drinks or water every hour

Gases, glues and aerosols

These are sniffed or breathed into the lungs.

The effects
- Users feel thick-headed, dizzy, giggly and dreamy
- It can be hallucinogenic
- The effects disappear after 15–45 minutes
- Afterwards, users may feel drowsy and may suffer from a headache

The risks
- Use of gases, glues or aerosols can cause instant death – even on the first go
- Squirting the products down the throat may cause the body to produce fluid that floods the lungs. This can be fatal
- Abusing gases, glues or aerosols can lead to nausea, vomiting, black-outs and fatal heart problems
- Accidents can occur when the user is high because their senses are affected
- There is a risk of suffocation if the substance is inhaled from a plastic bag over the head
- Long-term abuse can damage the brain, liver and kidneys

Please note: Sniffing gases, glues or aerosols kills one person every week

GHB

This is sometimes known as GBH, and is short for gammahydroxybutyrate.

It is a colourless liquid and is sold in small bottles or in capsules. The liquid is measured out in capfuls and then swallowed. It has no smell but has a salty taste. GHB is used as an alternative to anabolic steroids.

GHB is a Class C drug carrying a maximum penalty of 2 years in prison and/or a fine for possession and 14 years and/or a fine for supply.

The effects
- GHB has sedative properties and can produce a feeling of euphoria
- The effects have been known to last a day

The risks
- Excessive hits could lead to sickness, stiff muscles, fits and even collapse
- If incorrectly produced, GHB can badly burn the mouth
- It is very dangerous and can be fatal when mixed with alcohol or other drugs
- The long-term effects of GHB are not yet fully known

Heroin

Otherwise known as Smack, Brown, Gear, Horse, H, Junk, Skag or Jack.

Heroin is a painkilling drug made from morphine, which is derived from the opium poppy. It comes in the form of a white powder when pure. Street heroin is usually brownish-white. It is snorted, smoked or injected.

It is a Class A drug carrying the maximum penalty (possession – 7 years in prison and/or a fine; supply – life imprisonment and/or a fine)

The effects
- In small doses, heroin gives the user a sense of warmth and well-being
- Higher doses can make them drowsy and relaxed
- Excessive amounts can result in overdose, coma and in some cases death
- First-time use often leads to side-effects like dizziness and vomiting

The risks
- Heroin is very addictive. Getting the next fix can dominate a user's life
- Tolerance develops, which means the user needs more heroin to get the same effect
- Users who form a habit may end up taking the drug just to feel normal
- Those who start by smoking or snorting heroin sometimes switch to injecting to maximise the high
- Injecting can damage veins and lead to gangrene
- Sharing needles or syringes puts users at risk of dangerous infections like hepatitis and HIV
- Withdrawing from heroin can be very hard
- Many people do manage to wean themselves off heroin although mentally it can take years before you are completely free of it

Ketamine

Also known as Special K, Vitamin K or just K.

Ketamine is an anaesthetic with painkilling and psychedelic properties. It comes in tablet form or as a powder snorted up the nose. Ketamine is a prescription-only medicine. Although possession is not illegal without a prescription, supply is against the law.

The effects
- It makes users feel that the mind has been separated from the body. This creates *out of body* and hallucinatory experiences for up to three hours
- Like LSD, the effects are influenced by the user's mood and environment. In some instances a user may be physically unable to move

The risks
- As ketamine numbs the body, users risk serious injury without feeling the pain
- The effects can be quite alarming if the user isn't expecting them
- Excessive doses carry some risk of breathing problems and heart failure
- Ketamine is very dangerous when mixed with alcohol and other drugs
- The long-term effects of recreational use of ketamine are still not really known

LSD (Acid)

Other names include: Trips, Tabs, Blotters, Microdots and Dots. Its chemical name is Lysergic acid diethylamide.

LSD usually comes in tiny squares of paper often with a picture displayed on one side. The picture has no relevance to the effect or strength of the drug.

LSD is a Class A drug carrying the maximum penalty (possession – 7 years in prison and/or a fine; supply – life imprisonment and/or a fine)

The effects
- LSD is an hallucinogenic drug which has powerful effects on the mind
- The effects of LSD are known as a *trip* and can last as long as 8–12 hours. Whilst a user is tripping they will experience their surroundings in a very different way
- The effects depend on the user's mood, where they are and who they are with
- Sense of movement and time may speed up or slow down. Objects, colour and sound may become distorted
- Users experience trips differently every time

The risks
- Once the trip starts, there is no way of stopping it
- A bad trip can be terrifying. Users may feel very threatened and can even forget that the drug is responsible
- It is impossible to predict a bad trip, but it is more likely to happen if the user is feeling anxious, nervous or uncomfortable
- Feeling paranoid or out of control can leave users shaken for a long time afterwards
- Accidents may happen whilst users are hallucinating
- Users may experience flashbacks, where parts of a trip are briefly re-lived some time after the event
- LSD can complicate mental problems such as depression, anxiety and schizophrenia

Magic mushrooms

...Or 'shrooms and mushies. There are several types of magic mushrooms that grow wild in the UK. The main type is the Liberty Cap mushroom. However, there are two species that look similar to magic mushrooms but which are poisonous. Magic mushrooms are eaten raw, dried, cooked in food or stewed into a tea.

Although it is not illegal to possess raw magic mushrooms, it is an offence to possess any preparation of them (e.g. when they're dried or stewed). Magic mushrooms when prepared are Class A drugs. The maximum penalty for possession is 7 years in prison and/or a fine, and for supply is life imprisonment and/or a fine.

The effects
- Magic mushrooms have a similar affect to LSD, but the trip is often milder and shorter
- Magic mushrooms can make users feel very relaxed and 'spaced out'. The effects depend on the user's mood, where they are and who they are with
- They may cause hallucinations – objects, colour and sound become distorted
- A trip tends to last about four hours

The risks
- Magic mushrooms often cause stomach pains, sickness and diarrhoea
- Eating the wrong kind of mushroom can also cause serious illness and even fatal poisoning
- If users feel sick, they should go straight to hospital with a sample of the mushroom and explain what has happened
- Bad trips do happen and can be very frightening. Once the trip has started, there is no going back
- Like any hallucinogen, magic mushrooms can complicate mental problems

Poppers (or alkyl nitrites)

Trade names include: Ram, Thrust, Rock Hard, Kix, TNT and Liquid Gold.

Poppers is a term used for the group of chemicals known as alkyl nitrites. Poppers come as a clear or straw-coloured liquid in a small bottle or tube. The vapour is breathed in through the mouth or nose. Over recent years the use of poppers has become more common, especially in the dance culture. Amyl nitrite is prescription-only medicine and although possession in not illegal, supply can be an offence.

The effects
- Users get a very brief but intense *head rush*. This is caused by a sudden surge of blood through the heart and brain. Blood vessels enlarge, resulting in a flushed face and neck

- Some users say that they experience the impression of time slowing down
- The effects fade 2–5 minutes after use

The risks
- It can make some people feel faint and sick, especially when taken whilst dancing
- Users often experience a headache afterwards
- Regular use causes skin problems around the mouth and nose
- Taking alkyl nitrites is very dangerous for people with anaemia, glaucoma and breathing or heart problems
- If spilled, poppers can burn skin
- Poppers may be fatal if swallowed

Speed (amphetamines)

Other names include: Whiz, Uppers, Amph, Billy and Sulphate.

Speed is usually a grey, white or dirty white powder, or sometimes it is in tablet form. It can be snorted, swallowed, injected or smoked. Speed is the most impure illegal drug in the UK.

Amphetamines are Class B drugs but carry Class A penalties if they are prepared for injection. The maximum penalty for possession is 5 years in prison and/or a fine, and for supply is 14 years in prison and/or a fine.

The effects
- Speed is a stimulant; it quickens the heartbeat and breathing rate
- Users may feel confident
- Minds may race and the user may feel energetic
- It suppresses the appetite but does not satisfy the body's need for nourishment
- Some people also become tense and experience feelings of anxiety

The risks
- The comedown (tiredness and depression) lasts for one or two days and sometimes longer
- Sleep, memory and concentration are all affected in the short term
- High doses repeated over a few days may cause panic and hallucinations
- Long-term users may become dependent on the buzz speed gives them
- Tolerance can develop, which means the user needs more to get the same effect
- Long-term use puts a strain on the heart. Overdose can be fatal
- Use of speed can lead to mental illness such as psychosis

Tobacco

Tobacco contains a drug called nicotine, which is very addictive.

The effects
- Nicotine is a powerful and fast-acting drug
- When smoke is inhaled the nicotine effect hits the brain about 8 seconds later
- Nicotine speeds up the heart rate and increases blood pressure
- First-time users may feel sick

The risks
- It is very easy to get hooked
- Smoking is expensive. Ten cigarettes a day will cost upwards of £500 a year
- Tobacco smoke contains over 4000 chemicals, many of which are harmful to health
- Smokers are more likely to suffer coughs and chest problems. A long-term tobacco habit can lead to cancer, emphysema and heart disease – all of which can kill
- Passive smoking can cause breathing difficulties, asthma and even cancer
- Tobacco contributes to at least 2000 limb amputations and 111,000 premature deaths in the UK each year

(Information on knowing your drugs is reproduced from *The Score: Facts about Drugs*, published by the Department of Health (2004)).

How do you know that you have a problem?

Many people experiment with drugs and many either stop after a while or become recreational users. Unfortunately, this pattern of behaviour is not universal, alcohol and drug abuse can just sneak up on you. From being a recreational user, one can slip into a cycle of dependency. Nobody plans to do this, and many individuals are not even aware when it occurs. For this reason, it is good to keep a check of your drug habit so you are aware of when you may be becoming a bit extreme. The following set of questions can be used as a checklist:

- Do you have a favourite drug you use?
- Do you ever use drugs when you are alone?
- Do you use drugs because you are bored, lonely or anxious?
- Do you think a lot about drugs and drug use?
- Do you plan your day to make sure you can use drugs?
- Do you need to use more and more drugs to get the effect you want?

- Do you feel irritable or anxious if you do not get to use drugs?
- Do you miss your favourite drug if you do not use it for a while?

The more 'yes' answers you give, the more likely it is that your drug use may have become excessive. It is worthwhile reassessing your level of drug intake and pattern of usage to maintain control for yourself.

Drugs help some people to cope with stress and this can sometimes lead to them becoming reliant on them. It is also worth remembering that when you are stressed you are more likely to take more drugs or consume more alcohol which has serious implications for your health. If you feel that you may benefit from professional help and guidance, refer to 'Helpful resources' at the end of the chapter or go to Appendix 2 of the handbook for a list of services and helplines you can contact.

Know your limit – get assertive!

Whether you experiment with drugs or not is your choice, so it is important that you are taking drugs for the right reasons. That is, because you want to, and not because of peer pressure.

However, one of the biggest problems with just saying *no* is that it is not always that simple! Being the sensible voice of reason and caution in many ways can be badly received by your new experimenting friends. So how do you keep your friends and make the choice that's right for you? By being honest with yourself and by being assertive!

Assertion is a fantastic skill that can be used in many tricky situations. It's basically the skill of getting the balance between being a complete push over and being a ranting preacher. Being assertive puts you back in control and makes sure you do what is best for you.

Assertion is said to be linked into one's own levels of self-esteem. People with lower self-esteem and feelings of self-worth are less likely to state what they honestly feel and may end up resentfully following the crowd. However, an assertive individual is likely to be more confident and have a higher level of self-worth as they are more in control of what they want to do.

Assertion is something which takes time and practice to acquire, but remember you have the right to:

- say no
- to consider your own needs as being important
- to take responsibility for your own actions
- to do what you feel is right for you

Acting assertively helps you to maintain your rights and give you the confidence to do what is right for you. An example of assertion is illustrated in the model below.

The three-step model

This model can be used in any situation, but especially if you are feeling intimidated or under pressure to comply to other people's demands. Using this model you can make your point in an assertive manner, without offending and, more importantly, without drifting off the point you want to make or becoming emotional.

Step 1 – Actively listen to what the other person is saying and demonstrate to the other individual that you have heard and understood what they have said.

Step 2 – Say what you think and feel (a good linking word to use between steps 1 and 2 is 'however').

Step 3 – Say what you want to happen (a good linking word to use between steps 2 and 3 is 'and').

Using the same peer pressure example as above, the technique can be used in the following way:

Step 1 – *Okay I get the point. If we are all tripping it will make the evening more of a laugh.*

Step 2 – *However, I'm too much of a control freak to give it a go.*

Step 3 – *And so I think I'll give it a miss this time.*

For more information on assertion techniques look at Chapter 5, section 1.

Chapter summary

Taking drugs is a choice, so it's important that it is *your* choice. The aim of this chapter was not to condone the activity of drug taking, but to provide you with information on the following aspects of drug use:

✓   The effects of drugs and alcohol

✓   Awareness of when you may be over-indulging

✓   The effects of drugs

✓   Assertion techniques to use when you know your limit

Learning points from the chapter

Use the space provided below to note down anything you have found useful in this chapter.

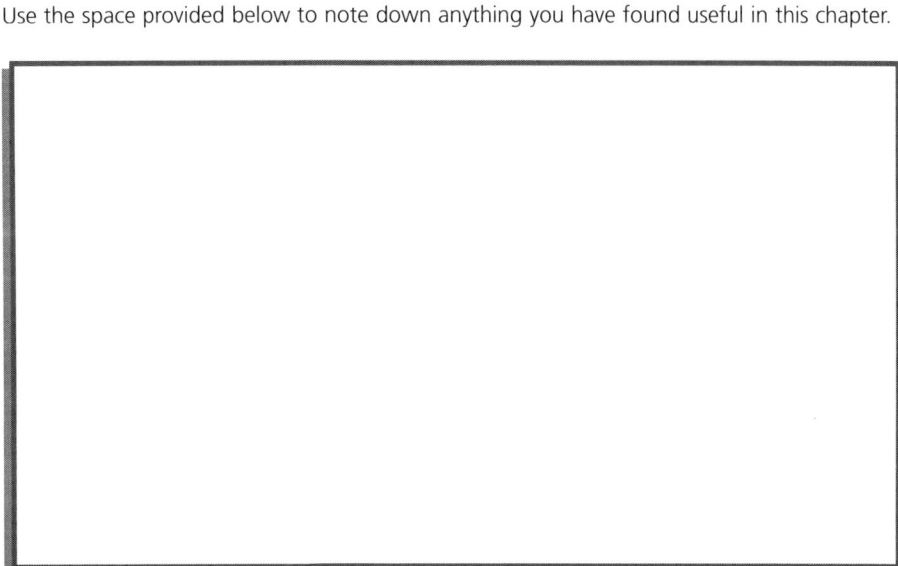

Helpful resources

Alcohol Concern

Waterbridge House, 32–36 Loman Street, London SE1 0EE
Helpline: 020 7922 8667 (Monday–Friday 1pm–5pm)
Email: contact@alcoholconcern.org.co.uk
Website: www.alcoholconcern.org.uk

Gives information, guidance and advice for those worried about their own drinking habits or somebody else's. It also contains publications and a directory of local alcohol services.

Alcoholics Anonymous

PO Box 1, Stonebow House, Stonebow, York YO1 7NJ
Helpline: 0845 769 7555 (24-hour service, calls charged at local rates, calls are redirected automatically to an AA member in your region)
Email: aanewcomer@runbox.com
Website: www.alcoholics-anonymous.org.uk

FRANK

Helpline: 0800 77 66 00 (24-hour service)

Text phone: 0800 917 8765

Email: frank@talktofrank.com

Website: www.talktofrank.com

Offers free and confidential advice about any drug issue, whether it is information you require, advice or a chat. The website also contains facts, guidance and support information.

13 Managing Your Money

STEPHEN PALMER AND ANGELA PURI

What is covered in this chapter
This chapter looks at how to manage your finances. Money mismanagement is one of the key stressors at university. This chapter highlights the different sources of income that a student may have coming into their account, such as student loans and parental contributions, and highlights a number of methods that can be used to budget your finances, such as using a budget calculator, choosing the right bank to open your account with and listing your expenses. It also offers advice on how to deal with a friend who always wants to borrow money from you without repaying the loan! Some practical tips on how to cut your costs are also available at the end of the chapter.

Keeping track of your finances

The trouble with being poor is that it takes up all your time.
(William De Kooning, b. 1904)

Being short of money at university is not that uncommon a story. In fact, it is one of the few times in your life that being broke is quite acceptable, and to a great extent it's expected!

However, having to count your pennies all the time can become frustrating and stressful. It is important to keep track of your expenses as you have to make sure that your money lasts you through each term. But before we can analyse where all your money goes, it is useful to look first at what money is coming into your account.*

---

*Please note that although this chapter has been written with the most up-do-date information on student finances, we are aware that governments may change their policies so it is advisable to stay informed via your student finance adviser or Local Education Authority.

Student loan

Currently, for students who are living in England or Wales and studying in the United Kingdom, the Government offers a loan to assist with the expenses of living at university (such as accommodation, food and course material). From 2006, there is an additional loan to cover the cost of your tuition fees, so full-time students will no longer need to pay their fees before they start their course. Instead, the student loan that covers the cost of the tuition fees will be paid directly to their university on their behalf.

The student loans that are available are much cheaper than any loan you may be given from a high street bank as the interest rate charged is linked to inflation. This means that the amount of money you end up repaying is equivalent in real terms to the amount of money you borrowed originally. How much money you get will depend on a number of factors, including where you're going to study (students living in London are likely to get more money) and where you will be living (at home or in halls/renting). 75 per cent of the maximum loan is available to all eligible students regardless of any other income they have. However, the remaining 25 per cent of the loan amount will depend on your own income and/or that of your family. This will be assessed by your Local Education Authority (LEA). The repayments on the loan do not start until you start earning an income of £15,000 or more and the monthly repayments will also depend on the amount you will earn as opposed to the amount you have borrowed.

Other financial support

Assistance is also available to certain groups of students who may require additional help. Currently, support is available for

- Students with dependent children
- Students with dependent adults (partners, parents or other members of your family)
- Disabled students
- Students with additional travel costs
- Students who have been in care

Your university or college may be able to provide additional support for students who are having financial difficulties (hardship funds). Additional money may also be available through sponsorship from organisations or via bursaries, access funds and grants. The amount of money given varies enormously but the grants and funds are usually one-off payments and do not have to be repaid.

- Access to Learning Fund – provides extra financial help for students on low incomes who are experiencing financial difficulties.
- The Parent's Learning Allowance – to help with course-related costs for students who have dependent children. Contact your LEA.
- Child Tax Credit – students with children can claim the tax credit which is paid to parents regardless of whether they are studying or working. Contact the Inland Revenue for further information.
- Childcare grant – for full-time students with dependent children in registered or approved childcare. Contact your LEA for more information.
- Adult Dependants' grant – students with partners or other adult members of your family who depend on you financially may be able to get additional financial support. Contact your LEA for more information.
- Disabled Students' Allowances (DSAs) – additional support is available and the amount you receive is not dependent on your income or your households. The assistance given does not have to be repaid. Contact your LEA for further information.

Parental contribution

The majority of students do receive some level of support from their parents, guardians, partners of other family members (85 per cent). If you are fortunate to be supported by your parents, it's worth doing your maths to calculate approximately how much money you will require from them. This will lessen the need to keep going back to them and having the stress of grovelling for more when you hit a shortfall.

Also, the more thought you have put into the amount of money you need, the easier it is to justify it to your parents. If possible, get a set amount each month, as opposed to one lump sum. This will help you to budget and prevent you from blowing your whole term's money in the first few weeks!

Jobs

There is nothing quite like the independence of having your own source of money? Getting a job gives you a regular income and can also boost your career prospects after you graduate. It can give you confidence in the workplace and keeps you in touch with the world of work. However, juggling commitments can be stressful so be careful that you do not take on too many hours as it may end up affecting your performance on your course. Universities tend to recommend that you do not work more than 15 hours a week.

Dealing with your finances

Avoidance doesn't help!

When you get your student loan in one go it can seem like a lot of money but remember it has to last you the whole term. A common cause of stress is money mismanagement, which not only causes concern now, but can create debt for your future ... do remember this fact! It does not take long to shift from not having enough money to go out, to accumulating high levels of debt that you have no way of paying off.

One of the common ways of getting into a high level of debt is **avoidance**. This is when you push the problem to the back of your mind, maybe because you are having such a good time or you just don't want to deal with the consequences. You avoid thinking of the debt you are incurring and stick your head in the proverbial sand!

'Looking back I can't believe I did it. My girlfriend was in my room one night and saw this pile of unopened letters. She asked me what they were and I just shrugged my shoulders in embarrassment. We opened all my bills, one by one, and I cringed every time I saw what was owed – most of it was interest. My girlfriend couldn't believe the situation I had got myself into. I guess I knew I was in trouble, I just didn't want to know how much!'

Nick, 25 years, Oxford

It is not surprising that just under half of all students (49 per cent) believe that having little money is the worst aspect of student life (MORI, 2005). Yet, it seems to be part and parcel of the student experience, and one that is unlikely to change! In this chapter we will concentrate on ways of managing your finances, to minimise the stress that the lack of money can cause.

Staying positive – staying in control

Unlike Nick in the quote above, problems are a lot easier to solve when you believe you have some level of control over them. By believing that you can have an effect on the outcome of a situation you ensure a much more proactive approach and improve your chances of dealing with the situation more effectively. Yet many of us go for the '*I don't want to think about it*' approach. By refusing to acknowledge of the problem, you are likely to increase your levels of stress as you see yourself as *helpless* in the situation and let the problem get the better of you.

Budgeting

Surviving university without a certain level of budgeting can be financially hazardous! However, it can be quite hard to keep track of what your money is being spent on unless you start off getting into good financial habits. Once you start budgeting it soon becomes quick and easy to keep tabs on what is coming into your account and also reduces the stress of debits from your account! Below are a few techniques to help you budget more effectively.

Listing your expenses

This may seem a bit tedious to begin with, but it is great way of staying aware of how much money is being spent and on what. It also highlights areas where you can cut down on spending and sometimes (when you're lucky) show you when you may have a little bit of extra cash to play around with!

Begin by listing your income and expenditure. Compile a list with two columns. In the first column write down what money you are expecting to come in during the month, for example your student loan, money from home, pay from your part-time job and so on. In the second column, list the payments you have to make throughout the month, such as accommodation (the biggest expense for most students!), bills (e.g. electricity, gas, mobile phone and any other direct debits), food expenses, credit card payments, toiletries, clothes, money for books or stationery, money for going out, travel expenses, music and any other miscellaneous expenses. It's worth noting down all your costs, big or small, as this all helps to give a better picture of how you spend your money.

To make your expenses list even easier the Department for Education and Skills come up with an interactive web tool called a budget calculator. You can access the calculator by going to the following web address: http://www.aimhigher.ac.uk/student_finance/cost_of_living_calculator.cfm. This tool makes budgeting a lot easier as all you need to do is put in the amount of money you spend on various living costs during a term and during a week. It then calculates your weekly and per term expenditure and the balance you have, based on the figures you have put in. It is a simple and fast way of giving you an overview of your financial situation.

Being assertive with friends

'I'm broke, can I borrow some cash?'

It is all too easy to be over-supportive of our friends. Many students find themselves a bit strapped for cash and in need of some financial assistance from friends. But the problem arises when friends are perpetually broke and in consistent need of your money!

Even if you enjoy their company, having a mate who never repays money you have lent to them soon begins to wear your friendship down. You may find it useful to consider what choices you have in dealing with such a situation:

1. Continue to give them free credit and whinge about it.
2. Continue to give them free credit and don't whinge about it.
3. Avoid their company and run a mile in the opposite direction when you next see them.
4. Become resentful.
5. Become assertive and calmly state, *'I'm not prepared to give you any more money'*, when they next make a request. You may need to repeat this a few times to get the message over.

In the long term, option 5 is probably the best approach if you want to maintain your friendship and not be resentful of their behaviour. Section 1 in Chapter 5 offers advice on assertion techniques and provides a number of assertiveness methods which you can practise. In the end, if your assertive attitude is not well received, then may be it is worth asking yourself whether that person was a real friend anyway.

Smart banking

When you open an account at a high street bank, resist the goodies until you have found out what the account itself actually offers. The interest rate they charge is one of the main things to look out for:

- Which bank gives you the highest interest-free overdraft?
- Who has the best authorised overdraft interest rate?
- Compare different banks' interest rates on unauthorised borrowing.

Once you have done this, then go for the most appealing extras that they are offering! Some students also find it useful to open a second account. By doing this, you can put all your incoming money in to one account (e.g. your student loan and other incoming monies which you may receive at the beginning of term) and transfer a set amount of money each month to the other account for your day-to-day expenses, which would cover your living and social expenses. This is likely to help you budget more effectively.

Cutting your costs

This may not be fun, but by showing a bit of restraint and discipline, you will reduce your stress by making your money last longer. Here are a few tips on how to manage your money more effectively:

- Learn how to cook. There are plenty of simple cook books to help you create healthy food cheaply and quickly.
- Carry your student union card everywhere. It can get you discounts on all sorts of things (such as 10 per cent discount in some high street retailers).
- Buy a Young Persons Railcard or bus pass if you do a lot of travelling.
- Buy the supermarket's own brands.
- Limit the amount of money you have on you. Some students find it helpful to withdraw all the money they are going to spend in the week and stick to that amount. This way you can see how much you have got left and whether you can afford that extra pint or not.
- Avoid the use of credit cards or use them in emergency situations only.
- Rather than buying all the books on your reading lists, take some of them out of the library or search out second-hand books. This can save you a small fortune. A good place to find second-hand books is at your course or departmental notice boards. Some universities also have a second-hand book shop on site which will sell you books from last year's students at very reasonable prices. Alternatively, get together with other students on your course and buy one book each from the reading lists – then share the books between you.
- Limit your nights out – it's easier to resist temptation to spend that way.
- Check you are not paying tax on your savings if you are not going to be earning any money during the financial year.
- Keep store point cards and collect points to get savings on products or cash back (e.g. Club cards or Advantage cards).
- Get student discounts on prescriptions, dental care and health checks.

Chapter summary

Managing finances is a stressful business, especially as you have the time, the places and the energy to enjoy your money but just don't have the income! This chapter emphasised the need to budget and highlighted some tips on how to make your money last.

✓ Money coming in: this includes your student loan, other financial support you may be entitled to, parental contributions and income you may receive if you take on a part-time job

✓ Money going out: this looked at ways you can manage your finances and included information on budgeting, smart banking and easy tips to cut down your costs

Learning points from the chapter

Use the space provided below to note down any useful hints or advice you have found in this chapter for reducing your stress levels.

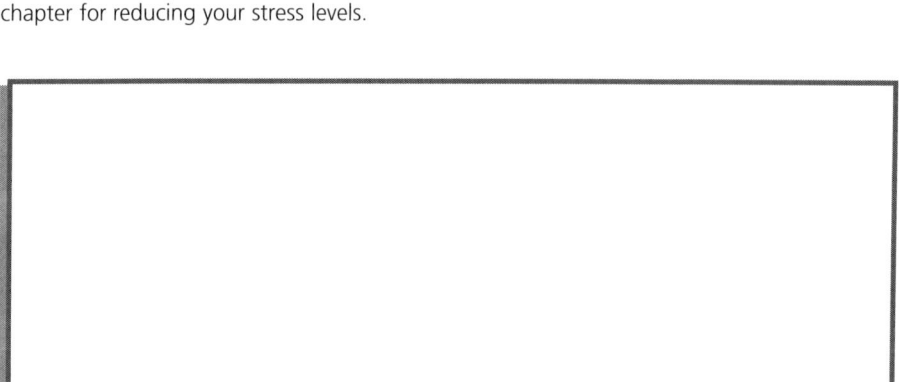

Helpful resources

Student Loans Company (SLC)
100 Bothwell Street, Glasgow G2 7JD
Tel: 0800 405010
Website: www.slc.co.uk

Department for Education and Skills
Link to details about student loans and financial support available
at: www.dfes.gov.uk/studentsupport/students/index.shtml

Consumer Credit Counselling Service
Wade House, Merrion Centre, Leeds LS2 8NG
Helpline: 0800 328 1813 (Monday–Friday 8am–8pm)
This is a dedicated helpline for students worried about debt and
money problems. Calls and advice given are free.
Website: www.cccs.co.uk

Free Stuff
Website: www.freestudentstuff.com
A website containing free information and offers such as free
cinema tickets, free ringtones, cash for completing surveys, discount
offers and much more 'free stuff'!

Part 4

OVERSEAS STUDENTS

14 English Language Requirements

GARETH DAVEY

INTRODUCTION

After reading this chapter, you should be able to:

☑ Know about English language entry requirements
☑ Understand The International Language Testing System (IELTS)
☑ Understand the features of Academic English
☑ Choose and use an English language dictionary

Courses in the UK are taught in English. This chapter describes the English language qualifications required for study at university, and the alternatives for students who do not have them. There is information about Academic English, the type of English language support you can expect to receive during your studies, and a guide to using an English dictionary.

English language qualifications

If English is not your first language, you may need to have an English language qualification to prove that you have a sufficient level. The preferred language test accepted by universities is the International English Language Testing System (IELTS), which is managed by the British Council and other organisations. A number of other qualifications from around the world, including the Test of English as a Foreign Language (TOEFL), are also accepted. Note, however, that a few universities or departments only accept IELTS and not alternatives. Contact your university for information about their requirements.

The university will need to see official certification or transcripts of your qualification, along with evidence of your other entry requirements (if the certificates are not in English, you will need to arrange for them to be translated). English language qualifications need to be recent, such as within the past two years. Many universities offer in-house English tests (i.e., tests they organise themselves), which they consider equivalent to (and therefore accepted in lieu of) the IELTS and other tests.

The IELTS score that you need depends on the course and university. The majority of undergraduate and postgraduate courses accept an IELTS score of 5.5–7.0, which is roughly equivalent to 213–250 on the computer-based TOEFL. Lower level courses, such as foundation programmes, have lower requirements, whereas others require higher scores. Check the entry requirements before you apply for a course.

Note that nationals of selected countries do not need to provide evidence of their English language ability. Also, some universities will be willing to waive the English language requirement for certain students whose academic record demonstrates their ability to study and be examined in English. Further, universities might admit students without an English language qualification on the condition that they complete an English course or test within a specified time.

The International English Language Testing System (IELTS)

The IELTS assesses whether non-native English speakers have sufficient English language skills to study and succeed on university courses. There are two versions of the test; the 'Academic module', for students who wish to study at university, and the 'General training' format for those who are going to the UK to work, attend a training programme, or complete secondary school. This chapter refers to the former.

Test structure

The IELTS probes the four basic language skills – listening, reading, writing, and speaking.

The listening paper examines listening skills in social and educational contexts. It includes recordings of a single speaker, conversations between two or more speakers, and a university lecture or talk. The passages cover a variety of accents and dialects, and increase in difficulty as they progress. Students are allowed to listen to the passages only once. A range of listening skills are assessed, including the ability to:

- listen for general and specific information
- listen for main ideas, details, and keywords
- understand gist
- understand speakers' opinions.

The reading part has three passages (between 2,000–2,750 words each) taken from non-specialist books, magazines, and newspapers. The reading skills that are assessed include the ability to:

- skim for general understanding
- scan for specific information

- identify writers' views, including a detailed argument
- understand how a process works
- use different written styles.

The writing paper consists of two tasks. The first task requires students to write a descriptive report (at least 150 words) based on data that is presented in a graph, table, or diagram. In task two, students must answer a short essay question (at least 250 words) that includes a point of view, argument, or problem. Writing skills that are checked in the test include the ability to:

- use appropriate content and vocabulary
- describe and explain data
- compare and contrast
- present a point of view or problem, with supporting evidence
- write in a variety of styles, and use a logical structure
- summarise main features
- discuss abstract issues and describe a process or how something works.

In the speaking section, there is a face-to-face interview with an examiner. Students are expected to answer short questions about themselves and their life, to speak at length about a familiar topic, and discuss issues and ideas. Speaking skills you need include:

- good pronunciation, intonation, and fluency
- ability to describe personal details and talk about everyday issues
- ability to express opinions and views and interact with the examiner
- keep the conversation flowing
- discuss topics

The listening, reading, writing, and speaking papers each have a different number of sections and questions (see Table 14.1). There is a range of question types, including multiple choice, short-answer questions, completion of sentences and diagrams, and choosing suitable paragraph headings.

Table 14.1

Module	Approximate test duration (minutes)	Number of tasks/sections	Number of questions
Listening	30*	4	40
Reading	60	3	40
Writing	60	2	2
Speaking	11–14	3+	variable

*10 minutes is provided for students to transfer their answers to an answer book

How can I prepare for the IELTS test?

There are several things you can do to prepare for the test.

- *Apply for the test.* To apply to take the test, you will need to complete an application form and hand it in to the test centre along with passport-sized photographs and proof of identity.
- *Become familiar with the test.* Being familiar with the test format, including its structure and the types of tasks and questions, will enable you to focus more on your English skills to improve your score. Information about IELTS, as well as preparation notes and test materials, can be downloaded or purchased from the IELTS website.
- *Attend a preparation course.* Some colleges offer courses to coach students for the test. They explain the test system, provide practise, and offer mock tests and feedback.
- *Read books about the test.* There will be books in your local bookshop that are designed to help students prepare; they provide exam strategies and tips, vocabulary, practice tests, and model answers.
- *Identify the skills being tested.* As the IELTS examines certain English skills (not only English proficiency) in each question, try to identify those being tested, and demonstrate your ability at them.
- *Take a mock test.* Taking a mock test will help you to practise your exam skills and judge your current level.

Taking the IELTS test

The IELTS test can be taken at many places around the world; there are more than 300 centres in over 100 countries. Your teacher or college can let you know the nearest one. Most centres offer the test monthly. The Listening, Reading and Writing tests are taken on the same day, whereas the Speaking test is taken on the same day or a few days before or after. Previously, students had to wait three months before they could re-sit the IELTS test; now there are no restrictions.

In the exam room:

- *Attend on time.* Make sure that you know the date, time, and place of the test. Do not be late, otherwise you may not be allowed to take the test.
- *Take proof of identity.* You will need to show appropriate proof of identity. Check the type of identification that should be taken.

- *Read and listen to the rules and regulations.* Follow the exam instructions carefully, otherwise your test could be disqualified. Only take items that are permitted in the test room, such as a pen/pencil and eraser. Note that your mobile phone and other belongings should be placed outside the room. Do not talk to other candidates after the test has started.
- *Read the test paper carefully.* Read the instructions and questions so that you know what needs to be done and how. Ensure that you have the correct test format (i.e., the Academic module). Fill in the details required on the front of the paper.
- *Write your answer.* Take care when you write the answers. Poor spelling and grammar, and illegible handwriting may be penalised. For the listening and reading tests, make sure that you transfer your answers onto the Answer Sheet. If not, they will not be marked. Think carefully about the correct answer; for example, when filling in a blank, only write down the missing word(s) and write no more than the word limit. When writing an answer, do not copy sentences from the exam paper, use your own words to paraphrase the information and never go above the word limit.
- *Check your answers before you finish.* Check that your answers make sense and are grammatically correct. Do not take any test materials away from the room. If you have a problem, raise your hand and ask an invigilator for assistance.

Test results

The results are issued on a 'Test Report Form' by the centre thirteen days after the test. The form will also include your name, nationality, first language, and date of birth. Your performance will be rated as a score for each module, known as a Band Score, on a scale of 1 (non-user of English) to 9 (expert user). The four scores are then calculated to produce an 'Overall Band Score' (see Table 14.2). The band scores reflect the ability to use and understand English at university level.

The Band Score required for entry on to a course reflects the level of English language needed, as courses vary in their linguistic demands. In addition to the Overall Band Score, some courses require a certain score in a particular paper.

Test of English as a Foreign Language (TOEFL)

Another test is the TOEFL. It is managed by the Educational Testing Service in the USA, and is an American test of English as a foreign language in university settings.

Table 14.2

IELTS Band Scores and their meaning
9 Expert user
8 Very good user
7 Good user
6 Competent user
5 Modest user
4 Limited user
3 Extremely limited user
2 Intermittent user
1 Non-user
0 Did not attempt test

Many universities also accept TOEFL as an English language qualification; however, a number do not accept it, so you should check before applying. TOEFL has had different formats during recent years; the most commonly taken test is the Internet-based version, in which students answer questions using a computer at test centres. The precise format of the paper can differ depending on the country the student lives in.

Below is a rough comparison of TOEFL and IELTS scores to help you judge your level. However, there is no official comparison and it is not possible to match them precisely as the two tests have many differences, including the skills they test. For this reason, different universities will cite slightly different IELTS and TOEFL comparisons as entry requirements. Again, check with the university before you apply.

Table 14.3   A rough comparison of IELTS and TOEFL scores

IELTS Band	TOEFL score (internet-based test)
7.0	100
6.5	90
6.0	80
5.5	70
5.0	60
4.5	50

What if I don't have the English requirements?

There are several things you can do if you need to improve your English language skills before you start your course.

Study English!

Learn English intensively, either in your country or in the UK. The advantage of studying in the UK is that you will be surrounded by English all of the time! The amount of time you will need depends on your current level and also your ability to learn a language. A wide range of English courses – for all ages and levels – are available, and you can study at a private language school, college, or university. Your local British Council office will be able to provide details of accredited courses in the UK. Key points to consider when choosing a course include the level, number of class hours, class size, course fees, and accommodation costs.

Pre-sessional (or Pre-entrance) Programme

Universities offer short intensive English programmes for students who want to improve their language skills or for students who have been offered a place on a course but have narrowly missed the English Language requirement. Programmes are held 1–2 months before the beginning of the course (e.g., in the summer for a course that begins in September). They help students to:

- develop language skills
- improve vocabulary and grammar
- practise study skills
- learn about life in the UK.

Successful completion of the programme at a university usually satisfies the English language requirement of their degree courses (you should check if this is the case).

International Foundation Programme

An International Foundation Programme is a one-year course designed for students who have completed high school and want to increase their level of competence in the English language. Students whose high school qualifications do not meet the required level may also be able to take the course. The main focus of the course is to improve English Language and study skills; there may also be the option to specialise in a subject of your choice. Students who pass the course may be guaranteed a place on an undergraduate or postgraduate degree at the same university.

Pre-Masters programme

This course is similar to Pre-sessional and Foundation Programmes but focuses specifically on preparing students for Master degree level. The length of the course depends on your English language level and other qualifications.

Studying in English at university

The level of English used in university is different to conversational English. It is more demanding and complex. You will need to understand and discuss issues at a deeper level; express issues clearly and coherently; think critically about ideas; and use a variety of styles.

Before you begin your studies

You must have a standard of English that will enable you to benefit fully from the course. Therefore, it is very important to consider carefully whether your English level is sufficient (as already noted, you can find out your English ability by taking a test such as IELTS). Courses vary in the demands they make on your English; those that are linguistically demanding require a higher language ability. For example, some subjects in the humanities and social sciences may have a higher IELTS requirement than those in science, engineering, and mathematics.

English language support during your course

Universities provide English language support to their students, arranged in regular classes, workshops, language labs, or as individual tuition. They are likely to take place in a language centre or department. You may be asked to undertake an English test at the beginning of the semester to determine if you need language support and to assign you to an appropriate class. Bear in mind that not all universities offer free English language support.

Academic English (English for Academic Purposes)

English that is used in academic contexts is advanced and is known collectively as 'Academic English' or 'English for Academic purposes'. A good grasp of academic English is essential for success at university. The main features of Academic English are:

1   *Formal.* Academic English uses formal vocabulary and is free from grammar errors. The use of slang (informal words and expressions) and colloquialism (conversational expressions that are spoken by people every day) is avoided.
2   *Clear, concise and precise.* Academic English uses fewer words to express something and gets straight to the point. The argument and line of reasoning can be followed easily. Hesitation (e.g., er, um, well) is common in conversational English but not in university.
3   *Impersonal and objective.* Another feature of academic English is its impartiality, which means that it does not usually reflect your view. There should also be no bias and subjective reasoning. Instead of stating personal opinions, you should look for viewpoints in books, published articles, and other sources. Personal pronouns, such as 'I, me, my' are usually omitted.

4   *Logical structure and use of evidence*. There should be a clear and logical structure and progression between ideas. Sentences should link into paragraphs, and each paragraph should follow from the previous one. Arguments have an introduction; development of a main idea; a conclusion; and are supported by evidence and examples.

5   *Use of difficult and full words*. Shortened forms of words and phrases are common in spoken English, but avoided at university level. This includes abbreviations (a shortened form of a word or phrase) and contractions (words that have been shortened; e.g., 'it did not = didn't' and 'they are = they're'). Vocabulary used at university level tends to be more complex than that used in everyday language, and can include jargon (specialist or technical words).

6   *Generalisations and caution*. In academic English statements and conclusions are careful or tentative to make them less definite. This gives allowance for other people's viewpoints. It is also common to generalise (infer general comments) about something.

7   *Style*. Academic writing can follow different styles, such as descriptive, argumentative, and evaluative.

8   *References*. Academic work lists books, articles and other sources to show where the facts came from.

9   *Advanced skills*. During your studies you will develop a range of skills such as how to write assignments, listen to lectures, give presentations, read and summarise articles, etc. These skills are an integral part of using academic English.

Note that the distinction between academic and non-academic English is not always clear-cut. The characteristics described above are not always included in academic English, and usage and style varies across disciplines. For example, non-academic English can also be very formal.

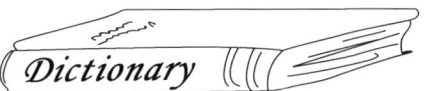

Using an English language dictionary

A dictionary is a very useful tool to help you to study your course in English. A good dictionary will enable you to do the following:

- look up the meaning and spelling of a word
- translate a word you see or hear
- find several meanings of a word and how they fit a particular context

(Continued)

- know how to pronounce a word
- look up grammar usage
- find example sentences about how a word is used.

Choosing a dictionary

There are different types of dictionary, and each one has good and bad points. Your choice depends on your English level, and what you want the dictionary for. There are generally two types – an English–English dictionary that defines and explains words in English, and a bilingual dictionary for translating words. An English–English dictionary is better for finding English definitions and English phrases but it will not give the meaning in your first language. Below is a list of points to consider when choosing a dictionary:

- Level of difficulty.
- Number of words, phrases, and examples.
- Amount of detail for each word. Some dictionaries give short definitions, whereas others provide detail and give examples.
- Type of dictionary. (e.g., for general use; specific aspects of the English language such as idioms, verbs, pronouncing; or related to a degree subject).
- Monolingual or bilingual.
- Layout and structure
- Some dictionaries contain additional facts such as units of measurements and conversion scales.
- Size/weight. Some dictionaries are desk-size (large and heavy), whereas others are pocket-size.
- British or American English (or both). Obviously, a British English dictionary is suitable for studying in the UK.
- Price. Dictionaries vary in price.

Some dictionaries are designed specifically for advanced learners of English as a second language. They are likely to be more suitable for non-native speakers; they contain less complicated definitions, more example sentences, and commonly used words. Examples are:

- *Cambridge Advanced Learner's Dictionary*
- *Collins Cobuild Advanced Learner's English Dictionary.*
- *Oxford Advanced Learner's Dictionary*

Using a dictionary

Take time to familiarise yourself with your dictionary and to understand how it works. It is also a good idea to practise finding words quickly. Dictionaries are arranged in alphabetical order, and there are words printed at the top of each page to guide you to the correct page.

Meaning

Many English words have more than one meaning. When looking up a word, read through all of them and find the one that fits the situation and makes most sense. Go back to where you found the word – such as a textbook – and re-read the sentence or paragraph. It is good practice to keep a record of all new words that you come across and to write down details of its usage, such as collocations (words that often go together) and different forms (e.g., nouns, verbs, adjectives).

Spelling

To find the spelling of a word, you will need to know the first few letters. When you have checked it in the dictionary, look at variations of how the word is spelt. If you need to find out the English translation of a word in your own language, you may find that there is more than one translation. Do a back translation to check it. Some dictionaries list the frequency of each word (commonly and least commonly used words). Another useful tool is a thesaurus, which lists related words and concepts.

Examples

Some dictionaries provide sentences to show how words are used. They are useful because they give you some grammatical usage about a word, enable you to see if you understand its meaning and show how to use a word in sentences. They also help you to use correct English sentences.

Pronunciation

A good dictionary will have details (using a phonetic symbol system) about the pronunciation of a word. As there are various phonetic systems used around the world, choose a dictionary that uses one that you are familiar with (the International Phonetic Alphabet is a common system). Some dictionaries provide an explanation of the pronunciation system.

Electronic dictionaries

Many dictionaries are now electronic, either as a hand-held device, a CD-ROM, or an online version. They help to look up information quickly, and have additional functions such as recordings to help you pronounce a word, and photographs or movies to help explain concepts. However, they may not be allowed in exam halls.

An example of an entry

The figure on the next page illustrates the information given about a word in a typical dictionary. Each dictionary has a different layout, features and conventions, and there will be an introductory guide which explains how to use it.

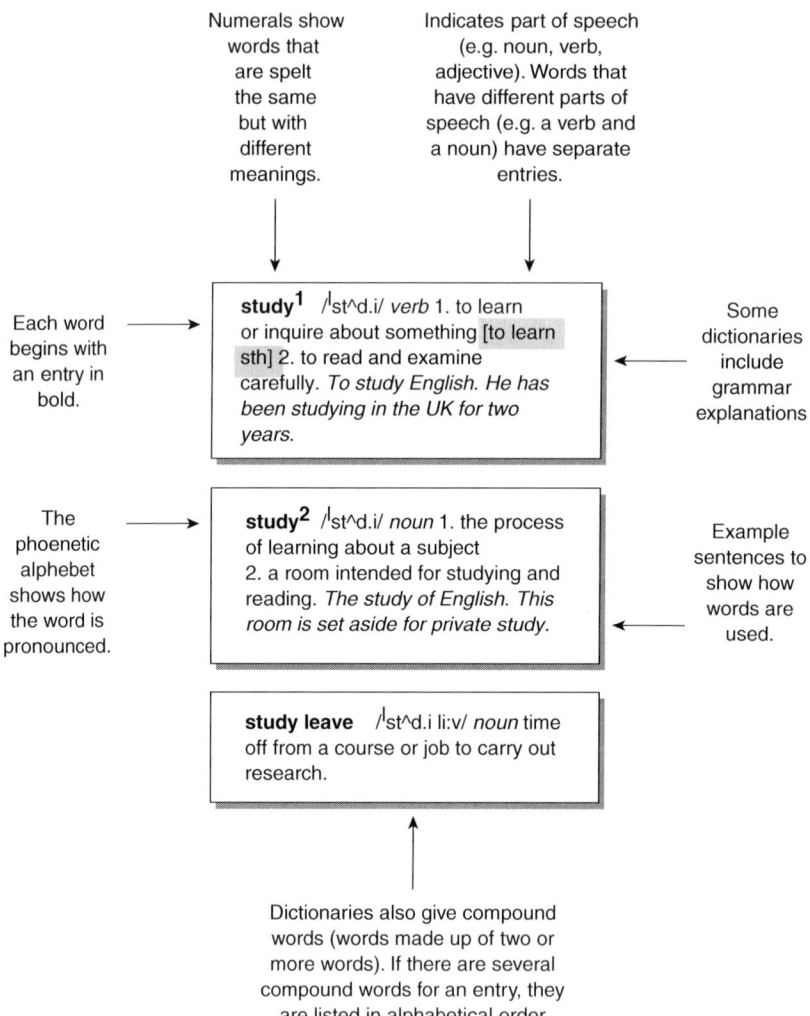

Numerals show words that are spelt the same but with different meanings.

Indicates part of speech (e.g. noun, verb, adjective). Words that have different parts of speech (e.g. a verb and a noun) have separate entries.

Each word begins with an entry in bold.

study¹ /ˈstʌd.i/ *verb* 1. to learn or inquire about something [to learn sth] 2. to read and examine carefully. *To study English. He has been studying in the UK for two years.*

Some dictionaries include grammar explanations

The phoenetic alphebet shows how the word is pronounced.

study² /ˈstʌd.i/ *noun* 1. the process of learning about a subject 2. a room intended for studying and reading. *The study of English. This room is set aside for private study.*

Example sentences to show how words are used.

study leave /ˈstʌd.i liːv/ *noun* time off from a course or job to carry out research.

Dictionaries also give compound words (words made up of two or more words). If there are several compound words for an entry, they are listed in alphabetical order

A word entry in a dictionary

15 Speaking English at University

RICKY LOWES, HELEN PETERS AND MARIE TURNER

AIMS

By studying and doing the activities in this chapter you should:

◆ think about what it means to communicate in another language;
◆ develop your communication strategies;
◆ be able to participate effectively in a seminar;
◆ develop your skills for group work; and
◆ learn how to develop your English-speaking skills.

GLOSSARY

These key words will be useful to you while reading this chapter:

Assertive: Someone who behaves confidently and is not frightened to say what they want or believe.

Challenge: Something needing great mental or physical effort in order to be done successfully and which therefore tests a person's ability.

Challenging: Difficult, in a way that tests your ability or determination.

Convey: To express a thought, feeling or idea so that other people understand it.

Discourse: Communication in speech or writing.

Dynamics: Forces or processes that produce change inside a group or system.

Interlocutor: Someone who is involved in a conversation.

Rewarding: Bringing benefits, especially by making you feel satisfied that you have done something important or useful, or done something well.

Submission: Giving in a piece of work.

Succinct: Said in a clear and short way; expressing what needs to be said without unnecessary words.

Communicating in another language

While you are studying at university in the UK you will be spending much of your time communicating in English. This gives you the opportunity to learn to speak English really well, a skill that will be useful for the rest of your life. However, it can be quite a challenge to communicate successfully in another language. Communication is a complex process and involves knowledge of the language at a number of levels. To communicate effectively a person has to have a good command of each of these levels. In our own language we are not normally aware of these levels as we use them without thinking. Speaking in another language is different because things do not necessarily come naturally, the way they do in our own language. Let us have a look at what is involved:

- *Phonological level*: this involves making the sounds of the language in the right way and also speaking with the right rhythm and intonation.
- *Lexical level*: this means using the vocabulary of the language to express meaning.
- *Grammatical level*: this is the system of combining words into phrases and sentences.
- *Discourse level*: this is the way the other elements are combined to create continuous pieces of language – that is, written text or dialogue.

You need to operate effectively at all these levels in order to be a really good communicator. It is important to be aware of each level and to develop your abilities in each.

Signpost

If you know you need to make improvements in some areas of your language, you should make a study plan. Turn to Chapter 2, pages 34–5, 'Being an effective learner', for ideas on how to do this.

Here are some other parts of this book that could be helpful:

- For pronunciation, see the section, 'Developing your speaking skills', later in this chapter.
- For vocabulary, see Chapter 4, 'Building vocabulary'.
- For discourse, see Chapter 9, 'Writing'.

Task 1

Complete the table below as honestly as you can to indicate where you need to make improvement:

	None/very little improvement needed	Some improvement needed	A lot of improvement needed
Pronunciation: Can people understand my speech easily?			
Vocabulary: Do I have the right word for each occasion?			
Grammar: Are my sentences correctly formed?			
Discourse: Can I link ideas effectively, in order to communicate, including linking my ideas to those of others?			

It is important to remember that you can compensate for any difficulties you have by being aware of the problem and trying to use other ways of putting your message across. For example, if you know your pronunciation is poor but you have a large vocabulary, then when you see that someone doesn't understand something you have said, you can substitute another word with a similar meaning.

Saying the right thing

As well as being correct in the sense of using the right vocabulary and grammar, it is also important to say the right things, to the right person and to speak in the appropriate style – that is, with the right level of formality. If you use very formal language in relaxed social situations, you will sound odd and perhaps unfriendly. If you use informal language at the wrong times, you may sound rude or as if you are not taking things seriously. So it is important to think about what kind of language to use in each situation.

It is also important to be aware of what you can and cannot say or ask. For example, you might ask a fellow student for their home telephone number, especially if you were working on a joint project with them, but it would not be appropriate to ask your teacher for their telephone number. People from different cultures have different ideas about what is acceptable to talk about, and you will have to be sensitive to discover what these are for your fellow students and for the society in which you are living:

> *In my country, people discuss money very openly but I find here that my friends do not like it if I ask how much money they have or how much money their parents earn.*
> **(Chinese student)**

> *I don't normally have problems communicating with other students or teachers, but sometimes there are problems with international students because we come from different cultures and our jokes and the way we see things is different.*
> **(Turkish student)**

Levels of formality vary according to the situation, the speakers and their relationship. A lecture, especially a large, public lecture, is likely to be more formal than a seminar, and a conversation between students is obviously less formal than a conversation between a student and a teacher. Of course, a lot depends also on what is being talked about and how well the people know each other, and there are a number of factors that determine the level of formality appropriate in any particular situation.

Formality in English is expressed by the following:

- The vocabulary used (e.g. 'return' rather than 'come back').
- The grammatical structures (e.g. the passive – 'the houses have been demolished' rather than 'they've demolished the houses').

Task 2

Look at the quiz below and decide:

◆ Is it acceptable to say such things at all?
◆ Is the language right for the occasion?

Tick the box that best describes the use of the language in that particular situation:

	Completely appropriate	Acceptable	Inappropriate
A student says 'this is bullshit' in a presentation	☐	☐	☐
A student calls her teacher (Mary Smith) 'Mrs Mary'	☐	☐	☐
A student calls her teacher (Mary Smith) 'Smith'	☐	☐	☐
A student calls her teacher (Mary Smith) 'Mary'	☐	☐	☐
A student writing to apply for a course begins the letter 'Highly Esteemed Professor'	☐	☐	☐
Student to teacher in a seminar: 'I can't agree with you on that point'	☐	☐	☐

Student to another student in a seminar: 'I can't agree with you on that point'	☐	☐	☐
A student corrects another on a mistake of fact he or she has made in a seminar: 'I'm sorry to correct you but General Motors were not the market leaders at that time'	☐	☐	☐
A student corrects another on a mistake in his or her English in a seminar: 'Excuse me, but it isn't "putted", it's "put"'	☐	☐	☐
A group of English friends are talking and use one word ('paradigm') repeatedly. You don't understand. Should you ask them to explain?	☐	☐	☐
Your teacher speaks too fast. You say: 'Slow down. We can't understand you'	☐	☐	☐
A student thanks a teacher who has been particularly helpful and friendly by saying 'Cheers, mate'	☐	☐	☐

Key

For comments on this task, see 'Key to tasks' at the end of this chapter.

- The level of personalization ('It is believed' rather than 'I think').
- The use of tentative language (*might, would, could*).
- The length and complexity of sentences.

Differences in style can be due to the following:

- *The relationship between the speakers.* For example, speaking to a friend you might say: 'I didn't catch a thing you said. Just slow down and speak up.' To someone you didn't know so well you might say: 'I'm sorry but I can't understand what you're saying. Could you speak a little slower and louder, please?'
- *The formality of the situation itself.* Talking to friends while preparing a presentation on change within a company you might say: 'It's incredible. They changed the system five times in four years. What a mess. No wonder the people who worked there were pissed off.' In the presentation you would be more likely to convey the information in a more formal style: 'Many changes to the system were introduced in a short period of time, with five new methods of operating brought in within a four-year period. Naturally, this caused confusion and some discontent in the workforce.'

English does not tend to use a lot of flowery language, such as 'Highly Esteemed Colleague, your most worthy and illustrious institution', etc.; this is regarded as old-fashioned and awkward. Even formal English tends to be quite simple and direct but it avoids the use of slang and colloquial language.

It is not a question of formal or informal language being easier or more difficult – it all depends what you are used to. Some students find speaking to young people who use slang and informal language much easier than speaking using more formal English. For others it is the opposite:

> *The common words used by young people are more familiar to me and it is not difficult to communicate with them. I feel easy with them. With older people you have to think before you speak.*
> **(Greek student)**

> *Young people tend to speak faster and use more slang. Older people tend to speak more clearly and are more formal. It is easier to speak with them.*
> **(Korean student)**

It is important to be able to communicate using both formal and informal language appropriately.

[...]

TALKING TO YOUR TUTORS

> *The tutors here are very helpful and friendly and they treat you in a friendly way. I call my tutor by her first name. But I still don't speak to her as I speak to my friends. However, it is not so formal as in my country.*
> **(Korean student)**

Often students find it difficult to determine exactly how to speak to their teachers, as the relationship between teachers and students in English-speaking universities may seem less formal than in their own countries. The key is to be friendly without being familiar. Do not be surprised if your teachers expect you to call them by their first name and are quite happy to provide help and guidance in a fairly informal way. They will not expect there to be a big distance between staff and students and will treat you in many ways as an equal. In return, they will expect you to be respectful and to be conscientious in your work. In order to have happy relations with your tutors here are some helpful guidelines:

- Check how they would like you to communicate with them – by phone, by email or in person.
- Find out if it is necessary to book tutorials in advance or if they have a drop-in system. If it is the second, find out the times and stick to them. Do not disturb your tutor outside tutorial hours unless the matter is urgent.
- Make sure your tutor has a way of contacting you if they need to. If your telephone number or email address change, let your tutor know.
- Ask your tutor any questions you need to in advance of deadlines. Do not leave it until the day before submission to get help with a piece of work and do not expect your tutor to provide you with a reference without notice. (You should always ask a tutor's permission before giving their name as a referee).

Speaking in seminars

Generally, classes at college or university fall into three types: lectures, seminars and tutorials. Let us look first at what lectures and tutorials are in order to see how they are different from seminars.

Lectures

Lectures are talks given by teachers or guest speakers, who have particular expertise on the topic, to groups of students, usually large groups. There may be as many a several hundred people present in a lecture. There may be time for questions and discussion at the end of the lecture but, generally, the role of the lecturer is to present knowledge and information, and the role of their audience is to listen and absorb what is being said.

Tutorials

Tutorials are classes where a small group of students discuss a subject or subjects with a tutor. Some tutorials may consist of the tutor and only one or two students. These classes may be less formal and may centre on topics the students have suggested or problems they are having with their work.

[…]

Seminars

A seminar is a class at a college or a university in which a group of students discuss a subject with a teacher. The size of the group may vary (usually between 10 and 20 students) but generally a seminar will have more participants than a tutorial and fewer than a lecture. The dynamics are different from either of the other two types of classes as well. Students are expected to be active participants – that is, they are expected to speak up, unlike in a lecture. On the other hand, the class is more formal than a tutorial, as it centres on focused discussion of a topic that the members of the seminar group are expected to have prepared. A seminar often allows students to discuss in depth issues that have been presented in a lecture and which they will have explored through their reading. It is a very valuable part of the teaching and learning experience.

What makes a good seminar?

A really good seminar is one in which ideas are actively explored in depth. Participants leave with a feeling of satisfaction that they have learnt something new, that they have been able to express their ideas, that they have listened to other people's views and have perhaps expanded or changed their own views as a result.

Active participation

The value of a seminar is in direct proportion to the contributions of the participants. It is important that all the students taking part in the seminar are able and willing to contribute. This means they must be *willing to speak* (see below), and they must have *something to say*. It is also important that all the students participate. If the seminar is dominated by a few of the more confident and talkative students, it will be much less interesting for everyone. Having a range of different views and approaches to the topic makes the seminar more interesting and a better learning experience. It is important to remember that even quite a small or apparently minor point may start off a really good discussion. Each person's contribution, however small, helps the rest of the participants to develop their ideas. This may be because it supports their own thoughts or, on the other hand, because they are in disagreement and it forces them to think more clearly about what they believe. So, remember: don't be shy – by sharing your thoughts you are helping the whole group to participate.

Having something to say

It is important to prepare for seminars because it is more difficult to come up with ideas and to express them clearly without any preparatory work. At the very least, you should:

- find out what the topic of the seminar is in advance;
- do some thinking about it;
- consider what you already know about the topic;
- think about what you do not know;
- do the reading your teacher has recommended; and
- think of questions to ask.

You might find it helpful at this point to work with another student who is in the same group as you. Together you can share what you already know and brainstorm ideas around the seminar topic or question (some seminars focus on a question). You should use the library, the Internet or other resources to do some research on the topic. This will mean that you go to the seminar with some knowledge of the subject, which will help you to feel more confident.

Example: preparing for a seminar

We could consider what thinking we could do before going to this seminar on a first-year Business and Management course, where the following task has been set:

Consider the main functions, in relation to the provision or administration of tourism, of any public sector organization, e.g. regional tourist authority, national tourist board, district council.

Questions that could be considered in this case are: 'What are these organizations exactly?', 'How far do their functions overlap?' and 'Whose interests are they promoting?' How could the student find the answers to these questions? Possible sources of information are recommended textbooks, the websites of the various organizations or even a telephone call to the organizations themselves. For example, a visit to the website of the Zambian National Tourist Board will provide you with a detailed list of its functions (http://www.zambiatourism.com/zntb/).

Task 3

Find out what the topic of your next seminar is. Write the title of the seminar at the top of a piece of paper. Underneath list anything you know about the topic. Then think about what you don't know and write some questions. Speak to a fellow student and see if they agree with your list and if they can answer any of the questions. Then write down at least three resources you could consult to research this topic and commit yourself to looking at them before your seminar.

Students are usually asked to read particular texts in preparation for a seminar. Very often your tutor will be happy to recommend extra reading you can do to prepare yourself for classes and most courses give lists of recommended readings for teaching sessions.

HOW CAN I BUILD UP MY CONFIDENCE?

I find speaking groups difficult. Sometimes I don't manage to say anything in my seminars.
(Korean student)

Be prepared

As we noted above, the first step to build up your confidence is to prepare. The way to do this is to:

- make sure you know the topic of the seminar;
- reflect on what you know/don't know;
- think of questions you would like to ask; and
- read around the subject.

Being prepared should give you more confidence to speak and make it easier for you to understand other students' contributions. You will find that you are not only more familiar with the ideas related to the topic but also with the language you will need:

If you have prepared beforehand it is easy to describe something or to understand the vocabulary used. I have more difficulties in explaining what I cannot understand in the subject.
(Brazilian student)

Analyse the difficulties

Sometimes it can be difficult to manage to speak, even if you want to and have something to say. The way conversation works differs greatly between cultures, so it may be difficult to participate even if you understand what is being said and you are
informed about the topic. In order to feel comfortable about speaking in class in an English-speaking environment, you may need to adopt a different approach to discussion. Two aspects to consider are 'wait time' and level of emotional expression.

Wait time

The time left between one person finishing speaking and the next person beginning to speak.

Some students find it difficult to enter the discussion as there never seems to be a pause long enough for them to take their turn. This may be because of shyness but it may also be because of different cultural expectations about the appropriate amount of time to wait after one person has finished speaking before the next person begins to speak.

Wait times can vary considerably between cultures (including between different cultures within the same country). People who have a very short wait time often start to speak as soon as their interlocutor has completed his or her final word. British, American, Australian and many European cultures tend to have short wait times. They often use a pattern of overlapping speech, which for them is a sign of involvement and interest. However, speakers who come from cultures where a significant pause between speakers is needed may perceive them as over-assertive or dominant. Speakers from cultures with long wait times may get frustrated at being interrupted and find themselves unable to join in a discussion. A teacher with short wait time may think a student has completed a response when the student only intended to pause.

For people from certain cultures it is natural to express emotional involvement in a discussion, for example by expressing personal convictions or raising their voice, whereas other cultures consider this to be inappropriate. If members of a group involved in discussion come from different cultural backgrounds, this can have an impact on their communication. Students for whom assertive communication comes naturally may tend to dominate in a conversation with students from more reserved cultures.

No one particular way of speaking is right or wrong but, for seminars to work well, those involved need to find a way of communicating comfortably without misunderstanding. It is important to devise strategies for effective participation that will allow you to listen attentively to other students and to speak effectively to communicate your views.

DEVISE STRATEGIES FOR PARTICIPATION

Getting an opportunity to speak

If you are a shy student, or you come from a culture with a longer wait time, you may need to make an extra effort to make sure you are heard in discussion. Making eye contact with the person who is speaking or the chair of the discussion, leaning forward slightly or slightly raising a hand are all ways to signal you wish to speak.

Try to speak early on in the seminar. This will get you into the habit of speaking and let the others know you are willing to participate.

The phrases below are useful ways of entering a conversation. You may have to raise your voice more than you feel at first is appropriate. Don't be shy – assertiveness is valued in English-speaking educational institutions as a sign you are attentive and keen:

- Could I just make a point?
- Could I say … ?
- Ah – I'd like to say …
- Yes, that's quite right and I'd like to add …
- May I add something?
- May I come in here?
- Can I ask … ?

You might even simply ask someone to repeat what he or she has said or to explain it a bit more.

If you find it easier to speak to just one other person at a time, you should make an effort to practise joining in conversations with groups of people. This is generally more difficult, even in one's own language, so be prepared to find it challenging. You have to listen to several people and follow more than one idea. If you can practise as often as possible in informal situations, you will build your confidence and skills to cope in the classroom.

Task 4

Arrange to meet with a group of people you feel comfortable with to discuss topics of interest to you all. You might like to form a study group to continue discussion of seminar topics outside class. Practise being appropriately assertive and try to use the expressions listed above to make sure you participate fully in the discussion.

Giving opportunities to speak
If you are from a culture with a short wait time, if you are a confident, fluent speaker and if you have lots of experience of speaking out in groups and you know that it is not a problem for you, you can have a crucial role in helping other students to speak.

Remember that having a range of different views and approaches to the topic makes for a better seminar. It will benefit everyone if the quieter students participate. There are various things the more confident members of the group can do:

◆ Make your point succinctly – don't continue talking for longer than necessary.
◆ Speak clearly, explaining vocabulary if necessary, so you are sure everyone understands.
◆ Address everyone in the group rather than just the seminar leader or one or two other students.
◆ Encourage others to talk by making eye contact or asking questions.
◆ Listen attentively while other students are speaking.
◆ Have an encouraging manner, showing that you welcome other people's ideas.

Task 5

Set yourself the goal of getting one other student to participate in your next seminar discussion by using any or all of the strategies above.

Asking questions
Asking questions can be a very positive way to contribute to a group discussion. It is a good strategy for active but limited participation and so this is a particularly useful way to begin to build up your confidence. This is where the questions you prepared in advance can be very helpful. Questions that require an elaborated response (i.e. those beginning with 'why', 'how', 'what', 'when', etc.) tend to stimulate better answers than questions that can be answered by 'yes' or 'no'. Other speakers will welcome your questions as they give them a chance to participate as well.

Task 6

Look at these seminar topics. (Degree programmes that such a seminar might be related to are given in brackets after the topic.) How many questions can you think of for each topic? If you do not know much about the topic, don't worry; you will probably have more questions! You may like to do this exercise with another student:

- Globalization and its effect on the labour market (International Studies/ Business).
- China's financial markets and Chinese economic reform (International Studies/Business).
- The effects of climate and climate change on fish and fisheries (Environmental Sciences/Biology).
- The place of European law in the English legal system (law).
- The European Union, enlargement and reform (European Studies/Politics).
- The impact of tourism on the environment and society (Social Studies/ Business).
- The political participation of ethnic minorities in multicultural cities (Sociology/Politics).

Key

You may want to compare the questions you have thought of with those suggested in the 'Key to tasks' section at the end of this chapter.

Signpost

If you have not already looked at Task 3 above, you could try it now.

Responding to other people's views

You can also ask questions in response to what other people say in the seminar. This allows you to clarify what they have said and gives them the chance to expand on or elaborate their views.

Example: asking questions in a seminar

In a degree programme in Environmental Science, there might be a seminar, 'The Antarctic peninsula: a vulnerable ecosystem'. A student expresses the view: 'All commercial and most scientific activity in the Antarctic peninsula should be stopped, due to its impact on the ecosystem'. Before getting into a debate on whether this is right or wrong, it would be interesting to ask more questions, such as:

◆ What do we know about the impact of these activities on the ecosystem?
◆ Is the research reliable?
◆ Should activity be stopped indefinitely?
◆ What would the consequences of that be?
◆ What kind of scientific activity would be excluded from the ban?
◆ How would a ban be enforced legally?
◆ Who would ensure this was done?

These questions could be answered by the original speaker or by others in the seminar. This kind of interaction makes the seminar more dynamic.

Task 7

Now think of one or two questions that could be asked in response to the arguments stated below:
◆ It is economic common sense that multinational companies should locate production in areas where labour costs are low.
◆ The benefits of tourism are greater than the negative effects.
◆ Growth in membership of the European Union will be a positive thing because it will bring diversity.
◆ Ethnic minorities are inevitably at a disadvantage when it comes to participating in politics.

Key

For suggested questions, see 'Key to tasks' at the end of this chapter.

Tell me more

You can also participate by inviting the speaker to expand on his or her point. This is a useful strategy if you feel you need more information or you have not fully understood what the person means. You should feel able to ask for further explanation if you have not understood a point.

Useful expressions are as follows:

- Could you tell us more about … ?
- That's interesting, can you say more?
- I'm sorry, I didn't get that, could you go over it again?
- I don't really understand your point, could you explain further?
- That's quite difficult to understand, can you give us more explanation/some more examples?

This can be a way of getting information even if you do not have a precise question to ask. Make sure you use one or more of these expressions in your next seminar to get someone to expand on their point.

Working in groups

All that we have said about speaking in seminars can be applied to speaking in less formal groups, such as when you are a member of a study group or when you are preparing a piece of group work with other students. You may also be asked to work in groups within a classroom setting.

The important thing to remember is that, for a group to work together successfully, all members have to be willing and able to participate. You will be working with people who come from other areas of the world, and their English and their ideas about studying may be different from yours. This means it is especially important to make an effort to communicate effectively.

There are tremendous benefits to working in groups: you can share ideas and knowledge, give each other support and confidence and be constructively critical of the work produced, leading to a higher standard of work. There are also challenges, and cross-cultural communication can be one of them. It is important for you to use your listening and your speaking skills well.

[…]

Simple rules for successful group work are as follows:

+ Be organized – make sure you arrange meeting times and that you have each other's contact details.
+ Include everyone – make sure all members of the group get the chance to contribute.
+ Consider everyone's feelings – be encouraging of contributions, especially from quieter members.
+ Allow time for discussion – make sure you understand everyone's point of view.

[…]

Group work is often a good opportunity for you to develop your speaking (and listening) skills, as the situation is less formal and less stressful than a seminar. If you take the opportunity to participate fully in group work, you may find that you are more able to take an active role in your seminars.

Developing your speaking skills

SPEAKING CLEARLY

You will feel more confident and be able to contribute more effectively to seminars if you are clear and easy to understand when you speak. You may feel that you are at a disadvantage because you have an accent when speaking English but this, in itself, is not necessarily a problem. Everyone speaks with an accent, including English native speakers, who have their own personal or regional accent. The important thing is to articulate sounds clearly so that you can be understood and to use rhythm and stress to convey your meaning effectively.

PRONOUNCING SOUNDS

Certain sounds in English may not exist in your language or may be slightly different. A typical example is the 'th' sound in words like 'think' or 'truth' /θ/ which does not exist in a number of other languages such as French or Turkish. Some languages do not make the same distinctions that English does between vowel sounds, such as /I/ (the vowel sound in 'ship') and /i:/ (the vowel sound in 'sheep') or between consonant sounds such as /r/ (in 'right') and /l/ in ('light'). An added complication is that English has a large number of vowel sounds (20 vowels and diphthongs) and distinguishing between them causes problems for many students (Japanese, for example, has only 5 vowel sounds). However, with careful study and plenty of practice, these distinctions can be learnt. English has certain combinations of sounds that do not occur in some other languages such as those that appear at the end of 'crisps' (/sps/) or 'grounds' (/ndz/).

If you find that particular sounds or sound combinations are difficult for you, you can help yourself by using pronunciation exercises available on tape and in books, which you should find in the language laboratory or the language centre of your college or university.

Signpost

If you are not sure which sounds to practise, you can consult a book such as *Learner English* or *Sounds English* (see the 'Useful resources' section at the end of this chapter). These books will tell you the sounds that speakers of your language have problems with in English. A dictionary with a CD-ROM (see the 'Useful resources' section at the end of Chapter 4) will give you the pronunciation of the sounds of English, and you can use this to check which sounds are difficult for you.

STRESS, RHYTHM AND INTONATION

These are three areas that contribute greatly to clear speaking and so are useful areas to work on in English. If you have not learnt to use the English system of stress, rhythm and intonation, English native speakers will find you difficult to understand and you may also find it difficult to understand what they are saying.

Task 8

Look at the phonemic chart taken from *Collins Cobuild English Language Dictionary* and, working from your own knowledge or with the help of one of the books mentioned above, make a note of the sounds that you find difficult:

Vowel Sounds

ɑː	calm, ah	ɒ	lot, spot	
ɑːʳ	heart, far	oʊ	note, coat	
æ	act, mass	ɔː	claw, maul	
aɪ	dive, cry	ɔʳ	more, cord	
aɪəʳ	fire, tyre	ɔɪ	boy, joint	
aʊ	out, down	ʊ	could, stood	
aʊəʳ	flour, sour	uː	you, use	
e	met, lend, pen	ʊəʳ	lure, pure	
eɪ	say, weight	ɜːʳ	turn, third	
eəʳ	fair, care	ʌ	fund, must	
ɪ	fit, win	ə	the first vowel in about	
iː	feed, me	əʳ	the first vowel in forgotten	
ɪəʳ	near, beard	i	the second vowel in very	
		u	the second vowel in actual	

Consonant Sounds

b	bed, rub	s	soon, bus
d	done, red	t	talk, bet
f	fit, if	v	van, love
g	good, dog	w	win, wool
h	hat, horse	ʰw	why, wheat
j	yellow, you	x	loch
k	king, pick	z	zoo, buzz
l	lip, bill	ʃ	ship, wish
ˈl	handle, panel	ʒ	measure, leisure
m	mat, ram	ŋ	sing, working
n	not, tin	tʃ	cheap, witch
°n	hidden, written	θ	thin, myth
p	pay, lip	ð	then, bathe
r	run, read	dʒ	joy, bridge

Now choose the one you think is the most important and set yourself the goal of improving your pronunciation of that particular sound.

Stress

When a word or syllable is pronounced with more force than the surrounding words or syllables.

A feature that is very important in English is 'stress timing'. This means that the rhythm of speech depends on the number of stressed and unstressed syllables in the sentences. Many languages stress the syllables fairly equally, which produces a regular rhythm. English speakers stress the words that carry most meaning so that listeners know what to pay attention to. They make these words clearer by using a different pitch and by making them longer and louder. The less important words receive less emphasis and so a rhythm is created of strong and weak beats, like music (e.g. '*I remem*bered to *post* the *let*ters'). Stress typically falls on nouns, verbs, adjectives and adverbs, as these are the sorts of words likely to communicate the meaning of what someone is saying.

In addition, you should remember that the stress is always on a particular syllable in a word. To know which syllable this is, you can look at a dictionary. The stress will be marked on the phonemic transcription of the word. The symbol | is commonly used by dictionaries to indicate that the following syllable is stressed. For example:

> **adversity** /əd'vɜː.sə.ti/ ⓤ /-'vɝː.sə.ti/ *noun* [C or U] a difficult or unlucky situation or event: *She was always cheerful* **in** *adversity.* ○ *The road to happiness is paved with adversities.*

A dictionary definition of the word 'adversity'
Source: Cambridge Advanced Learner's Dictionary (2003)

However, some dictionaries may underline the stressed syllable instead:

> **ec|lec|tic** /ɪklektɪk/ An **eclectic** collection of objects, ideas, or beliefs is wide-ranging and comes from many different sources. [FORMAL] ❑ *...an eclectic collection of paintings, drawings, and prints.*

A dictionary definition of the word 'eclectic'
Source: Collins Cobuild English Language Dictionary (2004)

So this is another way the dictionary can be of great help with pronunciation. If the dictionary has a CD-ROM, listen to the recording of the word. Some dictionaries have a facility for you to record your voice and compare your pronunciation with the original word.

Task 9

Look at the passage below, which has the stressed syllables marked by capital letters. Try reading it aloud to get a feel for the rhythm. Remember not to put emphasis on the unstressed syllables:

The IBErian LYNX is on the VERGE of exTINCtion. Its NAtural HAbitat is the CORK forests of SPAIN and PORtugal but these FORests are now under THREAT because the deMAND for CORK is FALLing. There has been an INcrease in the USE of SCREW-top and PLAStic STOPpers by WINE proDUcers.

Task 10

Now look at the passage below and highlight or underline the words you think a speaker should stress. It may help you to read the text aloud as you do this. If there are any words where you are not sure of the syllable where the stress falls, consult a dictionary:

Recent figures show that there are one hundred and fifty Iberian lynx left. Of these, thirty are breeding females. The lynx has been classified as 'critically endangered'. The World Wide Fund for Nature has given warning that unless something radical is done, the lynx will become extinct within a decade.

Key

For suggested answers, see 'Key to tasks' at the end of this chapter.

INTONATION AND PAUSING

To speak clearly and be understood easily you need to use English rhythm. The rhythm of speech is affected not just by stress but also by where you put pauses and whether your voice rises, stays level or falls (this is intonation).

Generally, pauses come between ideas, with longer pauses ‖ marking the end of an idea and shorter pauses │ marking breaks between related ideas, rather like full stops and commas in punctuation:

> I'm going shopping ‖ I'll buy meat │ tomatoes │ eggs │ and spaghetti ‖ and then I'll come home and cook.

Intonation is an important guide to meaning in English. Intonation patterns are not fixed according to grammar or vocabulary but are used flexibly to communicate what the speaker wants to say on a particular occasion. However, there are some simple, approximate guidelines that you can follow to help you. Your voice should fall ↘ to show that an idea is complete or that you are certain of something. It rises ↗ to show that an idea is incomplete or there is uncertainty. It stays level → to indicate an item in a list:

> I'm going shopping ↘ I'll buy meat → tomatoes → eggs → and spaghetti ↗ and then I'll come home and cook ↘
>
> Are you going out? ↗ Yes, ↘ and if you wait ↗ I'll take you with me ↘

(*Note*: The *amount* the voice rises or falls is determined by how the speaker feels about the information he or she is communicating. The voice rises most in surprise or disbelief and falls most to show complete certainty or that an idea is totally finished.)

So, by using a rising or falling intonation, you can use your voice to show how you feel about what you say and that you have or have not finished what you want to say.

Example: Intonation

In the first sentence below the speaker is expressing one idea. In the second this becomes the first part of a more complex idea and the voice shows there is more to come:

Developed countries should be prepared to take responsibility for global warming ↘
Developed countries should be prepared to take responsibility for global warming ↗ but developing countries also need to play their part ↘

Task 11

Look at the text below (which is unpunctuated) and mark where you think the voice rises and falls and where the pauses are. You may find it helpful to read the text aloud as you do this:

In my talk today I'd like to explore three regimes of pre-school education I shall look at the situation of children educated in their home language that of those educated in the national language and that of those educated in bilingual programmes while it is still too early to draw definite conclusions there are indications that these different regimes are not equally effective in promoting bilingualism.

Key

For a suggested answer, see 'Key to tasks' at the end of this chapter.

All this information on pronunciation is only a very basic guide. You should consult any of the books suggested to understand the subject in more depth and to find exercises to help you practise. You can practise by:

- using a book such as *Speaking Clearly* to develop effective stress, rhythm and intonation;
- speaking aloud on a topic to a friend and asking him or her to say how clear you are; and
- speaking on to a tape and then playing it back to yourself.

You may also find it useful to listen at the same time as you read a text. There are websites that have these facilities (the BBC's Reith Lectures are a good example of this) and this allows you to notice the stress, intonation and pausing of good speakers.

Signpost

Details of *Speaking Clearly* and the BBC's Reith Lectures can be found in the 'Useful resources' section at the end of this chapter.

Conclusion

There are many different aspects of developing your speaking skills and, by putting the ideas in this chapter into practice, you can become a more effective speaker.

One last thing you should think about is the principle of co-operative communication. This was described by a linguist named Grice and was simple:

Say what is necessary to say, in the most appropriate way, for that particular point in the conversation (or discussion).

He clarified this into four 'rules', which are called 'Grice's maxims'. Here they are below in a simplified form:

1 *Be clear*: this means to speak in a way that your interlocutors can understand you. This may mean you have to work on your level of English.
2 *Be truthful*: this means you must not say that which you know to be false and you must not say things that you lack evidence for.
3 *Be brief*: do not say more than you need to (but don't say less than is necessary either!).
4 *Be relevant*: do not go off the point. Make sure what you are saying is related to the general direction of the conversation or discussion.

Much of this is common sense. However, if any of these 'rules' are broken the result is poor communication and frustration for the interlocutors.

One more 'rule' we should add is: *be confident*!

Confidence is key to success in speaking. So remember to be confident in your own abilities and be willing to do whatever is necessary to make sure you are understood. Shyness does not help in communication! Prepare before, when you can, and then speak up and get your message across!

REFERENCE

Grice, H.P. (1975) 'Logic and conversation', in P. Cole and J. Morgan (eds) *Syntax and Semantics*. Volume 3. New York, NY: Academic Press.

USEFUL RESOURCES

General
http://www.uefap.co.uk/speaking/spkfram.htm
> This is part of the website for the University of Hertfordshire and it gives helpful advice on aspects of speaking in academic contexts.

http://pweb.sophia.ac.jp
> This site is written for Japanese learners of English but the advice it gives is sensible and helpful for students of all nationalities.

Anderson, K. and Lynch, T. (1992) *Study Speaking*. Cambridge: Cambridge University Press.

Swan, M. and Smith, B. (2001) *Learner English*. Cambridge: Cambridge University Press. Although this book is written for teachers of English rather than students of English, you should find helpful indications of where your language is different from English and what you should therefore study.

Pronunciation
http://www.ennglishclub.com/pronounciation/index.htm
> This site gives a clear and simple guide to where emphasis goes in the sentence, and gives a clear and fairly comprehensive guide to word stress in English.

http://www.bbc.co.uk/radio4/
> This is the Radio 4 home page of the BBC website. There are many interesting programmes you can listen to, some of which have transcripts that you can read at the same time. You will also find the link to the Reith Lectures (recommended above) here.

Baker, A. (1981) *Ship or Sheep*. Cambridge: Cambridge University Press.

Hancock, M. (2003) *English Pronunciation in Use.* Cambridge: Cambridge University Press.

Haycraft, B. (1994) *English Aloud 1 & 2*. Basingstoke: Macmillan ELT.

Headway Pronunciation Course (four levels: elementary to upper intermediate). Oxford: Oxford University Press.

O'Connor, J.D. and Fletcher, C. (1989) *Sounds English*. Harlow: Longman.

Rogerson, P. and Gilbert, J. (1990) *Speaking Clearly*. Cambridge: Cambridge University Press.

KEY TO TASKS

Task 2

- It would be totally inappropriate to say 'this is bullshit' in a presentation. This is vulgar, informal language that would only be used in very informal situations with people you know well, probably students of your own age. More appropriate expressions could be: 'This is wrong/untrue/misleading/false. I don't agree with this', etc.

- Generally, the appropriate way to address a member of staff you know is by his or her first name, so 'Mary' would be the right way to address the teacher. It is unacceptable to call a teacher by his or her surname only, although Ms Smith for a female teacher or Mr Smith for a male teacher you do not know well is fine. Titles such as Ms or Mr are not used with the first name. Although not likely to cause offence, it sounds very odd.

- The correct way to begin a letter to a person you know is 'Dear + his or her name'. If you do not know the name then use 'Dear Sir or Madam'.

- There is nothing wrong with a student openly disagreeing with a teacher or another student in a seminar as long as the disagreement is expressed respectfully and backed up by argument. Disagreement can often be the basis of some stimulating discussion.

- A student corrects another on a mistake of fact he or she has made in a seminar. This is perfectly acceptable and in fact helpful if the first student is wrong.

- A student corrects another on a mistake in his or her English in a seminar. Unless the mistake leads to misunderstanding, correcting someone's English is unnecessary and could lead to embarrassment, so it is better not to do it.

- A group of English friends are talking and use one word repeatedly you don't understand. Should you ask them to explain? If the word is repeated several times it is probably important and so worth asking about. However, in general it is best not to ask people to explain things too often as this can disrupt the conversation.

- It is good to ask the teacher to slow down, but this is not the most polite way. 'Excuse me, could you speak more slowly, we are finding it difficult to understand.' would be better.

◆ 'Cheers, mate' is too informal. 'Thank you very much' is neutral and appropriate.
◆ It is totally inappropriate to ask a teacher to change a mark. Marks are given based on a teacher's professional judgement, not on what a student wants or expects. The only thing the student can do is ask to know why they got the mark they did, and hopefully the student will then be able to apply what the teacher says in order to do better in their next essay.

Task 6
These are some possible questions. The list of questions is not supposed to be complete.

Globalization and its effect on the labour market (international studies/business):

◆ What are the main effects?
◆ Are the effects felt equally all over the world?
◆ Are they regarded as positive or negative? By whom?
◆ Are the effects likely to be long lasting?

China's financial markets and Chinese economic reform (international studies/business):

◆ Where are China's main financial markets?
◆ What kind of reforms have there been/are there planned?
◆ How long-term is the reform?
◆ What else is affected by the reforms?
◆ Who is most affected by these reforms?

The effects of climate and climate change on fish and fisheries (environmental sciences/biology):

◆ What climate change has taken place? In which areas?
◆ Are all fish equally affected?
◆ Are the effects negative or positive?
◆ Are the changes permanent or temporary?
◆ How have fisheries adapted so far?

The place of European law in the English legal system (law):

◆ In which areas are there most differences between European law and English law?
◆ How far does European law complement English law?

- How do English legal bodies/the British government feel about the relationship between European and English law?

The European Union, enlargement and reform (European studies/politics):

- How has the EU responded so far to enlargement?
- What future enlargement is planned?
- How do the member states feel about this?
- In what areas is reform needed?
- Are member states in agreement on reform?

The impact of tourism on the environment and society (social studies/business):

- Which parts of the world are being considered?
- Is the impact the same in different places?
- Are some areas more vulnerable? Why?
- Are the effects of tourism positive or negative?
- How is the impact measured?
- Who makes the assessment?

The political participation of ethnic minorities in multicultural cities (sociology/politics):

- Which cities are considered to be multicultural?
- What is the definition of multicultural?
- How is political participation measured?
- Which factors have most influence on their political participation?

Task 7

Here are some questions we have thought of. There could be many more.

It is economic common sense that multinational companies should locate production in areas where labour costs are low:

- Do you think there are other factors that should be considered?
- What is the effect on the areas where production starts up/closes down?
- What are the long term/short term effects?

The benefits of tourism are greater than the negative effects:

- What are the benefits/negative effects?
- Are they affecting the same people?
- Are they of the same type?
- How are they measured?
- Are they long- or short-term?

Growth in the European Union will be a positive thing because it will bring diversity:

- How will this diversity express itself?
- Is diversity always positive?
- What will the concrete effects be?

Ethnic minorities are inevitably at a disadvantage when it comes to participating in politics:

- Is this shown in all cases?
- What are the major obstacles?
- Are there any ways of avoiding or lessening the disadvantage?

Task 10
REcentFIGuresSHOWthatthereareONEHUNdredandFIFtyIBERianLYNXLEFT,OfTHESE, THIRtyareBREEDingFEmales.TheLYNXhasbeenCLASSifiedas'CRITicallyenDANgered'. TheWORLDWIDEFUNDforNAturehasgivenWARNingthatunLESSsomethingRADicalis DONE, the LYNX will become exTINCT within a DEcade.

Task 11
In my talk today↗ | I'd like to explore three regimes ↗ of pre-school education ↘ || I shall look at the situation of children educated in their home language ↗ | that of those educated in the national language ↗ | and that of those educated in bilingual programmes ↘ || while it is still too early ↗ to draw definite conclusions ↗ | there are indications ↗ | that these different regimes ↗ are not equally effective in promoting bilingualism ↘ ||

16 Coping with Life as an International Student

RICKY LOWES, HELEN PETERS AND MARIE TURNER

AIMS

By studying and doing the activities in this chapter you should:

- gain some understanding of social life at university in the UK;
- find out information on the kinds of sporting and leisure activities available;
- get an idea of what facilities are provided for students to assist them practically;
- start thinking about financial aspects of being a student, including part-time work; and
- discover some hints on how to make the most of your time, and enjoy yourself too!

GLOSSARY

These key words will be useful to you while reading this chapter:

Affiliated: Part of or in a close relationship with another, usually larger, group or organization.

Bursary: A sum of money given to a person by an organization, such as a university, to pay for him or her to study.

Culture shock: A feeling of confusion felt by someone visiting a country or place he or she does not know.

Excluded: To be kept out of something.

Extra-curricular: Activities which are not part of the usual school or college course.

Lobby: To try to persuade a politician, the government or an official group that a particular thing should or should not happen, or that a law should be changed.

Socialize: To spend the time when you are not working, with friends or with other people in order to enjoy yourself.

Voluntary: Done willingly, without being forced or paid to do it.

Social life at university in the UK

Many UK students, especially those who go to university straight after leaving school, see their time there as a time to enjoy themselves, meet new people and try out activities they have not done before, as well as a time for study. Universities in the UK have a number of different facilities which cater for students' social life, such as places to eat, sports facilities, leisure facilities and clubs.

SOCIALIZING

There are cafes and bars where students meet to eat and drink and there are often events organized with live music or discos. There is usually a lot of drinking of alcohol, but there are always people who do not drink alcohol and there are plenty of other drinks available, so if you do not drink alcohol you will not feel out of place. However, if you come from a society where it is not customary to drink alcohol, you may not be used to seeing people drinking all around you.

One thing which you may find surprising is that teachers sometimes organize parties for students, especially at the beginning or end of the year or at Christmas. They may also go out with groups of students for a meal or for a drink in a pub. Students and teachers relate to each other more informally in the UK than in some other countries. They usually call each other by their first names, for example, and some students from overseas find it strange or embarrassing at first when they find they are expected to socialize with teachers:

> At first, I did not love party-life. I thought it would not be good for me to be in a party. I can remember, in the international student party arranged by the university, I could not participate in the funny game where my teachers were dancing, poking fun, enjoying. However, after participating in two or three parties I realized I was wrong ... it is a challenge to adapt to different social customs. Party-life gives me a chance to meet many new people and to be sociable.
> **(Bangladeshi student)**

> After the lecture, since it was the last class, the lecturer invited us all to go to a pub for a drink with another group of students on MA courses. About 20 people, we occupied two tables and all the boys drank beer. We chatted, laughed, made fun of one

another including the teacher. He was very kind and smart and good at dealing with our curiosity and nosiness. It was a really nice party and we all enjoyed it very much. **(Chinese student)**

[…]

If you do not feel like socializing there is no obligation to join in this type of activity and nobody will mind if you choose not to. However, by participating, you can get to know people and improve your knowledge of the language and culture.

CLUBS AND SOCIETIES

As well as eating, drinking and music there will also be many different clubs and societies for students to join. At the beginning of the academic year in September there will be a 'freshers' fair'. This is an event organized for students who have recently started studying at a college or university. It is held before classes start and events are organized by the students' union for new students to inform them about all the activities available. Every student is automatically a member of the students' union and it is free of charge. Student unions in all the different universities are affiliated to the National Union of Students (NUS), which is a powerful lobby for student rights across the country. Many student unions produce a regular newspaper which gives information about issues and activities. The students' union will give you an NUS membership card which will entitle you to discounts in museums, art galleries, cinemas, theatres, travel agents and some shops.

Here are some examples of clubs and societies. Different universities will have different ones:

- The Christian Union.
- The Creative Writing Society.
- The Drama Performing Society.
- The Fine Art Club.
- The Hindu Society.
- The International Students' Society.
- The Lesbian, Gay, Bisexual and Transgender Society.

◆ The Muslim Women's Society.
◆ The Computing Society.
◆ The Rock Society.
◆ The Utopia Society (Politics and Modern History).
◆ The Pan African Society.

As you can see from the list above, they cater for a very wide range of interests, so there should be something for everyone.

There may also be societies for students from particular countries, for example a Chinese Students' Society, or a Greek Students' Society. Joining one of these, if there is one for students from your country, will obviously be enjoyable and reassuring for you, as you will meet other students who speak your language and who may share your ideas and interests. However, it will also be a good idea to join other clubs or societies which interest you because in this way you will meet students from the UK and other countries, discover new activities or develop your existing hobbies, and learn a lot of English. Even if you are already a fluent speaker you will learn the local ways of speaking, specialist language and colloquial expressions which will be new to you if you are new to the country or the region.

Sport and leisure activities

Universities will have sports facilities either on campus or further away if the university is located in the middle of a big city like London or Birmingham. It is quite common for Wednesday afternoons to be left free of lectures so that students can participate in team sports. If the playing fields are not on campus, buses will be arranged to take students to play football, rugby, cricket, hockey, netball and so on, and there will be matches against teams from other universities which may involve travelling around the country. Playing a team sport is a very good way to meet people and keep yourself fit and healthy. If you have played in a team at home, the university will be very happy to have you as a player and if you are a beginner, you will be able to get training. There will probably be some sports facilities on the campus wherever it is (for example, a gym, squash or badminton courts or perhaps a swimming pool if you are lucky). You can find out about sports at the freshers' fair or through the students' union, which will have an office somewhere on the campus where you will find friendly fellow students who will give you any information you need.

There may also be activities which involve short trips away from the university such as rock climbing or caving, bird watching or environmental projects. These will be a great way for you to get to know more of the country.

Here are some examples of sport and leisure activities:

- ◆ *Team sports*: basketball, cricket, football, hockey, netball, rugby, volleyball.
- ◆ *Individual sports*: badminton, squash, tennis, athletics.
- ◆ *Outdoor activities*: canoeing, climbing, horse riding, rowing, parachuting, ski-ing.

Task 1

If you are already in the UK, find out what activities are available in your university and make a list of those you would like to join.

If you have not yet arrived but have access to the Internet, look at the website of the university you are planning to attend and find out what is available. If you do not have access to the Internet, write to the university and ask them to send you information about extracurricular activities.

Adjusting to your new surroundings

Studying and living in a new country is an exciting and rewarding experience. Nevertheless, there may be times that you feel anxious or homesick because there are many things around you that are unfamiliar. Do not worry – it is quite usual to experience some sort of 'culture shock'. Make sure you keep in touch with friends and family at home, but also find out about and join in the social life at your new university. There will be many people around you who will be able to offer you explanations, friendship and support.

Student services

You will find that all universities have a range of services to deal with any problems or difficulties students might have during their time there. These will include specialists in the following:

ACCOMMODATION

They will help you get a place in a university hall of residence or find a 'homestay' with an English family. They may also be able to give you lists of other accommodation if you want to live independently.

FINANCE

They will help you open a bank account and sort out your fees and accommodation expenses and give you any other financial advice you need.

CAREERS

They may be able to help you to find part-time work while you study and will advise you about future career opportunities and work placements.

DISABILITIES

They will help you if you have any special needs while you study because of any disability or medical condition. There is now legislation in the UK that says that universities must provide for the needs of disabled students. If you are blind or partially sighted, deaf, use a wheelchair, have a hidden disability such as epilepsy or diabetes or suffer from any form of mental illness, contact the disability adviser in your university and he or she will help you get any assistance you need for your study. It is best to tell your adviser what you need well in advance of your arrival so that he or she can have arrangements in place for when your course starts, but he or she will help you at any time.

COUNSELLING

Universities have counsellors to help students who become unhappy or upset for any reason. These counsellors will talk to you about your problem in confidence and give you support and advice.

Most universities will also have a special adviser for international students who will help you with applications for visa renewals, advice if your family want to visit you or if you want to visit other European countries.

Task 2

Look at the website or the prospectus of your university or any university where you think you may be studying and find out which of the services listed above they offer.

Finance

EXPENSES

Often the biggest problem students from other countries face in the UK is finance. Of course, everybody knows how high the fees are for international students, but on top of that the cost of living is also very high. Everything is expensive: food, clothes transport, books. If you are studying Architecture, design subjects or Fine Art you will need to spend a lot of money on materials. You will also have to pay for printing work that you do on the computers at the university, for any photocopying you do and for fines if you keep your library books out too long. One thing that is free, though, at university is unlimited access to the Internet. You will find that prices in London are higher than in the rest of the country, especially for accommodation and transport. On the other hand, you can find markets in London where you can buy everything you need cheaply, but you need to know where to find them.

GRANTS AND SCHOLARSHIPS

Find out before you start at university whether any scholarships, grants or discounts are available for you. Some universities offer special discounts for students who have had a member of their family study at the university. Some have scholarships for people from specific countries. There are also lots of grants and bursaries offered by other organizations for specific groups of people, sometimes based on religion, gender, age, country of origin or subject of study. These are usually small sums of money up to a few hundred pounds but everything helps. You can find out about these either from the financial adviser or the international adviser of your university, or from UCKOSA.

Signpost

See the 'Useful resources' section at the end of this chapter.

PART-TIME WORK

Many students in the UK have part-time jobs. As an international student you will have the right to work for 20 hours per week maximum. Students often work in supermarkets, fast-food outlets, restaurants, hotels or bars because they can fit the hours in with their studies by working in the evenings and at weekends. Bigger chains are more flexible in their hours than smaller restaurants with fewer staff. It is harder to work in a shop or an office because these are usually daytime jobs. However, you may find that your timetable gives you one or two free days a week on which you can work in a job. Remember, though, that it is important to attend your lectures and seminars and to do all your coursework and preparation. As a student this must be your first priority because your success depends on it, and so does your visa.

The careers adviser in your university may be able to help you find part-time work. You can also go along the nearest high street and ask in the different shops and restaurants if they need any help, or look in the local newspaper for advertisements. If you have relatives or friends they will also be able to help you. There may be some part-time work in the university, putting books back on the shelves in the library or helping to welcome new students or show visitors round. However, there is usually a lot of competition for these jobs and you will be more likely to get one in your second or third year, when you know the university better. It is a good idea to get involved in voluntary work, either at the university or for charitable organizations, because this gives you work experience in the UK and helps improve your knowledge and confidence. It could also help you find paid employment.

Task 3

Work out a budget for one year at university. Include all the expenses you will have to pay: fees, accommodation, transport, food, books and materials, clothes, entertainment, mobile phone.

Now work out where the money is going to come from.

Plan carefully. If you fall behind with payment of your fees or payment for university accommodation you may be excluded from the university. This could seriously affect your studies and also your right to stay in the UK.

Health care

If you are planning to study for more than six months you will be entitled to free health care from the National Health Service (NHS). The first thing to do when you have found your accommodation is to register with a doctor (called a general practitioner or GP). You must do this straight away, not when you get sick, because often they are full or have waiting lists and you do not want to be searching for a doctor if you are feeling unwell. Also it will be important to get a medical certificate from your doctor if you miss any coursework deadlines or exams because you are ill. If you are living in a university hall of residence, they will inform you of where to find a doctor. If you are living with a family, you will be entitled to register with their doctor. If you are living independently, you can go to the nearest public library and they will give you a list of doctors (GPs) in your area. Then you should go there and register with the doctor, taking evidence that you are a student with you. You will not pay to see the doctor but you will have to pay a charge at the chemist for any medicine the doctor prescribes. If you have an accident or fall ill when the doctor is not available, you can go to the nearest hospital which has an accident and emergency department.

Transport

As a full-time student you may be entitled to a discount on travel. Some students in London can get a 30% reduction in fares. In order to get this you need to apply to your university for a special card.

All students up to the age of 25 can get a card for cheap travel on the railways all over the UK. This is called a 'young person's railcard' and costs £26 for a year. With this card you will get a third off rail fares. You can get the card at your local station or at www.youngpersonsrailcard.co.uk

All students up to the age of 25 can also get a discount 'Coach card' for travel on coaches all over the UK. This costs £10 and also gives you a 30% reduction in fares. You can find out about it at www.GoByCoach.com

Safety

Always be careful of yourself and your belongings. If you go out at night, go where there are plenty of other people and use public transport or official cabs. Don't get into a car unless you know the driver or it is marked as a cab, with a light on top and a registration number. Do not carry large sums of money and do not walk about talking on your mobile phone, as someone may try to take it. If anyone does grab your bag or phone, let them have it. Do not get into a fight. If you do have a bad experience, go to see the counsellors at your university. They will help you and give you advice.

Making the most of your time

It is very exciting to go abroad to study in a new country, and there is a lot to discover both in your studies and in life outside the university. There will be many aspects of life which are different from home, some of them we have mentioned in previous chapters. Expect things to be different. Expect to be surprised and to have to get used to a different kind of life. Then you will not be disappointed. It is not easy to be far from home for the first time and you may find it difficult to get used to the climate, especially in winter, the food and, most importantly, the people and customs. You may find these very strange but be sure that, if you do, they probably find you a bit strange, too. Be tolerant of people's differences and they will be tolerant of yours.

If you are unhappy for any reason, be it practical, because you don't understand something or can't find a solution for something, or emotional because you are homesick or lonely or confused, talk to someone about it. You can go to any of the advisers in student services, you can go to one of your tutors or you can talk to a relative, a friend or a fellow student, but make sure you talk to someone and get the help you need. There will always be someone to help you if you can find that person.

USEFUL RESOURCES

The British Council publishes a free information sheet for international students on 'Tuition fees and the cost of living'. Phone 020 7389 4383 or email educationenquiries@britishcouncil. org.

www.nusonline.co.uk

The National Union of Students (NUS) is a very useful source of advice and information.

www.skill.org.uk

Skill – the National Bureau of Students with Disabilities has an information sheet for international students.

17 Daily Life and Culture

GARETH DAVEY

INTRODUCTION

After reading this chapter, you should:

- ☑ Know about the UK's geography and climate
- ☑ Understand British customs, manners, and etiquette
- ☑ Be prepared for daily life such as eating out and shopping
- ☑ Consider extra arrangements and support for your family

This chapter introduces the UK and its people, geography, climate, customs, and governance. There are details about daily life, including British food and drink, shopping, using public transport, and socialising. There is also an overview of the arrangements and support to consider if your family will accompany you to the UK.

Introduction to the UK

People in different countries use a variety of names to refer to the UK, such as Britain, the British Isles, or England. However, the official name is the 'United Kingdom of Great Britain and Northern Ireland', which is commonly abbreviated to the 'UK'. The UK is located in northwest Europe, and consists of a large island called Great Britain, a region known as Northern Ireland, many small islands, and overseas territories. The country is separated from the rest of Europe by the English Channel in the south and the North Sea in the east. There is a channel tunnel that connects England to France via a train called the Eurostar.

Characteristics of the UK

Population	60.6 million; third largest country in Europe
Area	244,820 sq km
Climate	Generally mild and temperate. Cool summers and fairly mild winters.
Languages	English is the dominant and official language. Welsh is common in parts of Wales; Scottish Gaelic is spoken in areas in Scotland; and Irish Gaelic in some places in Northern Ireland. Ethnic groups also use other languages.
Religion	Christianity is the most common religion. Other prominent religions include Islam, Sikhism, Judaism, Hinduism, and Buddhism.
Major cities	The capital city is London. Other major cities include Birmingham, Manchester, Sheffield, Liverpool, Bristol, and Nottingham. In Scotland, the capital city is Edinburgh, and the largest city is Glasgow. The capital city of Wales is Cardiff, and the capital city of Northern Ireland is Belfast.
Highest mountain	Ben Nevis (1,343 metres), located in Scotland.
Longest river	The Severn.
Largest lake	Loch Morar (310 metres deep), located in Scotland.

Regions

Great Britain consists of three regions: England, Scotland, and Wales. Northern Ireland is located to the north east of the Republic of Ireland. The largest and most populous region is England. It consists mostly of a lowland landscape, particularly in the south and south west; mountainous terrain and limestone hills in the north; and chalk hills in the south. The highest mountain in England is Scafell Pike, located in the Lake District National Park. The main rivers and estuaries include the Severn, Thames, Trent, Tyne, and Humber.

Scotland is located in the north, and it is the second largest and most populous region. It's capital city is Edinburgh. There are rural highlands in the north and west, uplands in the south and east, and many offshore islands, including two large groups of islands known as the Orkney and Shetland islands. Scotland has many mountains, lakes, firths and lochs. The largest rivers are the Tey, Spey, and Clyde. Some people in Scotland speak a language called Gaelic.

Wales is located in the west, and it is generally mountainous, particularly in the north and central areas. The majority of the population, and the capital city Cardiff, is located in the south. Other big cities include Swansea and Newport. The highest mountain is Snowdon, located in Snowdonia. There are many waterfalls, including Pistyll Rhaeadr in Powys. About 20 per cent of the population speak a language called Welsh. The national game of Wales is rugby.

Northern Ireland is mostly mountainous, and has many drumlins (small hills). There are uplands and lowlands, such as the uplands of County Antrim in the north east. The main river is the Shannon. There is Lough Neagh, the largest lake in the UK, and Lough Erne, which is a lake and network of islands. The capital city of Northern Ireland is Belfast.

Population

More than 60.6 million people live in the UK, mostly in major cities. The population is predominantly made up of the English, Scottish, Welsh, Irish, and immigrants who live and work in the country. People move around the four regions of the UK more than they used to, but there are regional differences, such as accent and traditions. For example, many people in England, Scotland, Northern Ireland, and Wales speak English using a regional dialect, which includes a different pronunciation, and unique words and grammar.

The UK welcomes and celebrates cultural diversity. British society is ethnically diverse, and there is a wide range of cultural, racial, and religious backgrounds. The main ethnic groups are Black African and Caribbean, Bangladeshi, Chinese, Indian, and Pakistani. There are also significant numbers from Australia, Canada, Italy, Poland, and the USA. There are equal opportunities in areas such as education, employment, and health care, and there are laws to protect people from discrimination.

Climate

The climate is generally mild and temperate, with cool summers and fairly mild winters. There are four seasons: winter (December to February), spring (March to May), summer (June to August), and autumn (September to November). The weather is changeable, and can vary widely from day-to-day. Temperatures rarely fall below -10°C (14°F), or rise above 32°C (90°F). There is abundant rainfall throughout the year, although autumn and winter are the wettest seasons. There

Tip

Your country may have a different climate to the UK. Remember to bring or buy adequate clothing, such as a warm jumper, a waterproof coat, and an umbrella.

is snowfall in some areas during winter and spring. In recent years there have been summer heat waves.

The UK consists of England, Scotland, and Wales (Great Britain) and Northern Ireland.

The weather also depends on the location. In general, the east is drier than the west, and the south is the warmest. The weather tends to be more extreme in mountainous hilly areas; for example, there tends to be more snow in Scotland than in the south.

Government, politics, and law

The UK is a parliamentary democracy, which means that parliament makes legalisation. Parliament consists of elected representatives (known as Members of Parliament, or MPs), the House of Lords (in which non-elected members propose, amend, and revise legislation), and the Queen.

MPs belong to different political parties. The largest political parties are the Labour Party, Conservative Party, and Liberal Democrats. The party with the majority of support forms the government, and its leader, known as the Prime Minister, is the head of the government. MPs meet in a room called the House of Commons, where they discuss legislation. A group of senior ministers, known as the Cabinet, make important policy decisions and head departments. The second largest political party forms the Opposition party that challenges government decisions and suggests alternatives. The Opposition also has a leader and a shadow cabinet.

The UK government is a constitutional monarchy, which means that the Queen is the head of state. Her duties include opening parliament, closing parliament before a general election, and approving legislation.

Although parliament makes legalisation, a number of issues are decided at the regional level, in the Scottish Parliament, National Assembly for Wales or, when it is sitting, the Northern Ireland Assembly. They are responsible for regional issues, including development, education, health, and social services. For more information about the UK government, visit the Houses of Parliament website.

The UK is a member of the European Union (EU), which is a confederation of different countries. The countries pool some of their sovereignty to work together on economic, judicial and security issues. The EU proposes and passes laws which also become law in the UK.

Economy and money

The UK is a leading financial and trading centre, and has one of the world's largest economies. The economy is stable, and is experiencing continuous growth and low inflation. It is a free market, and based primarily on private enterprise; many state-owned enterprises have been privatised since the 1980s. The currency is pound sterling, represented by the symbol £.

The UK was the first country to experience the industrial revolution. The economy focused initially on heavy industry and manufacturing. However, heavy industry has declined throughout the 20th century, and is being replaced by the service sector. Financial services, business services, and insurance companies now dominate the economy. Tourism and agriculture play an important role. Although heavy industry is declining, they are still important, especially coal, oil, and agriculture. Creative industries – such as advertising and television production – are also significant.

Royal Family

The UK has a royal family that dates back over ten centuries. Queen Elizabeth II has been on the throne since 1952. She is married to Prince Phillip (the Duke of

Edinburgh), who is the son of Prince and Princess Andrew of Greece and Denmark. The Queen has three children, including Prince Charles (The Prince of Wales), who is the heir to the throne. Prince Charles has two sons – Princes William and Harry. Other members of the Royal Family include the Queen's other children, grandchildren, cousins, and their spouses. The Queen lives in Buckingham Palace in London, and in other residences such as Windsor Castle in England, and Balmoral Castle and Holyroodhouse Palace in Scotland.

The Queen and the Royal Family play an important role, and participate in ceremonial roles, public duties, and charity work. The Queen also approves legislation passed by parliament, and acts as the Head of the Church of England and the Armed Services. There are many royal traditions, such as 'Changing the Guard' at Buckingham Palace, in which new guards change duty. To learn more about the Royal Family and royal traditions, visit the Buckingham Palace website.

British food and drink

There is a wide range of cuisine to choose from. There are traditional dishes, as well as many foods from around the world. Traditional British dishes include fish and chips, English breakfast, roast dinners, Yorkshire pudding, and afternoon tea. Although traditional dishes remain popular, nowadays many foods from around the world are commonly available. Popular ethnic cuisine includes Chinese, French, Greek, Indian, Italian, and Thai.

Meals

People eat three or four meals a day; breakfast, lunch, dinner, and sometimes supper. Breakfast cereal, or toast with marmalade or butter, is commonly eaten for breakfast. A traditional English breakfast is made up of bacon, egg, sausage, mushroom, and tomatoes. A range of dishes is eaten for lunch and dinner. Main meals are often followed with a sweet dessert.

> **Tip**
>
> It is safe to drink tap water in the UK. Also, bottled water is available from shops.

Popular drinks include tea and coffee (served with or without milk), herbal teas, fruit juices, and soft drinks. In addition to small meals, snacks such as sandwiches, biscuits, chocolate, and crisps are popular.

It is traditional for a family to eat together for Sunday dinner, which includes beef, roast potatoes, brussel sprouts, Yorkshire pudding, and gravy.

Food ingredients

Ingredients for cooking are widely available from local shops and supermarkets. Shops sell fresh food, as well as ready-made meals in tins and plastic containers that can be warmed by microwave oven. Organic food (food produced without use of synthetic fertilisers or pesticides) is increasing in popularity, although it is more expensive. An increasing number of people are vegetarian, which means that they only eat vegetables and vegetable products. Vegetarian food is widely available in supermarkets and restaurants.

Many foods are labelled with nutritional contents, including the number of calories they contain, and whether they are suitable for vegetarians.

Eating out

You will be spoilt for choice when eating out. The university campus and nearby areas have many places to dine. They include cafes (which serve tea and coffee, and small dishes), pubs (which sell alcohol and basic dishes), fast food outlets, and restaurants. Traditional British take-away food includes fish and chips, sausage in batter, steak and kidney pie, and mushy peas. Other popular take-away includes pizza, American-style fast food, Chinese meals, kebabs, and ethnic dishes. Opening hours of food outlets vary, and generally open at meal times and late at night. Many offer a delivery service and charge extra for it.

Traditional British dishes

Main meal	
Fish and chips	Fish that is deep-fried in batter, served with chips that are sprinkled with salt and malt vinegar.
English breakfast	A substantial breakfast that includes bacon, baked beans, eggs, fried bread, mushrooms, and tomatoes (it can also include other dishes). Often served with tea and coffee. In Scotland, the traditional breakfast may include lorne slices (sausage) and Ayrshire bacon.
Hot pot	A meat and vegetable stew that is cooked slowly in the oven.
Shephard's Pie	A pie that consists of lamb and vegetables, and is topped with mash potato. Cottage pie uses minced beef instead of lamb.
Toad in the hole	Roasted sausages covered in batter.
Yorkshire pudding	A savoury dish made from baked batter. Often served with roast beef and gravy.
Sausage and mash	Good quality sausages served with mashed potato and onion gravy.

(Continued)

Bubble and squeak	Chopped vegetables (usually cabbage and mashed potato) that are shaped into patties and fried.
Ploughman's Lunch	A cold meal or snack. Includes a thick slice of cheese, crusty fresh bread, pickle, pickled onions, and sometimes a salad.
Afternoon tea	Tea or coffee that is served with a snack, such as sandwiches, cream scones, or assorted pastries. Served at 4 o'clock.
Desserts	
Rhubarb crumble	Baked rhubarb topped with crumble (a mixture of sugar, flour, and butter). Served with custard or cream.
Trifle	A cake that includes fruit, sponge, jelly, and custard. Ingredients are arranged in layers, with sponge at the bottom, and cream and fruit at the top.
Bread and butter pudding	Baked buttered bread slices and raisins.
Spotted dick	Steamed pudding with dried fruit (sultanas and raisins).
Strawberries and cream	Fresh strawberries served with whipped cream.

There are regional variations in traditional food. For example, in Scotland the national dish is Haggis, and game (wild animals hunted for food) and salmon are popular. In Wales, traditional foods include laver bread (seaweed rolled in oatmeal and fried), Welsh Rarebit (melted cheese on toast), leeks, and Welsh cakes. Traditional food in Northern Ireland includes the Ulster fry, which consists of fried bacon, eggs, sausage, mushrooms, soda bread, and potato farl.

Manners and etiquette

Every country has social rules about correct and polite behaviour. Good manners show politeness, appreciation, and give a good impression. Below are examples of good manners and social skills in the UK.

- *Greetings*. It is usual to say 'Hello' or 'Good morning/afternoon/evening' when greeting people. More formal greetings include a handshake and 'How do you do?' or 'Nice to meet you'. People use the first name to greet people informally, and the title (Mr, Mrs, Miss, Dr, etc) with the surname formally. Cheek kissing as a social gesture is not as common as in other European countries, but it is an acceptable greeting for two friends and family members of the opposite gender to greet each other in this way.

- *Timing*. Be punctual! It is generally polite to arrive on time, and rude to be late. Arrange a time in advance before visiting someone, as it is impolite to turn up unexpected. It is a good idea to inform others in advance if you are going to be late.
- *Queuing*. Queuing is very common. It is bad mannered to jump a queue!
- *Smoking*. Smoking is not allowed in university buildings, in public buildings, on public transport, and sometimes in other people's homes.
- *Listening*. Be willing to listen to others. Try not to make assumptions about what other people are thinking about.
- *Tipping*. It is common in restaurants to leave extra money for the service (known as a 'tip'), usually 10–15 per cent of the bill. Some restaurants include the tip in the bill as a 'service charge'. A tip is not needed in a fast food restaurant.

Table Manners

Most food is eaten with cutlery (a knife, fork, and spoon). When you have finished eating, the knife and fork should be placed together.

- To show your appreciation, say thank you when food is served. If you eat at a friend's home, or as a guest in a restaurant, it is polite to say that the food is delicious (even if it is not).
- Begin eating only after everyone has been served and your host has started.
- Do not eat food too fast, and try not to finish before your companions.
- It is inappropriate to ask to take left-over food home.
- Do not play with food and try not to smoke when dining.
- Try not to cough, sneeze, or burp at the table. If you must, do so away from the table, and cover your nose with a napkin.
- Sit up straight, and do not rest elbows on the table while eating.
- It is rude to open your mouth, talk, spit, or make loud noises when eating.
- Do not use your fingers to remove food from your teeth.
- Ask someone to pass items to you if you cannot reach it easily.
- Napkins should be unfolded and put on your lap.
- Consider switching off your mobile phone as it could disturb others.

[...]

Making friends

Making friends in a different country and culture is not as difficult as it seems. There are many opportunities to do so.

- To make conversation, ask people about their course, hobbies, etc. Try to use open-ended questions (questions that cannot be answered with a yes or no answer). Always be polite and respectful to others.
- Do not worry too much about your English language ability. It is not necessary to have perfect pronunciation and grammar to be understood. If you don't understand others, ask them to speak slower or to explain it differently.
- It is easier to make friends if you participate in social activities and excursions organised by your university, including social events for international students.
- Go to the Student Union's bar, coffee bar, and other places to meet people.
- Consider activities such as attending church or helping with voluntary work.
- Keep in contact with people who you meet.
- If you want to travel on holiday, ask a travel agent about the possibility of joining a tour group.

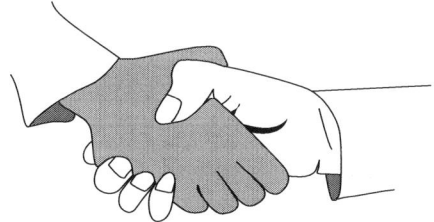

Getting around – public transport

There is a comprehensive public transport system which can be used to reach most locations in the country. Services include bus, coach, rail, taxi, and, for longer distances, air services. Public transport is generally reliable, safe, and comfortable.

Bus and coach

It is convenient and cheap to travel by bus. Timetables are available at bus stops, and bus company offices and their websites.

Longer distances can be travelled via coach, which link most cites and towns. The main coach operators include National Express and Scottish Citylink.

Coach tickets are cheaper than train tickets. You can save 30 per cent off National Express coach travel by purchasing a Young Persons Coachcard, which is available for full-time students and young people aged between 16 and 26.

How to catch a bus

Catching a bus in the UK might differ from your country.

- Queue at the bus stop, and wait your turn to board.
- The route number and destination are displayed on the front of the bus.
- Put your hand out to signal for an approaching bus to stop.
- It is polite to allow passengers to leave the bus before you alight.
- Inform the driver where you are going, and pay the fare. Try to give the driver the correct fare because they may not be able to issue change.
- Buy a single or return ticket. It is possible to buy a bus pass that can be used for a longer time, such as for a week or month.
- When you approach your destination, press the bell to signal the driver to stop.

Rail

Major train stations are located in large cities, and many town centres have smaller stations. Tickets should be purchased in advance at ticket offices, self-service machines in train stations, via telephone from National Rail Enquiries, or at certain travel agents. It may be possible to buy tickets on the train if a station does not sell them.

A train ticket can be expensive, especially for longer distances; the fare depends on the distance you travel and when you buy the ticket. There is usually a discount if it is bought in advance, if you use a discount card, or if you travel outside peak times. A cheaper ticket, however, generally has more restrictions concerning when it can be used.

There are different types of train tickets. Some are flexible and allow travel on any train at any time, whereas others are restricted to certain times or trains. The main types of tickets are:

- *Standard open and Standard day tickets.* Valid on the date shown on the ticket, and can be used at any time of the day.
- *Cheap day tickets.* Valid on the date shown on the ticket, and are limited to off-peak times.
- *Saver and super-saver tickets.* Cheaper and have more limitations, such as off-peak travel only.
- *Super advance and Apex tickets.* Booked in advance, and are cheaper, but are restricted to selected routes and the date shown on the ticket.

Information about train services and timetables is available from National Rail Enquiries, The Trainline, and Traveline.

Young Persons Railcard

People aged 16–25 (or aged 26 or over and in full-time education) can buy a Young Persons Railcard to receive up to 30 per cent off the price of certain types of tickets. To obtain a railcard, fill in an application form at a train station, and provide identification, photographs, and a fee. You will also need to show proof that you are a full-time student. If your application is successful, you will be issued with a railcard. The application form is available from a staffed ticket office, or online at www.railcards-online.co.uk

The London Underground

At first glance the London Underground (also known as 'the tube') may seem daunting. However, it is easy and convenient to use.

Planning your journey
Look at a map of the Underground to plan your journey. Maps are available at most stations and on trains. There are 12 train lines, and each one has a different name and is represented

by a different colour on the map. For example, the Northern Line, which runs from north to south London, is coloured black, whereas the Central Line, which runs from east to west, is red. Find the line you will start on and the station you are going to, and then see how many lines and zones you need to travel in to reach your destination.

Buying a ticket

Tickets are available from ticket offices or self-service machines at stations. It is quicker to use a machine; they should give change and also accept credit and debit cards. The price of the ticket depends on the zone you start and finish in (the Underground is divided into 6 zones; the city centre is Zone 1), and whether it is a single or return.

If you use the underground regularly you can buy travel cards for daily, weekly and monthly travel. They can also be used on some buses and railways services in the London area. Alternatively, you can buy an 'Oyster card', which is a plastic card that can be swiped across a card reader at the turnstile (it is often cheaper to use it instead of buying tickets).

Entering and leaving the station

To enter and leave a station you will need to pass through a turnstile. It opens when you put your ticket, with the black magnetic strip facing downwards, into a slot in the turnstile, and reappears when you pass through. Remember to collect your ticket after you pass through; if the ticket is for a single journey, it will stay in the machine when you leave the station). There are colour-coded directions to help you reach the line you want.

On the train

When a train arrives at the station, the doors should open automatically, or you may need to press the illuminated 'open' button. If you make a mistake and go in the wrong direction, don't worry; you can get off at the next stop and change to the opposite platform. There are also station attendants to give advice.

The Underground generally opens at 5.30am and closes around midnight. There is a limited service on Sundays. It is better to avoid busy rush hours (8am–9.30am and 4pm–6pm) and travelling alone at night. For more information about the London Underground, contact Travel Information Centres at several London train stations, Transport for London (www.tfl.gov.uk), and the London Underground website (www.thetube.com).

Taxis

Taxis can be expensive. It is customary to book a taxi via telephone, although traditional London taxis can be hailed in the street. Telephone numbers of taxi companies can be found in the telephone directory, or on university notice boards. Only use taxis that are registered with the local authority, and ask for the price of the journey before you depart, especially if there is no meter in the taxi. Taxi companies often give discounts to students.

Bicycle

A cheaper and quicker alternative is to use a bicycle to travel around your area. It is generally safe to cycle in the UK, although there are difficulties in certain places due to poor roads, heavy traffic, hilly terrain, and bad weather. A new bicycle can be bought from a bike shop; a cheaper option is to look for a second-hand one in local newspaper advertisements or university notice boards. There is the National Cycle Network, which is a set of cycle routes across the UK. For more about cycling in London, including route maps, visit the London Cycling Campaign website (www.lcc.org.uk).

Safety while cycling

- Be familiar with your route and look for cycle signs.
- Keep your bicycle in good working order. Regularly check the brakes, chain, and wheels.
- Use lights, and fluorescent/reflective clothing when riding at night.
- Wear a cycle helmet.
- Be aware of cars and pedestrians around you. Use mirrors to view traffic behind.
- Learn about the Highway Code. It is a set of rules that apply to all road users. More is available from www.highwaycode.gov.uk
- Always lock your bicycle when not in use.

Travelling by plane

The UK has a range of airports and airlines, including budget airlines that offer low prices. It is advisable to book as early as possible to obtain the best fare. Popular airlines include:

- British Airways
- BMI
- Bmibaby

- Ryanair
- EasyJet
- Flybe.

Owning and driving a car

The law and procedures for driving in the UK may be very different to those in your country. Before driving you must ensure that you meet all of the legal requirements that apply to you and your vehicle. For example, you will need to be over a certain age, have a valid driving licence, insurance, road tax, and proof that your vehicle is roadworthy. If you have a licence that was issued in your country, you may be able to use it in the

UK. Students from EEA countries are generally able to drive while their licence is valid, or exchange it for a British one. Some students from other countries may be allowed to use a valid licence issued in their country for a certain time period, and then apply for a UK driving licence. Check the legal requirements before you drive. For up-to-date information about the rules and regulations, contact the DVLA in England, Wales, and Scotland, and the DVLNI in Northern Ireland.

If you don't have a valid licence, you can learn to drive. Lessons are available from driving schools and approved instructors (look in your local telephone directory for their details). Before learning, you will need to apply for a provisional licence; applications can be made at your local Post Office. You are not allowed to drive on your own until you pass the driving test.

There are various motoring organisations you can join that provide services such as breakdown and recovery services and advise about owning and driving a car. They include the AA and the RAC.

A list of car hire companies is available in a phone directory. National companies include Hertz, Thrifty Car Rental, and the National Car Rental.

Shopping

Everyday items such as food and household goods can be bought from local shops, newsagents, and supermarkets. The university campus will have shops.

The high street is the focal point of shopping and most national chain stores are located there. Big cities such as London, Cardiff, Birmingham, Manchester, and Edinburgh attract shoppers from around the world. There are also shopping centres on the outskirts of towns and cities that offer shops, restaurants, cinemas, and sports facilities.

> **Tip**
>
> Keep receipts for goods that you buy. You may need them if you want to return faulty or unsatisfactory goods.

Department stores are large retail stores that sell goods such as clothes, household items, electrical appliances, furniture and furnishings, and gifts. Major department stores include:

- Primark
- Debenhams
- Harrods
- John Lewis
- Marks and Spencer
- Selfridges
- Woolworths.

Supermarkets are large food stores located in towns and cities. Large supermarkets sell household goods, computers, mobile phones, and even financial services. Major supermarkets include:

- Asda
- Safeway
- Sainsbury's

- Marks and Spencer
- Tesco
- Waitrose.

Street markets sell goods from farmers and local producers, including fresh food, clothes, and shoes. Their goods are often cheaper than supermarkets. Famous markets in London include:

- Camden Market
- Spitalfields
- Portobello Road Market
- Berwick Street Market
- Greenwich Market.

Newsagents are smaller shops that sell newspapers, magazines, stationary, and snacks.

Other shops include bakers and patisseries, booksellers, charity shops, chemists, electrical goods shops, florists, gift shops, health shops, off-licences, pet shops, and petrol stations.

Opening hours are from 9am to 5pm (and a shorter time on Sundays). Shops, such as supermarkets, are open until the evening, and a few are open 24 hours a day. Internet shopping is increasing in popularity.

In recent years there has been increased awareness of ethical issues among shoppers. More and more people are buying products from companies that ensure that producers receive a good deal for their goods. Supermarkets sell Fair Trade products.

Buying and washing clothes

Clothes can be bought from department stores or clothes shops. Cheaper clothes are available in supermarkets or in charity shops. Bear in mind, however, that British clothes and shoe sizes could differ from your country.

Major clothes shops include:

- Gap
- House of Fraser
- Next
- Oasis

- River Island
- Topman
- Topshop.

University accommodation such as a hall of residence should have washing machines for their students. If not, you can wash your clothes in a launderette, which is a shop that has self-service coin-operated washing machines and dryers.

Practicing your religion

A range of religious faiths is represented in the UK and on the university campus. The most common faith is Christianity (the UK is a Christian country), and the second is Islam. Most Christians are members of the Church of England, or the Catholic Church (Roman Catholics); there are also other denominations nationwide. Other prominent religions in the country include Sikhism, Judaism, Hinduism, and Buddhism.

Everyone in the UK has the right to practise their faith. There are many opportunities to follow your religion and to be part of a religious community. Your options include:

- *The university chaplaincy.* A service that offers advice and support to students of all faiths and provides information about religious groups on campus. They also help to arrange religious services.
- *Student societies.* University societies and clubs where people of the same faith meet.
- Places of worship in the local area. All towns and cities have churches, mosques, synagogues, and prayer rooms.

Note that a large proportion of people do not have a religious affiliation, and church attendance is generally declining. Even so, people who do not regularly attend church do participate in religious ceremonies for births, marriages, and deaths.

Bringing your family to the UK

In normal circumstances it is possible for your spouse and children to stay with you in the UK while you are a student. You will need to consider the financial implications, as well as support for your family.

Immigration rules and employment

Immigration rules change regularly, and you should consult up-to-date information. There are different immigration rules for EEA nationals and non-EEA nationals. Generally, EEA nationals should be able to accompany you to the UK with no or few restrictions whereas non-EEA nationals will need to apply for permission, and will need to meet certain immigration criteria. For example, you may need to provide evidence that you and your spouses are married or in a civil partnership, and that you can financially support your family. There are also requirements for your child. Check the up-to-date regulations that are applicable.

Accommodation and finances

Universities have limited accommodation for families. Therefore, try to book it as early as you can, or ask to be put on the waiting list. Alternatively, you can look in the private sector for housing. If a suitable place to stay cannot be arranged before you leave your country, it might be easier and cheaper for you to arrive alone to find somewhere. In addition, bear in mind that accommodation arrangements may need to be booked first in order to satisfy your family's immigration regulations.

Living in the UK and supporting a family is expensive. Extra costs include family accommodation, childcare, and living costs. Be realistic about these extra costs. You and your spouse may be allowed to work, and you need to check if any restrictions exist. The stamp in your passport will also state whether or not employment is prohibited.

Childcare

Childcare for young children is expensive. The average price is about £120 per week, although state-run primary and secondary school is free. Childcare options for young children include a childminder, nursery, or playgroup. Your university should have a nursery on campus.

Further information about childcare options is available from the Childcare Link and the Daycare Trust, which are organisations that provide details of childcare providers.

Children older than 4 or 5 should attend school. Children aged between 4 and 11 attend primary school, whereas those between 11 and 16 attend secondary school. You have the option of sending them to a state-owned school, which is free, or a private (independent) school that charges fees. To obtain a place in a state school, contact the education department of the local government.

> **Tip**
>
> Ofsted is the official body for inspecting schools and childcare providers. You may wish to choose childcare providers that are registered with Ofsted.

School places are allocated according to where you live (called the 'Catchment Area'), though it may be possible to choose a school in another area. You can apply for a school place after you arrive in the UK, as it is necessary to have an address.

There are many factors to consider when choosing a school, such as its performance, how students are selected, whether the school is affiliated to a religion, and the travelling distance between school and home. Before you make a decision, it is advisable to visit the school, and to discuss your needs with the Head Teacher. Possible questions to ask are whether there are other international children at the school and the availability of support for children whose first language is not English. Do bear in mind, however, that your choice of school could be restricted if places are limited, especially if the school is not in your local area.

Performance data for different schools is available from:

- England: Department for Education and Skills
- Wales: National Assembly for Wales
- Scotland: HM Inspectorate of Education
- Northern Ireland: Department of Education.

The school year runs from September through to July. There are holidays at Christmas, and Easter, and one-week holidays in October, February, and May. Holidays roughly coincide with university holidays, but you might need to make child care arrangements in the school holidays or after school.

Children older than 16 can either continue with their education or take employment. Further education is usually not free.

Health and welfare

Think about how your family will adapt to the UK lifestyle and culture. It will be different to what they are used to, and they will not have access to the same advice, support, and facilities at university as you (because they will not be registered students at the university). Ask your university to see what support they can provide for your family.

18 Mature, Part-time and Overseas Students

GORDON RUGG, SUE GERRARD AND SUSIE HOOPER

Feeling as if you don't fit in: before you start; mature students; juggling responsibilities at home and university. Part-time students: work–life balance. Issues affecting students from overseas. Other students from minority groups.

If you're a part-time student, a mature student or a student from overseas, then there's a small word which you're likely to hear quite often when you deal with the university system. It's 'Ah.' You'll often hear it when you ask an administrator what the situation is for part-time, mature or overseas students; it usually means either 'Damn, we forgot about them when we wrote that set of regulations' or 'Damn, I'll have to dig out the regulations about this.' That's a bit better than 'Ha, this regulation will make them unhappy', but not much better in practical terms. If you're in one of these categories, or a similar one such as year-abroad students and sandwich-year students, then The System is likely to overlook you in ways that bring hassle and stress to your life.

As people who have been part-time, mature and year-abroad students in our time, we know what it's like to go through this, and we sympathise with anyone who's sharing that experience. There are some exceptions. Some universities specialise in part-time courses, often aimed at mature students, and do an excellent job with them, as we can testify from personal experience; some specialise in courses designed for overseas students, and do these so well that the overseas students stay in touch with the university even decades later, when they're government ministers back in their home country, as we can testify from knowing some of those happy students. However, the majority of undergraduate courses at British universities are based on an implicit simplifying assumption that all the students will be full-time, home-grown and straight from school. When a course is run both in full-time mode and also in part-time mode, then there is a tendency for the part-time version to be overlooked. This isn't done out of malice, prejudice or ignorance; it's simply a reflection of the time pressures put on British academics these days. The result is that you are likely to hit two main problems, and various minor problems.

FEELING AS IF YOU DON'T FIT IN

Lack of regulations

You will probably find sooner or later that the university's regulations either don't say anything about an issue which is affecting you, or that the university's regulations are inconsistent. For instance, if you are a part-time student and your company suddenly decides to send you to Switzerland for three months, there may not be any regulations covering this situation. Alternatively, there may be one regulation about being sent away on company business, and another regulation about absences of up to six months, and these may contradict each other. If this happens, then you're going to feel understandably angry or otherwise upset. If you're in this situation, do some calming exercises then think through the situation in terms of what outcome you want, and how best to get there, including which information you'll need to find out. Sometimes an emotional scene will produce the short-term result you want, but that comes with a price, in terms of how other people perceive you – not many people want to work with someone who becomes emotional whenever there's a problem, so it's inadvisable to use the emotional scene except as a last resort. A more effective strategy is usually to write a clear letter or email explaining the situation, quoting the relevant regulations, and asking the relevant person to tell you what you should do. This turns the situation from your problem into their problem, so you can get on with your life while they decide what to do. A useful addition to this strategy is to ask them whether you should do X or Y, where both X and Y are options that you'd be happy with. This tactic is usually worth a try – it doesn't challenge the decision-maker's authority, and it gives them a simple, clearly defined menu of options if they're overworked and rushed (which they usually are). There's a chance that they'll go for one of these options rather than spending a cheerless couple of hours wading through the regulations in case there's an option Z that you haven't mentioned. This doesn't always work – some bureaucrats know the relevant regulations without needing to re-read the documentation, and sometimes the options you've identified are actually storing up potential trouble for you later on – but it's worth having it in your repertoire.

Feeling marginalised

You will almost certainly feel marginalised at some point in your studies – you will get the impression that the university doesn't care about you, and is only interested in the money that you pay it in fees. It's an understandable feeling. However, that doesn't mean it's necessarily true. Most students feel marginalised sooner or later for one reason or another. First year undergraduates feel that lecturers view them as an anonymous mob, of little interest compared to second and third years. Final year students feel that the university doesn't pay enough attention to them in terms of support, such as making the first and second years keep quiet when it's revision time and the final exams are looming. If you ever end up working in a large organisation with responsibility for a number of people, then you'll soon discover that even the most caring organisations often give the impression of marginalising people for the simple reason that everyone is just too busy to think of all the human issues all the time. It's nothing personal. This may not sound very encouraging initially. However, there is one way in which it is very useful information, in relation to stress. The thing to remember is that if you are feeling stressed, miserable and lonely, then it's probably because The System is badly set up, not because there's something wrong with you. That may appear cold comfort when you're going through a bad time, but it's actually quite constructive, since it means that you probably don't need to contemplate a session of confronting your own shortcomings in addition to handling the immediate problem – you just need to work out how to live with The System. The following sections describe some of those areas where The System can cause you problems, and what you can do about them. We begin with a section on issues that affect more or less everyone. There's then a section for mature students, another for students on part-time courses, a third for students from overseas, and a fourth for students in categories other than those just mentioned.

BEFORE YOU BEGIN

This section begins with the question of whether doing a degree is the right choice for you at this time in your life; sometimes it's better to do so while you have the chance, but sometimes it's better to wait until a time that's better for you. The following sections work through preparations that you can make to give yourself more support during your time as a student, then some common stressors affecting the readers for whom this chapter is intended, and finally a section on what to do if the degree doesn't feel like the right thing for you.

Is a degree the right thing for you at this point?
It takes considerable commitment and good time management to follow a degree course; to do so whilst holding down a job or looking after a young

family takes great commitment and excellent time management; to do so whilst holding down a job *and* looking after a family takes the steely resolve and organisational skills of a nursing sister in a First World War field hospital. That's the bad news. The good news is that most students who go through this emerge feeling glad that they did it, and with good memories of their times on the course. After that reassurance, if you're in one of the categories above, then it's still wise to ask yourself right at the start whether this is the best time for you to be doing a degree. It may sound like a good idea in terms of enhanced career prospects and income, but the cost in terms of employer's goodwill and family relationships may be very high. However, don't assume it would be better to wait until your children are older or you're in a more senior job. Ironically, it's sometimes easier to take a degree when children are young. You are more likely to find someone who will entertain a couple of toddlers for an hour or two than to be able to find someone willing to explain to your child's school and the local constabulary how your teenager happened to be purloining goods from a shop when they were supposed to be in school, particularly when the teenager blames the crime on having a parent who is too busy studying to look after them properly.

Some things to check before you make your final decision to do the course

If you're planning to do the course while employed, then make sure your employer is aware of precisely what time commitment your course of study actually involves. This will have the added advantage of making *you* aware of what time commitment your course of study actually involves. Employers often like the idea of an employee engaging in a course of study; they end up with a better qualified employee at little or no cost to themselves and it can enhance their reputation as a company which empowers its workers. But you can be sure that, when faced with a choice between sending you to a vital European sales conference and allowing you a day's annual leave to finish an assignment, it is unlikely that the assignment will win. If you're in this situation then it's worth building up as much goodwill as you can before you start the course. If you're one of those valued people who covered for absent colleagues and came in for the weekend to move furniture during an office relocation, your application for support when studying will probably be viewed more favourably than if you have a reputation as an unhelpful clock-watcher.

Some employers already have formal arrangements in place for employees who are studying. Sometimes this is a good thing. It at least means you are likely to be allowed time to study. But you will need to check that the arrangements you need are the ones that the employer is offering. If the arrangements are based on what Engineering requested for Phil and Dave, who both needed to spend three months gathering data in the Far East, that may not fit in very well with your requirements for covering your English Literature modules at the Open University. If you can get your employer to agree to a sabbatical, or to a part-time contract whilst you complete the course, and you can afford to take a drop in salary, so much the better. Your stress levels will probably come within the normal range if you can do so.

WHEN YOU START

Support networks

Assuming that you have decided to go ahead with becoming a student, then the next step is to make sure that you have an adequate support network. The more relatives, friends and work colleagues you can rope into babysitting, running errands and covering for you at work, the better. Let your tutors and lecturers know as early as possible that you have work and family commitments, especially if you are a primary carer. Don't expect special treatment, since university staff are obliged to assess your work on the same criteria as all other students, but it will improve the chances of their being flexible when any problems crop up, particularly in relation to deadlines and emergencies.

Time-planning

If you're taking a degree course whilst working, or looking after a family, the chances are you have already done some long-term planning. You will need to keep reassessing your progress and your long-term plans from time to time, but your real challenge is going to be effective time and priority management in the short-term. Planning the year ahead is going to be much the same for you as for full-time students with no other commitments, except that you are going to have much less study time available. With regard to short-term planning, you will be in a very different situation to full-time students. You're not going to have the luxury of being able to tackle tasks one after the other, in order of urgency. It's probably just as well, because, unless your course involves a lot of practical work, you are better off dividing the work into chunks anyway, and leaving time for refreshment and reflection between tasks. It's tempting to carve out long periods like entire weekends or two weeks' leave in a writers' retreat in which to work. Resist this temptation unless you are sure that this is what you need, which it may be if you're tackling a lengthy piece of written work that requires complex coherent thought. An hour or two of study first thing in the morning before you go to work, an hour at lunchtime and a couple of hours in the evening after the kids have gone to bed, gives you five hours study time a day, which is more than most mortals can cope with. If you have a long drive to work, consider using public transport instead, so you can work whilst you travel. Commuter trains offer ample opportunity for study – you may be crammed in like cattle en route to the abattoir, but you'll be crammed in with people reading newspapers, catching up on paperwork, writing novels and preparing presentations, who take a dim view of those who want to share their taste in music or their telephone conversations with their neighbours, so there may be comparatively little distraction.

Priority management

This is different to time-management and almost everyone finds it difficult. It is a common problem for people working in matrix organisations, who have more than one immediate boss, or for students who are working and who have families, since you can find yourself in situations where each of the domains you operate in has thrown something at you that needs to be done urgently. There are various techniques to help with priority management, which you can find on page xx. Ask yourself questions about the task you have to prioritise. First *is blood involved?* Is there a health and safety issue? Second; *how important is it?* What are the consequences if I don't do it? Third; *how urgent is it?* If your child is rushed to hospital or your father has had a heart attack, then this takes priority over everything else. You may need to prioritise an important issue, such as getting your central heating fixed, over an urgent issue like meeting an assignment deadline.

Delegating responsibility

Going back to the previous example about priority management, don't assume that you are the only person who can look after your child or your father. Delegate that task to others if you can, once the initial emergency is over. Similarly in everyday life, it's often possible to delegate tasks such as tending the baby or undertaking the school run to your partner (allow a few weeks to get the routine running smoothly) or to a friend or relative, so you have some study time before you leave for work. You could try arriving at work early, or leaving late, so that you can study when the office is empty. Assignments can be completed effectively with carefully arranged support from a long-suffering partner and a network of friends and relations.

Motivation

Take one step at a time. Clichéd advice, but sound. You are not tackling an entire degree course at once, and by the time you are in your final year, your family circumstances and your work situation could have changed dramatically. Something that seems like an insurmountable obstacle now may not be an issue in a month's time. Plan ahead, but aim to get through one task, then another. Reward yourself when you complete each task. Exercise is an ally. You may be able to set aside time for a morning jog, or an evening or two at the gym each week, but a brisk walk round the park, or a regular stint in the garden are probably more realistic for most people. Activities like these not only compensate for a sedentary lifestyle, they also give you the opportunity to assimilate and reflect on your coursework, often at a subconscious level, where you can start to grasp the deep structure of your field of study.

If it's all too much

It's not the end of the world if you decide to postpone or drop out of the course. Your partner, your family, and sometimes your relationship with your employer, are not worth sacrificing for the sake of a qualification. You can take a degree at any time, but may not be able to find another partner, family or job like the one you have already. Obvious? Not if you're heavily stressed. A lot of students lose sight of this option when the stress levels are high. Sometimes postponing or leaving the course is the right choice. Knowing that you have this option can be a very reassuring safety net, and can help you get through bad times that are only temporary. Having said that, there's a difference between making a clear, informed decision to suspend or leave a course which isn't right for you, and giving up impulsively just because you happen to be having a bad day. If you're going through difficult circumstances, universities can be surprisingly accommodating and supportive in terms of offering ways for you to continue your degree when the emergency is over, and it's usually wiser to take this route, since it keeps your options open. If you do think you want to take time out or to leave the course completely, then don't make any drastic decisions about it for a week. If you still think it's the right decision after that week, then talk to your tutor about it, and take things from there.

MATURE STUDENTS

Specific problems

Some of the problems mature students with children encounter are specific, easily identifiable ones, which you'll discover soon enough. Here are some of the classics:

- You have a 9.00 am lecture which clashes with the school run.
- You have a lecture at 3.00 pm or later which clashes with the school run.
- All the car park spaces are taken by 9.30 am and you can't get in before 9.45 am because of the school run.
- You have a lecture at any time between 9.00 am and 6.00 pm during school holidays (including half terms).
- One of the children or an elderly parent is ill.

- There is a problem with the roof or the boiler and you need to stay home for the builder/plumber/electrician.
- There's a major family event such as Christmas and you have an assignment due in the day after you return to university.
- The children want your attention when there's an assignment to be completed by the next day.

The simplest first step to dealing with these is to share ideas with other mature students who have been through the same problem. What solutions have they found to the obvious problems about finding the right balance between noticing the children and doing the course; or making arrangements for when one of the children is ill? The university might helpfully arrange a talk about this for you, which often takes the form of a patronising lecture about time management from someone younger than you, who doesn't have children, and who knows much less about time management and priority management than you do. Since individual circumstances can vary widely, we can't offer foolproof solutions to these problems. However, the strategies we touched on earlier in the section on support networks and time-planning, are key here. If you are likely to face the kind of problems listed above, before you start your degree, make sure you have a good network of family, friends and neighbours who have agreed to help you out with childcare, walking the dog, or waiting in for plumbers. Secondly, make sure the university staff you'll be working with are well aware of your other commitments. If you think you will need an extension to a deadline for an assignment, ask about it as soon as you realise it may be an issue, and be prepared to provide doctor's notes, letters from employers and so on, as evidence that you have had a real emergency which has prevented you completing on time. Consider the possibility of taking a degree a module at a time, an option offered by, for example, the Open University.

In addition, you're likely to find that the younger undergraduates alternate between treating you as a primordial relic who remembers the Roaring Twenties and treating you as a source of wisdom and support when things go wrong in their lives or when someone needs to be student representative and complain about the lecturer that everybody hates. How to handle this depends on your personality. Some people enjoy hamming it up and playing the primordial relic; others simply ignore the age thing and get on with life; others again get a feeling of accomplishment from helping the younger students to blossom and grow.

Less well-defined problems

There are also problems affecting mature students which are more insidious because you have difficulty putting your finger on them. Some classics are:

- feeling that you just don't quite fit in somehow
- wondering if you're wasting your time
- feeling that you don't understand how the academic world works, or feeling stupid
- wondering if you'll manage to stick the course till the end.

There are a couple of common themes underlying most of the general and the hard-to-identify problems mature students face. One them is knowing the rules of the academic game, the other is self-doubt in various forms. Self-doubt usually arises either because you are in an unfamiliar situation, and don't know whether you are up to the task, or because you have been in a similar situation before, and didn't do very well. If you have previously failed exams, for example, you may experience a feeling of sick dread every time you enter a lecture theatre. Obviously, you need to replace the negative feelings with more positive ones. How do you do this? One way is to take a long, objective look at why you failed your exams, or didn't finish a previous degree course. Was it because you didn't understand the work, didn't manage your time effectively, or were there specific circumstances involved that are no longer relevant? Make sure you have addressed the problems this time round by using the strategies described in this book, or by discussing your concerns with your tutor. If you have addressed the problems, but still feel your stomach muscles knotting up every time you walk through the front door of the department, a simple strategy of positive reinforcement can help erase the negative feelings. Treat yourself to a cappuccino or download a track onto your iPod after every lecture, for example. (Hopefully, the feelings will soon disappear, or this strategy could get expensive!)

If you're worried about coping with the work, try reading through your lecture notes every evening, to make sure you understand them, and read up on, or talk over things you don't understand with other students or your tutor. If you don't get a good mark for your first piece of written work, make sure you find out why, and try to address any problem areas with the next assignment. Facing up to your weaker skills is not a sign of incompetence, but an opportunity to get better.

We've said a fair amount about the rules of the game throughout this book, but it's worth returning to the topic here since some aspects of it are more of an issue for mature students. More specifically, there are some questions about the rules of the game which mature students wonder about much more often than younger ones. For starters, there's the issue of why it's called a 'game' at all. That can make the whole process sound trivial and ultimately pointless. Games in the sense of sports in fact tend to be treated as something deadly serious by their players, and are often a major factor in players' decisions about life events and lifestyles, but that's a secondary issue. The key point about the game metaphor is that games have rules, and if you've ever tried playing a game where you don't know all the rules, you can end up in an embarrassing mess. Almost all games have a scoring system: some games have simple rules, whereas others have lots of complex rules; there are no prizes for guessing which of these categories the academic game falls into. It is also a game where the other players expect you to know the rules already or to pick them up as you go along. No one is likely to teach them to you. That's enough to make anyone feel stressed, so here are some of the questions and the corresponding unwritten rules that frequently crop up with mature students.

Why does this stuff have so little visible connection to the real world?
This is a particularly common question among students who have previously been in employment. There are several answers. The main one is that universities deal with knowledge about the deep underlying principles, so that you can work out for yourself from those principles solutions to apply to real world situations. Universities are pretty good at this on the whole. They're usually less good at explaining the intermediate steps you need to take to turn the principles into a practical solution – they'll probably assume that once you've grasped the concept, you'll be able to work out the implications for yourself.

Why do they waste their time on such weird things?
The work of academics often looks utterly unconnected with anything. Sometimes the reason is personal curiosity. More often, though, it's to do with the reasons that difficult problems are difficult. Academics get more prestige and research funding if they crack difficult problems than if they crack easy ones. With difficult problems, it's a pretty good bet that the actual solution isn't the obvious one (because if the obvious solution is the right one, then the problem won't remain unsolved for long). If you combine this with the point about underlying principles, the result is that the search for the answer can lead into some very unlikely places. It usually makes sense when the chain of reasoning is spelled out, but most academics have too heavy a workload to spend time explaining their research to students on taught courses.

Why don't they give us better training?
This question goes to the heart of a long-running polite division in academia. In brief, universities typically view their role as being primarily about education, and colleges' role as being primarily about training. What's the difference? In brief, training tells you what to do, whereas education tells you (a) a little about what you need to do, (b) a moderate amount about why you need to do it and (c) a lot about how to work out for yourself some better ways of doing it. So, for example, a university psychology course would typically cover the theory underpinning various forms of therapeutic technique, whereas a further education college might train students on its counselling course, to use a particular style of psychotherapy. Each type of course is fine and worthy, but serves different purposes. If you're doing a

university degree, then that means that you've signed up for education rather than just training, so listen and learn, even if you decide afterwards that you don't love it.

Problems affecting mature students who have spent time in the working world

Many of the classic problems affecting mature students who have previously been working also apply to mature students in general, and so have been covered above. There are, however, some specific problems which we deal with in this section. A classic difficulty is that you've changed from a senior member of staff in your previous organisation into a first year undergraduate, which is about as low as it gets on the academic status ladder. This can be seriously unsettling. It's not so bad if the lecturing staff show signs of recognising your situation, but if they don't, the transition can be stressful. A related problem is that you might find marked differences in values between academia and your previous role. The commonest manifestation of this is in writing style. You're used to writing clear, concise text that goes to the heart of the matter; they expect you to write something that unpicks obscure details. You're used to finding quick practical solutions that work; they're used to tackling the deep underlying principles, on a timescale of years or even decades. You're used to slick PowerPoint presentations; you find yourself listening to a lecture from someone in shirtsleeves sitting on a desk who occasionally scribbles something on a whiteboard.

So what do you do about it? The things to remember are that you chose to do the degree, and that the degree is about learning new things. Academia usually has reasons for doing things the way it does. If you don't know why, then it's a good idea to find out by asking an approachable member of staff over an informal cup of coffee, and making an effort to understand what they're saying, rather than trying to persuade them that they're wrong. It may be a frustrating experience initially, because you're starting from very different places, but if you can learn both viewpoints, then it puts you in a very powerful position. Industry and commerce are usually very good at the things that they do routinely; academia is usually very good at the things that industry and commerce find difficult. If you can perform effectively in both academia and the world of work, this is a significant and very useful ability.

PART-TIME STUDENTS

Conflicting practical demands

One obvious problem that affects most part-time students is the conflict between the practical demands of the day job and the studies. People tend to start off optimistic about being able to handle this, basing their judgements on carefully calculated timetables or on guesstimates of how much time everything will take. In practice, this usually works well until the first minor crisis, at which point everything falls apart in a messy heap. The underlying cause of this is lack of what is known as 'slack' or 'spare capacity.' It's like having your finances neatly organised so that you always have a little bit more income than expenditure; that's fine until you hit a big bit of unexpected expenditure. If you have enough money saved up, then you're all right; if you haven't, you suddenly acquire a significant debt, which is going to take a long time to clear. It's exactly the same with time. If your day job unexpectedly requires extra time, or if you're ill for a week, then suddenly you don't have any slack, your boss is hassling you, and you're behind in a couple of assignments simultaneously. There are various things you can do to reduce the risk of these problems, and to reduce their severity if they do occur. One is to make sure from the start that your boss and family are willing to be supportive during your degree; if they aren't, then you need to think seriously about whether to take on the degree. Efficient time-budgeting and priority management can help. We've described these skills earlier in this chapter.

Conflicting emotional demands

A related issue is the conflicting emotional demands of home and work. Your family will want you to be emotionally involved in their highs and lows; your boss will want you to be a good team player who is emotionally supportive in the ups and downs of organisational life; Christmas and summer holidays are likely to be a nightmare of conflicting loyalties. Again, time-budgeting and priority management can help; assertiveness can be particularly helpful for this problem. If it all gets too much, then it's worth stepping back and looking at the problem in perspective. If you leave your family, it's a major life event that's the topic of great literature like *Anna Karenina*; if you leave your job, you will have no income, and there's a number of books about being penniless and hungry; but if you drop out of a degree course, the world of literature will not give a damn. Blood comes first; if the tension between job, family and degree gets too much, then family is most important, followed by income.

STUDENTS FROM OVERSEAS

Before you start

If you're a student from abroad, you'll have many interesting experiences with stress before you even reach the university. You'll need to complete the admissions forms, which are often difficult to understand even if English is your first language. You'll probably need to have your certificates validated, and maybe translated as well. It's a good idea to get help from people who already know the British university system and who know how to complete the forms. After this, there will also be the emotional times of preparing for the journey, and of saying goodbye to friends and family, followed by the exhaustion of the journey itself. If you're feeling stressed by all of this, rest assured you are not unique; it's a feeling that everybody in your position goes through. The exercises in the second chapter of this book and in the appendices should help; also, you may find the chapter for new students useful.

During the journey to the UK, you'll probably focus just on getting to your destination. You might remember the welcoming photos of the campus on the university's website, with images of smiling students in bright sunshine against a background of beautiful gardens. What you might forget is that those photos are usually taken in summer, and you'll probably be arriving in autumn. You'll also quite probably be arriving late because of delays on your journey. The result is that many overseas students arrive at their university late at night, in the dark, in the rain and the cold, when everywhere appears to be closed. It's not a pleasant experience. So, what can you do about it? The simplest solution is to find out what you should do when you get here *before* you begin your journey. You can ask the university administrators what to do if this happens to you. They should then tell you where the 24-hour reception is, where you will at least meet a human being who will welcome you. It's also wise to ask the administrators about where you could stay if you arrive at your destination very late – they should be able to tell you about nearby hotels where you can stay overnight, so that you can get a good night's sleep, and then arrive at the university the next morning, when offices are open and the world is a more pleasant place. It's a wise idea to make sure you have enough cash in Sterling with you to cover expenses of this sort – it will reduce the potential stress considerably. We realise that this advice possibly comes too late for many readers of this book, who will buy it after they've already arrived here, but if one of your friends is thinking of coming to a British university, it's something you might want to tell them about.

Arrival

Once you have arrived, you will need to get yourself registered at the university. British bureaucracy is fairly simple compared with bureaucracy in some other places, so it shouldn't stress you too much. The university system is used to dealing with overseas students, and is usually friendly and supportive. You'll also need to find your accommodation. Most universities offer places in university halls of residence to overseas students and to first year students. There are many advantages in this, and we've assumed that you'll be staying in a hall for at least your first year. The first week or two will probably be eventful, including good things as well as bad things. After that, you'll be reasonably familiar with the university system, and will probably have a routine for your weekdays. That's the point at which problems can begin. For the first two weeks many students are too busy to think much about their friends and family at home, or to feel lonely. Once there is some free time, and you are used to Britain, then you start to miss things from home, and to feel like a stranger in a strange land. You'll miss family and friends; you'll miss familiar food and familiar smells and sights; you'll miss little things that sound silly when you tell people about them, like a familiar bell that you used to hear every morning on the way to work. It's perfectly normal to feel this way – almost everyone feels like this in a new country. It can hurt a lot, but for most people it gets better after the first few weeks.

Cultural issues

There are other problems which arise occasionally, such as when you're away from home and missing a festival or a family event, like a birthday, that usually brings the family together. There will be little things that suddenly remind you of home, just when you think you're used to being in Britain. There will be things that happen here which suddenly remind you of how much difference there can be between cultures – for instance, an item in the local news, or an event at the university, which shocks you but which is treated as perfectly normal by the people around you.

   Some overseas students react by finding other students from their home country and spending as much time as possible with them. This is understandable, but it isn't a good idea. It means that you won't be making good use of being in the UK at a British university. You might as well have studied at a university back home. It can also cause problems if your English isn't very good. Your exams will be in English, so you need to practise it as much as possible and speak it as well as possible. A better strategy is to have a mixture of friends. For example, you might have one evening a week when you socialise with students from your homeland, and another evening when you socialise with students from the UK. It's a good idea to find the university support services for overseas students, and to ask them what facilities are available to help you. There are usually societies for students from the same country, or from the same religion, and these will be able to give you friendship, advice and support. This is particularly useful for learning about differences in culture between your country and the UK, so that you don't accidentally cause offence or get into trouble.

Being an overseas student can be particularly difficult if you're a mature student with a partner and children and a senior post back home, but find yourself living in a hall of residence surrounded by noisy teenagers. Universities are often understanding about this situation. Some have special accommodation for mature students in a quiet area, so if this applies to you, then it's a good idea to ask the university whether they can offer accommodation somewhere more suited to your needs.

A frequent problem if you are a student from overseas is that you can't be familiar with all the social conventions in your new home, so you may worry about unintentionally sending out the wrong social signals to other people. A useful strategy is to make friends with at least one sensible, friendly British student of the same sex as yourself, and to ask them for advice when you're not sure about something.

There's one last problem which often affects overseas students just when they think that the stress is over. When you return home after a course at a British university, you'll probably have changed without realising it. You may have adopted some forms of British culture, and have got used to some British conventions. You'll also have experienced things that people in your home community haven't experienced. The result is that you may at times feel like a stranger in your own land. Again, this is perfectly normal, given what has happened to you, but it's a strange feeling. You may find it useful to find other ex-students who have been through the same experience, so that you can talk about it with someone who understands how you feel.

OTHER STUDENTS: TEMPORARY ABSENCES

There are various other types of student who are likely to face problems sooner or later because they don't fit neatly into The System. The issue might be an academic one, such as students doing a year abroad or a sandwich year. Or you may have had time out of your course due to illness or through switching courses in mid-stream. At a practical level, this can lead to being 'out of sync' with the regulations, if the university has changed some of its rules while you were away and has forgotten to allow for students who have been temporarily out of the system. There are similar issues if you've done a course or module that doesn't map neatly onto The System, such as modules you did on your year abroad which don't have an exact equivalent at home. At an emotional level, returning after time away can feel very odd. The places will look comfortingly familiar, but there will be a weird absence which is difficult to pin down at first. It's the absence of 'familiar strangers' – people that you see every day, although you may never have spoken to them. Many of them will have graduated and left during your year away. The result is that you can feel like a ghost, passing unnoticed through crowded places.

You can also feel like an outsider for non-academic reasons, such as being a member of a minority group, whether it's sexual, ethnic, religious or political. Ironically, a university is one of the best places to be in terms of social support if you're in a minority – you'll probably find it easier to meet others like you at university than anywhere else, and you're much more likely to be accepted in a university than in most other places. If this is the case for you, then you should find out about the university's support systems, clubs, and so on: you might be pleasantly surprised.

SUMMARY

If you're a mature student, an overseas student, a part-time student or are otherwise different from the standard-issue full-time home-grown undergraduate aged between 18 and 22, then you're likely to feel marginalised at university. If you have a family or a job, then you'll experience stresses from conflicting demands for your time and attention. You may also experience stress from starting again at the bottom of the status ladder as a new student. You'll also probably encounter culture clash between the academic world and your usual world. If you go through these feelings, that's normal, and we describe some ways of handling them; it's worth persevering, because the students reading this chapter are likely both to get the most out of a degree and also to give back most to the academic world. They're also likely to be the students most valued by the academic staff, even if the academics don't always show it until graduation day.

BIBLIOGRAPHY AND SUGGESTED FURTHER RESOURCES

The Open University has a lot of experience of mature students and part-time students; if you belong to one or both of those categories, it's well worth looking at their support material, and investigating their website.

Linda Pritchard and Leila Roberts's *The Mature Student's Guide to Higher Education* (Open University Press/McGraw-Hill Education, 2006) is what its title says. It works through the process of undertaking higher education, including career options at the end of your course.

If you are an overseas student, then you will probably find your university's student support material to be more useful than general books about studying in the UK. Most universities have online material which answers specific frequently asked questions such as 'How can I get from the airport to the university?' If your university doesn't answer a more general question, such as 'How do I apply for a student visa?' then another university's website might.

Part 5

WHAT'S NEXT?

19 Why do a Postgraduate Degree?

SIMON P. FELTON

Introduction

This chapter will look at the potential benefits and also the possible drawbacks of a postgraduate research degree enabling you to clarify your expectations and make an informed decision about whether this is the correct path for you. Spending time considering the challenges you may face and gauging the benefits you will accrue will contribute to your motivation to pursue this exciting course of action. This motivation will then contribute to a successful outcome and the realisation of those benefits.

Specifically, this chapter includes the following:

- Common reasons why people choose to do a research degree and what may lie beneath them
- Potential benefits to be gained from a postgraduate research degree
- Possible drawbacks of doing a postgraduate research degree
- Advice on how to clarify your own reasons and decide if this is the right course of action for you.

This chapter prompts you with questions throughout the text to help you to clarify your reasons, what benefits you expect and what drawbacks you anticipate. This will enable you to make a positive decision to pursue a research degree or not and be happy with whatever choice you make.

Common Reasons for Pursuing a Postgraduate Research Degree

> I really loved my subject and wanted to continue researching as I enjoyed research, I didn't have clear career aspirations so I chose based on my enthusiasm for the subject.
>
> (Research student, Cardiff University)

The reasons for individuals undertaking a postgraduate research degree are diverse because they are driven by personal needs and desires.

Two surveys published in the last few years have looked at the reasons why people pursue a research degree. One survey, by the National Postgraduate Committee (NPC 2002), that targeted all UK-domiciled postgraduate students found that nearly half (46%) of full-time students who were asked 'why they chose further study?' said their primary reason was to improve their career prospects. The next most popular primary reason was to continue studying (35%). The values for part-time students were similar; career prospects 41% and continuing study 34%. Part-time students were more likely to list personal development as a reason for pursuing postgraduate study (18% putting this as their primary reason compared to 9% of full-timers). A small proportion of both full- (2.8%) and part-time (3.8%) students listed the fact that they had secured funding as their primary reason for continuing to study.

A second survey conducted on behalf of the UK GRAD Programme called 'What Do PhDs Do?' (UK Grad, 2004), which is explored in depth in Chapter 22, found that the common reasons for pursuing a research degree were the following:

- Subject interest
- Desire for career progression
- Broader career choice or career change
- Personal benefit defined broadly in terms of a sense of achievement, a boost to self-confidence etc.

The key reasons deduced from both surveys therefore are as follows:

- Interest in a particular field of study
- Career motivations (better job, career change, necessary for chosen career etc.)
- Personal development and intellectual challenge
- Secured funding.

As well as these reasons, anecdotal evidence from talking to research students suggests that there are some other common reasons:

- To benefit some aspect of human life, for example, contribute to a cure for some disease, help to deal with global warming, etc.
- It was suggested to them as an option for their next step by a university lecturer
- To avoid entry into the job market
- Did not know what else to do.

I really enjoyed research and was encouraged by my tutor to continue onto a PhD. I wanted to continue my research and the opportunity to shape developments in biochemistry really appealed to me. It broadens the horizons, allows one to reach the peak of study and it can bring great intellectual reward and open many horizons. (Research student, University of Birmingham)

QUESTIONS TO CONSIDER

1   Do you share any of these reasons?
2   What other reasons do you have?

What Benefits May Be Gained by Studying for a Research Degree?

One of the significant benefits of a postgraduate research degree and the purpose of research is the generation of an original contribution to knowledge and the enormous personal and intellectual satisfaction this can afford you.

The research degree is an internationally recognised qualification. Additionally, the UK's positive reputation for research will add to that recognition. The UK remains second to the US on most measures of quality of research in an international context (such as citations and discipline strength by cited work) and benefits from younger research graduates as compared to other countries (King, 2004; UK Grad, 2004). You will share in that positive recognition.

The employment potential of a research degree lies in the research student having demonstrated the capability and tenacity in undertaking an extended piece of investigative work as well as in specific technical skills acquired. A research degree also develops important transferable 'life skills' and employ-ability skills such as public speaking, presentations, writing proposals, spe-cialist knowledge, self-reliance and responsibility. Research students having organised their own studies can be excellent project managers, experts at analysis, and capable of working through complex processes with confidence and autonomy; skills recognised by the Quality Assurance Agency (QAA) as those gained by masters and doctoral qualifications (see Chapters 14 and 23 and Appendix 2 for further information on skills).

My research was focussed on the developments in genetics and pushing the boundaries of knowledge while contributing to a wider project. The sponsorship by the company provided the means to complete the PhD and the route to a research career with the company. I was glad that the company was involved as the research was focussed for work in the sector and the company itself. (Research student, Imperial College, London)

What Are the Possible Drawbacks of Studying for a Research Degree?

> I'd got the academic 'buzz' during my Bachelors, the dissertation was the key factor, and I decided to go further than just my Masters where the 'buzz' got stronger. Some people thought it was just a continuation of being an undergraduate but it is not like that. There was a lot of work to do in a limited timeframe for my Masters and the PhD is really demanding, with not much time for relaxing – you need to be clear you really want to do this as it's costly in time, money and relationships.
>
> (Research student, Queen Mary College, London)

While there may be considerable benefits from pursuing a research degree there are also drawbacks, as Ben points out, such as the financial cost, the time commitment required and the possible impact on your personal life from taking on such a lengthy commitment. It is important these 'costs' are considered alongside the benefits before undertaking a research degree. The financial costs of undertaking a research degree maybe considerable, this is explored in detail in Chapter 4. This section highlights some of the other drawbacks.

The time required to complete a research degree, especially a PhD or equivalent, can cause a number of issues:

- Employers who are seeking young graduates may see a graduate with three-year work experience as more valuable than a student with research degree experience. You may have to work hard to convince them otherwise, although we believe you can.
- Maintaining the motivation to complete and therefore be successful in your studies can be very problematic over a number of years, especially if you are studying part-time. It is also very difficult to predict what any changes in your personal circumstances over this timescale may be and what impact any changes may have, either positive or negative.

The nature of a research degree may not suit you as an individual for the following reasons:

- Research students often experience loneliness or isolation in the process of conducting research. Remember that the uniqueness of the work you are doing may also mean there are few people around who may understand it.
- The autonomy that research gives may also be a burden to those who prefer structure in their working environments.

Although many research students suggested that a deep interest in the work was one of the reasons for undertaking the research degree, it may also become a drawback if your interest becomes an obsession that diverts your attention from other priorities in your life to the detriment of those priorities. You should be aware of this and those around should also be aware of this before you embark on a research degree.

Finally, others may not 'see' the benefits of a research degree that are obvious to you. For instance, employers may exhibit a stereotypical reaction that you maybe over-qualified. You may ultimately need to work hard to convince those around you (family, partners, friends etc.) as well as those who may employ you of why undertaking a research degree has been so beneficial.

Factors for Success

There have been a number of studies that have looked at the factors that affect the successful completion of research degrees, which have been discussed in a very interesting paper by Wright and Cochrane (2000). From their reading of this literature the factors break down into three broad categories:

1 Institutional and structural issues associated with research degrees themselves
2 Non-psychological individual issues such as availability of financial support
3 Individual resilience reasons such as motivation, self-confidence etc.

The study described in the paper focused on the second category and found that successful completion within four years of starting a PhD (full-time or equivalent timescale part-time) was more likely if a research student was:

• from a science, engineering or medical-based subject
• the holder of a first or upper second-class bachelors degree
• funded by a UK research council
• studying part-time
• an international research student.

The factors differed slightly for successful completion within 10 years (full-time only; the study did not extend to the equivalent part-time timescales). They were found to be:

• in science, engineering or medical-based subjects
• funded by a UK research council
• under 27 years of age
• international research students.

In their discussion of the results, Wright and Cochrane suggested that the inclusion of part-time and international students, in this 'ideal' mix of factors for success was perhaps attributable to the third category of reasons, that is individual resilience reasons. They go on to propose that these groups may have invested more in the process, in terms of money, time and effort, and were perhaps therefore clearer of what they would lose if they were unsuccessful.

Although this hypothesis was not tested in the research, it does sound logical from the way they present it. It is for this reason that we strongly suggest you be clear why you want to do a research degree which will give you a similar level of 'investment' in its outcome. It is this investment which will enable you to develop the perseverance and tenacity that are crucial attributes for any research student. Clarity of your motivations to undertake a research degree is explored in more detail in the next section.

What Lies beneath These Common Reasons?

If we were to ask a person who was considering undertaking a research degree why and were told one of the common reasons listed earlier in the chapter, we would probably follow up any of those answers with 'Tell me more' or 'Explain that in more detail'. In this section, we will try to delve deeper into the possible answers that this may elicit and present you with some questions to consider.

Interest in a Particular Field of Study

This is a highly motivating reason and is certainly a common one as we have seen. However, someone who does not share this interest would surely ask you to be more specific and to say exactly what is it about this subject that really warrants your attention. If this is your current reason for considering a research degree, it maybe worth examining this to understand what initially caused this interest to develop. For instance, was it an event in your personal life or the experience of being taught by a charismatic lecturer who was passionately interested in this subject or another similar event? If it is an external event, you do need to be clear that they have really led to a deep personal interest in the topic and are not the actual reason themselves.

QUESTIONS TO CONSIDER

1 Has your interest in this topic been stimulated by another event or person?
2 Is your interest in this subject strong enough to see you through what may be quite an extended period of study?
3 Can you study further in your field of interest through other routes without undertaking a research degree?

Career Motivations

> I couldn't have secured an academic post without a PhD. If you are starting a career in academia you MUST have a PhD.
>
> (Academic, University of Manchester)

> A research degree gives me a good grounding for the commercial and academic world. It has given me the confidence to discuss projects and I feel that I can achieve anything. I chose to do my research degree for career progression reasons – to develop myself and add value to me in the employment market.
>
> (Marketing Director)

If this is your reason then you should replace the title of this chapter with 'Why Do This Particular Career?' because that would be the nature of the follow-up questions to understand the reasoning in more detail. It is important to research the career you are interested in to understand how potential employers would view applicants with a research degree (start by talking to people who actually work in the field you're interested in). You therefore need to determine if you are really committed to this career choice and are sure that holding a research degree will help you to get that ideal job.

QUESTIONS TO CONSIDER

1 Have you researched this career fully to determine if it is right for you?
2 Have you looked at how the prospects for this career path will look like in one, three or more years?
3 Will a research degree really give you a competitive advantage over other job seekers in this area who do not have a research degree?

Personal Development and Intellectual Challenge

The personal development reason is again complex. It may elicit follow-up questions regarding the exact nature of the development you want to undertake. You may also then be asked why you feel it is necessary.

Initially the intellectual challenge reason is much easier to grasp, but doing original research is definitely challenging. However, follow-up questions along the lines of 'why test your intellect in this particular research area?' could produce some interesting observations.

QUESTIONS TO CONSIDER

1 Will a research degree provide you with the appropriate ways to develop yourself in the areas you have identified?
2 Why do you want to develop yourself in this way?
3 Why do you want to test your intellect in *this particular* research area?

Secured Funding for the Degree

The obvious follow up question with this reason is 'why did you look for funding to do this research?'; this is because this reason is not really a reason but a means by which you can undertake this research without undue financial hardship. If you are currently in this situation it would be wise to think clearly about your motivations to undertake your particular area of enquiry and not any other project that has funding attached to it.

QUESTIONS TO CONSIDER

1 What other areas of research also attract funding?
2 Would you be more interested in these areas?
3 What other reasons do you have for choosing to do this particular research project?

To Benefit Humankind

It is easy to see why this reason is extremely compelling and motivating. However, there are issues to consider here too. Is the impact or benefit of the research you will be undertaking achievable within the usual timescales of a research degree? Even though we have said that a research degree may take a significant investment of time it may still not be long enough to achieve the benefit you desire and it is likely to be only a small step in that process.

QUESTIONS TO CONSIDER

1 Will your passion to benefit humankind survive the disappointments if your research does not progress as quickly as you would like or the 'solution' to this problem is not as you had hoped?
2 Will you be satisfied with the contribution you can make within the timescales of a research degree?
3 Have you talked to other researchers about this?

Suggested as an Option

This reason is very likely to raise questions such as 'do you always follow the suggestions of others?', as it does suggest that you may not have thought long or hard about what you would like to do with the next few years of your life. If this suggestion has come from an academic, you may be seduced by the compliment. However, a research degree requires you to be an independent researcher; a person who thinks through issues and takes responsibility for a course of action. Therefore, you should look for your own reasons if you are currently in this situation.

QUESTIONS TO CONSIDER

1 What are your reasons for considering this option?
2 What other options are there that may interest you?

Avoid Entry into the Job Market

This reason again sounds as if you have not positively decided a research degree is for you. It implies that you know what you do not want to do. If eliminating all the things you do not want to do with the next few years of your life leaves you only with a research degree as the last option, have you really considered and explored all your options?

QUESTIONS TO CONSIDER

1 What other options have you considered other than a 'traditional' job and a research degree?
2 What really does interest you and make you excited in life?

Wright and Cochrane (2000) described reasons such as the last two as 'bandwagon' reasons, which implies that if these reasons apply to you then you are being taken through life rather than driving its direction for yourself. This could be viewed as a worrying trait for a person who is endeavouring to demonstrate that she or he is an independent, resourceful and professional researcher who can operate with a high degree of autonomy.

How Could You Go about Deciding Whether a Research Degree Is for You?

Before you commit to enrolling on a research degree, it would be useful for you to delve into your personal situation; what are your reasons?, what benefits do you expect to gain?, and which of the drawbacks may affect you?, is the research degree you are considering the right one for you? and so on (see Chapter 2 for more information relating to this final question). One useful way to do this is to be challenged to articulate these answers in a conversation with a friend. This person should be someone you trust and someone who is capable of asking those awkward questions that your initial answers may raise. This may also help you to see things that you had not thought of, which may either reinforce or reduce your commitment to this course of action.

QUESTIONS TO CONSIDER

Here are four key questions for you to answer in your conversation with your friend:

1 Why you are choosing this course of action?
2 What will you gain from pursuing your research degree?
3 What might you miss out on by pursuing a research degree?
4 What would happen if you were unsuccessful in your research degree?

This section attempts to draw all of the information presented so far together to help you prepare for this conversation. Remember that just like the viva neither you nor I will have predicted all the questions that you could be asked in this conversation, and this is the very reason why it is such a useful exercise to clarify your hopes, doubts and expectations of what lies ahead.

1   Why you are choosing this course of action?

    a   List your motivations for doing a research degree.
    b   Explain these motivations to someone you trust who will objectively and constructively challenge you to explain the detailed reasons beneath them with questions such as:

        i   Do you know what academic research is?
        ii   What previous experience of research do you have, did you enjoy the research?
        iii   Why will doing a research degree fulfil your ambition?

    iv   Could you do something else to fulfil your ambition?

    v   Can you maintain your passion and enthusiasm over the course of the research degree?

    vi   Are you doing it for personal, financial, career gains?

Capture the results of this conversation; it may produce information and reasons you have not considered before.

2   What will you gain from pursuing your research degree?

    a   List all the possible benefits that you believe you will gain from pursuing a research degree.

    b   Do some research to determine if the benefits you have listed are likely to be realised.

    c   Quantify the benefits you believe are realisable.

    d   Work out your order of priority for these benefits. This will give you your minimum level of benefit that must be gained from your research degree to call it a success.

3   What might you miss out on by pursuing a research degree?

    a   List all the other education/career/life directions you could take.

    b   What benefits would you gain from each scenario and quantify them all?

    c   Prioritise these benefits against those you are likely to gain from doing your research degree.

4   What would happen if you were unsuccessful in your research degree?

    a   What is the most important thing you will have lost if you don't obtain your research degree?

    b   Will you be able to take any of the other education/career directions you listed above?

    c   At what point in your research degree would you be unable to take each alternative course?

Once you have done this are you convinced that a research degree is for you? Do the benefits outweigh the drawbacks? Whatever the answer, you will have given yourself the best chance for success no matter what you decide to do.

    The clear message is that you should understand in detail your motivations for choosing to do a research degree. This is especially important for part-time study where you will need to maintain this motivation over a considerable length of time.

> [D]o not ignore or underestimate the commitment balancing part-time research with a full-time job. (Part-time research masters student)

A research student from the University of Leeds encourages you to think all this through:

> postgraduate study demands focus and determination, there are more dangers and potential areas for failure. You need to plan your studies and get support from fellow academics, colleagues and family if you are to succeed and enjoy it.

Conclusion

This chapter aimed to help you to answer the question 'Why do a postgraduate research degree?' You should now be clearer about your personal motivations for enrolling on a research degree and the benefits you are expecting from it.

It is crucial to consider why you want to undertake a research degree. It will help you to continue to generate the passion that will see you through the whole process. It will also be easier to see how doing the research degree is helping you to meet your goals. This will help you to shape the direction of the research and to develop into an independent researcher.

If you are confident about your reasons and the expected benefits and you are fully aware of the potential drawbacks, it will be easier to maintain your enthusiasm for your research degree and see it through to a successful outcome. From the growth in the numbers of people undertaking research degrees over the last few years it is clear that pursuing a research degree is an attractive and potentially, hugely beneficial course of action.

Hopefully, after this careful consideration you will make the positive decision to take a research degree (and therefore benefit from the rest of the chapters in this book!). If this is the case then you may also find it useful to periodically review and reflect on your initial reasons for your choice, the benefits you are accruing, especially those you had not foreseen and to understand how you are dealing with any drawbacks. This type of activity will make your research degree the true educational and developmental process it can be. Expect it to be challenging, but remember the most challenging situations are often those which generate the most significant benefits.

SOURCES OF SUPPORT

Bentley, P.J. (2006) *The PhD Application Handbook*, Maidenhead: Open University Press – The first chapter of this book explores the issues raised in this chapter in an accessible and lively way.

www.careerweb.leeds.ac.uk/downloads/Empress_LR_000.pdf – Employers' Perceptions of Recruiting Research Staff and Students. This research report provides useful background to what employers value when recruiting research staff and provides ideas on how to increase your employability if career issues motivate you to do a research degree.

www.cse.ucsd.edu/users/mihir/phd.html – This URL has been created by a US supervisor of research students to help his current and prospective students to understand the PhD process. It also includes some questions you need to ask yourself before choosing to do a research degree.

www.dartmouth.edu/~csrc/students/gradschool/artsci/ – The Careers Service of Dartmouth College (one of the 8 Ivy League colleges that also include Harvard and Yale) has some similar questions to help you to consider your options.

www.phd-survey.org/advice/advice.htm – This URL is again compiled for potential research students in the US. It contains questions to ask of yourself as well as sections with questions to ask of potential universities and supervisors.

www.prospects.ac.uk – Comprehensive website providing career advice and information on postgraduate study with sections on why do postgraduate study, choosing where to do it and advice on funding. For information relating to this chapter go to the home page, click on Postgrad Study and select 'About postgrad study' from the menu.

www.grad.ac.uk – Useful website giving guidance for researchers on completing a doctorate, skills training and national and regional events to support researchers.

References

King, D.A. (2004) 'The Scientific Impact of Nations', *Nature*, 430: 311–316, available at: www.dti.gov.uk/files/file11959.pdf (accessed 2 January 2008) – Nature journal article which explores the scientific impact of various nations to establish national research productivity comparisons such as citations and discipline strength by citation.

NPC (2002) *National Survey of Postgraduate Funding and Priorities*, Troon: The National Postgraduate Committee of the UK, available at: www.npc.org.uk/page/1083342227.pdf (accessed 5 October 2007).

The UK GRAD Programme (2004, 2006, 2007) *What Do PhDs Do?*, available at: www.grad.ac.uk/wdpd/ (accessed 5 October 2007) – Provides a useful introduction to why do a PhD, where PhDs work and on disciplinary differences.

Wright, T. and Cochrane, R. (2000) 'Factors Influencing Successful Submission of PhD Theses', *Studies in Higher Education*, 25(2): 181–195.

20 Putting Yourself on the Job Market

JOAN TURNER

warm-up exercise
Brainstorm for a couple of minutes on the skills you think you learn at university that can transfer to the job market. If possible, do this with others and compare what you come up with.

TRANSFERABLE SKILLS

When asked to reflect back on their own experiences of university, the well-known broadcasters Melvyn Bragg and Allan Little gave answers typical of independent learners. They emphasised the process of learning and the motivation to learn.

> ➤ I learnt what I wanted to do with my life. I knew that I wanted to write fiction and I wanted to keep learning stuff
>> (Melvyn Bragg – in *Guardian Higher*, 7 September 1999, in answer to the question, What did you really learn at university?)

> ➤ The intellectual discipline you acquire while studying is at the heart of what you do as a journalist – it is a continual process of assessing information, interpreting, making judgements about what matters, what doesn't and why.
>> (Allan Little in answer to the question: did your degree prepare you for the world of work? In *EdiT*, The University of Edinburgh Magazine, Volume, 2,2, 2000.)

University is not just about the content of what you study, it is also about the skills you develop through interacting with content. You can then go on being a learner, applying those skills to different kinds of content in different contexts throughout your life. This is often talked about as developing *transferable skills*, a buzz word with employers and with university administrators. What Allan Little talks about in the quote above as 'the intellectual discipline' of 'assessing information, interpreting, making judgements about what matters, what doesn't and why' may also be seen as transferable skills. They transfer from the process of being a student to being a journalist. You may find that in your student handbook, you have listed the 'key skills' or 'transferable skills' that studying your particular subject or subjects will help you to develop. Some may be practical such as creating statistical charts or tables, while others may be more abstract such as making judgements based on the evidence available.

This book has emphasised the importance of learning to become an independent learner. This in itself is a transferable skill. Whether you continue being a student and go on to postgraduate studies, get down to job-hunting right away, or have the freedom, time, and money to go 'travelling' for a year or so first, the myriad skills of taking charge of your learning and managing the study process should stand you in good stead. What I want to focus on particularly however, in this last chapter, is the process of getting a job.

PREPARING FOR WORK AFTER THE DEGREE

You may have already been in the workplace before you went to university, but you are a different person now and you present yourself for work as that 'new' person rather than as the pre-degree you.

For many of you, the process of job-hunting will already have begun in your final year. Your university careers office will have details of companies to apply to and often representatives from some of the larger companies will come to your university to give information and to offer interviews. Some lucky students therefore leave university with a job lined up.

Make sure you become familiar with your university careers office and the kinds of services it can offer you. This process can begin as early as your first year!

If you're reading this, as many of you will be, before your final year, and therefore the prospect of actively looking for a full-time job after your degree will seem some time off, think about how important it will be at this stage to have done the best you could during your degree. It will be too late if you only realise at the end of your degree that you could have done better.

Make a point of improving your study strategies and your approach to learning now, to maximise your chances of getting a good degree and having a head start in the employment market

THE JOB APPLICATION PROCESS

Here are three of the commonest ways of applying for jobs:

➢ through graduate training programmes;
➢ direct applications for advertised positions;
➢ sending out your CV on spec.

Applying for entry into a graduate training programme such as with a bank, or the National Health Service, the civil service, or the police, is most likely to be by means of an application form that these organisations have already prepared.

The candidate selection process may be held in several stages. After initial selection from the application forms, there may be preliminary interviews, then you may be asked to take particular psychological or personality tests, and then a further interview. So the whole procedure can take quite a lot of time.

If you fail to get selected for the first programme you try for, don't be too downhearted, pick yourself up and try for the next one. Don't just say exactly what you said on the previous application form, which would have been slightly different anyway, try to express yourself better, and tailor your abilities and experiences as well as you can to the kind of programmes on offer. There is more below on the kinds of questions you are asked on such forms.

Similarly if you get to an initial interview but no further, think of the opportunity of getting an interview as valuable experience.

ANSWERING APPLICATION FORM QUESTIONS

Here are some examples of types of application form questions.

➢ Can you give an example of when you worked well in a group?
➢ Can you give an example of something that you feel you did really well?
➢ Can you give an example of an instance where you felt you could have done something better?
➢ Can you say something about how you coped with a difficult situation?

Try and formulate what you say on the application form in a way that emphasises the skills you have gained through the experience you are telling your prospective employers about. Don't ramble on in storytelling mode, try and break down the episode from your experience, whatever it is, into the kinds of analytical categories that most employers think in terms of. Here are a few such categories to bear in mind (see also the section on linking experience with skills, below):

➢ taking up a *challenge*;
➢ showing *responsibility*;
➢ evidence of good *interpersonal skills* (working well with people);
➢ evidence of *customer service skills*;
➢ experience of *team work*;
➢ showing *initiative*.

PREPARING YOUR CV

TASK 1

Look at the first page of the three (fictitious) CVs below. How do they strike you as different? Which do you want to pay more attention to?

Curriculum Vitae
Iona Montague

Personal Details

Term Time Address:	**Home Address**	**Nationality:**	British
Halls of Residence	46 Cooks Road		
University	London	**Date of Birth:**	28 August 1979
Kent TN24 0NG	N16 5AR		
Tel: 01234 567 890	Tel: 020 8765 4321	**Email:**	i.mont@y.ac.uk

Education

1999–2001   University of Innovation & Excellence
BSc (Hons) Business Studies: Courses include international
marketing, corporate strategy, accounting and finance, and
management economics
Skills gained: team work, presentation skills, research and analytical
skills and time management

1997–1999   Inner City Comprehensive
A-Levels: Business Studies (C), English (C)
AS Level: French (C)

CV No 1

Curriculum Vitae

Full Name:	**Timothy George Buchanan**
Date of birth:	22/2/66
Place of birth:	**Sunderland**
	Tyne and Wear
	United Kingdom
Nationality:	**British**
Present Address:	**14 Cavendish Avenue**
	Norfolk
	NR6 6JD
Telephone:	**04776 897 990**
Education:	
1996–1997	**Access Course in Primary Education**
	Bramwell College of Further Education
1997–2000	**BEd (2:1)**
	University of Appleton

CV No 2

CURRICULUM VITAE

NAME: Ayse BILOGUN

DATE OF BIRTH: 26/06/80

PLACE OF BIRTH: Brighton, England

NATIONALITY: British

PRESENT ADDRESS: Saltmine Lane
                        Dundee
                        Scotland
                        Tel: 07301 148794

EDUCATION

1997–2000   Badminton University
                        BA (Hons) Fine Art (IIi)

CV No 3

Here is a checklist of points to remember in terms of how you present your CV:

- ✓ *Necessary personal details.* Usually name, date of birth, current address, telephone number and e-mail (if applicable) or where you can best be contacted.
- ✓ *Leave out unnecessary personal details.* It is not usually necessary to include a photograph, your marital status, your race or your religion.
- ✓ *Clarity of personal details.* Consider using a larger font size or different font from the following details of your educational history and the rest of your CV. Alternatively, set out your personal details horizontally across the page, as in CV no. 1 above.
- ✓ *Attention to layout.* Don't cram things too close together; make it easy for the reader to follow at a glance the information that is being given. Leave one and a half line spaces between each line, and use 12 or 14 point type. Leave double the amount of spacing between sections, and make sure each section has a heading, possibly in bold.
- ✓ *Sequencing of details.* Work backwards from the present.
- ✓ *Include grades* with A levels, etc.
- ✓ *Link work experience to skills gained.* For example, don't just say 'I worked in a flower shop', make it achievement orientated, as in: 'At A&J Flowers Ltd., I developed a creative flair making up floral arrangements, and learnt a lot about customer service'.

THINKING OF YOUR EXPERIENCE
IN TERMS OF SKILLS GAINED

TASK 2

Match the following study tasks and examples of work experience with the skills they develop. A list of possible skills is given, but you may think of lots more.

Work Experience	Skills
Working in a pub	
Stacking shelves in a supermarket	
Helping out at a riding stables	
Voluntary work at a sports club	
Babysitting	
Setting up a child care rota	
Giving a seminar presentation	
Studying as a mother/father with young children	
Working as a shop assistant	
Writing academic assignments	
Handling a large workload	

IT skills
Customer service skills
Interpersonal skills
Written communication skills
Spoken communication skills
Coping skills
Organisational skills
Administrative skills
Creative skills
Perseverance

Leadership skills
Problem-solving skills
Information-gathering skills
Synthesising information
Analytical skills
Handling change
Handling diversity
Reliability

The Covering Letter

When applying for jobs directly in response to an advertisement, you may not have to fill in an application form. In such a case, you need to include a covering letter along with your CV. A standard covering letter would simply say something like the following:

Dear Sir or Madam,

NAME OF POST YOU ARE APPLYING FOR

I am interested in applying for the above vacancy and enclose my curriculum vitae.

If you require further details please do not hesitate to contact me. (This is more like a routine formula than something that is absolutely necessary.)

I look forward to hearing from you.

Yours faithfully, (or Yours sincerely, if you have mentioned the person to whom you are sending the letter by name)

Your Signature

Your name in capital letters

The Covering Letter as Opportunity

A covering letter such as the above misses the opportunity to show clearly and succinctly how you fit the post offered. If you are applying directly for a vacancy which you have seen advertised, further details of what is required for the post are likely to have been sent to you. You should use these details to **structure** your covering letter. These details are known as the job specification.

Let's take a look at the following three fictitious posts. How might you structure your covering letter in relation to them?

FRESCO

Quality Controller

A quality controller is required to assess the quality of fresh fruit and vegetables as they are delivered to the store.

You will be required to monitor the delivery of fresh produce and make recommendations as to its quality, based on our company specifications.

You will be required to write up a report on each consignment and forward it to your line manager in the quality assurance office.

Initial training in quality assurance procedures will be provided.

Job Advert C

MIDDLETON MANOR
PRIMARY SCHOOL

Newly Qualified Year 3 Teacher

Middleton Manor is a bustling multi-cultural primary school in the Exminster area of the city. You will have:

⋏ Some experience of working in a multi-cultural school
⋏ The ability to work well with children from a variety of different backgrounds
⋏ The ability to work under pressure
⋏ The ability to work well in a team
⋏ Flair and initiative in dealing with young children
⋏ Good communication skills

Job Advert B

METROPOLITAN MUSEUM
OF ARTS AND CRAFTS

Retail Assistant

The Metropolitan Museum of Arts is a major public venue and receives over 10 million visitors a year.

A lively graduate is required to work in its large, busy, museum shop. Must have good interpersonal skills, broad knowledge of art history, and sound administrative ability.

Could be a good opportunity for a recent graduate in an arts related field.

Job Advert A

Here is an example of how the holder of CV No 3 above might apply for post A.

Dear Ms A:

RE: Retail Assistant in the Metropolitan Museum of Arts and Crafts

I am very much interested in applying for the above post and enclose my CV.

I think you will find that my experience and qualifications meet your requirements most satisfactorily.

Whilst still at school, I had a Saturday job at my local Arts Centre. I gained a good working knowledge of both the kind of retail business that was done and the kinds of people who visited. I was praised by the head of centre for my administrative ability, my good time-keeping and my open and friendly manner with everybody who came into the centre.

I have a degree in graphic design and my course included lectures on European art history which I very much enjoyed, and I did well in my assignments.

In the hope that I might discuss my knowledge and experience further with you at interview, I look forward to hearing from you.

Yours sincerely,

THE INTERVIEW

[...]

Very often if you are offered an interview, you will be asked to give a short presentation on a topic. You should give a lot of careful thought to this, prepare some OHP slides or PowerPoint slides (making sure that you've rung up in advance to request the appropriate equipment) and time yourself giving it.

Usually the amount of time that you are asked to speak for is specified and you should be careful not to overrun. Saying what you have to say in as succinct a manner as possible is always appreciated.

Anticipating Questions

It helps to try and think of the kinds of questions you might be asked in an interview. Here are some things you could do in preparation for this.

➢ Look back at the job specification. There is likely to be at least one question that is intended to bring out the kind of information that your interviewers can judge you on, with regard to each specification.
➢ You should always prepare something to say in answer to the question '*Why are you interested in this job?*'.

In order to answer the above question or a similar question well, it's a good idea to have as clear an idea as possible of what the job entails. Ask yourself:

➢ How big is the company or organisation?
➢ What are its main concerns?

Usually the information on the company or organisation is sent out with the letter inviting you for interview.

➢ Make sure you read this information thoroughly and well in advance.
➢ Don't just find out on the bus on your way to the interview that there's something you should have thought about before!

Overcoming Nervousness

Before you go into the interview room, take some deep breaths, walk in confidently (even if you don't feel it) and smile at everyone as you go in. Try not to be daunted by the number of people facing you, focus on them rather than think about them looking at you. It may help to have visualised yourself going through the interview in advance, rehearsing your presentation or the answers you might give.

Most interviewers are fairly sympathetic if you're a little bit nervous. Provided you have prepared yourself well and answer the questions in a coherent and relevant manner, it won't matter if you occasionally speak too fast, or run out of breath, or have to pause for a drink of water. You may even say at some stage: 'Excuse me. I'm a little bit nervous.' This will buy you a bit of time and you can begin again to answer the question or regain your composure.

In the Interview

Make sure that you have organised what you want to say or show in your presentation in sequence, so that you don't have to scrabble around to find things.

Take your time to get any papers or slides out of your briefcase. Don't give a sense of being in a hurry to get things over with.

After you have given your presentation, take time to sit down comfortably and try to appear relaxed. It might help if you sit well back in the chair rather than lean forward anxiously.

Listen carefully to the questions as they are asked. If you haven't quite understood any of them, don't worry about asking for them to be repeated.

Sometimes, when there is more than one interviewer, the questions can be a bit similar. Try to answer them in the terms that the questioner has used, and if necessary, refer back to what you said in answer to another question, but reformulate that answer. So you might begin: 'As I said in answer to a previous question ...'.

There is no harm in specific details of your experience, or your stance on a particular aspect of the job, being refocused as they relate to different questions.

[...]

ARE YOU LOOKING FOR SUCCESS @ UNIVERSITY ?

THEN THIS IS THE BOOK FOR YOU!

WITH ITS EASY-TO-USE, DIP IN, DIP OUT STRUCTURE, THIS BOOK COVERS ALL OF THE SKILLS YOU WILL NEED DURING YOUR DEGREE, INCLUDING:

· TIME MANAGEMENT
· NOTE-TAKING
· ESSAY WRITING
· RESEARCH SKILLS
· CRITICAL THINKING
· DOING PRESENTATIONS
· REVISING FOR EXAMS

Study Skills
the essential guide for students

BUY THE COMPANION TO UNIVERSITY LIFE: the essential guide for Students TODAY!

Printed in Great Britain by
Amazon.co.uk, Ltd.,
Marston Gate.